Morris Minor Restoration Manual

Morris Minor Restoration Manual

Ray Newell

✳ THE CROWOOD PRESS

First published in 2023 by
The Crowood Press Ltd
Ramsbury, Marlborough
Wiltshire SN8 2HR

enquiries@crowood.com

www.crowood.com

© Ray Newell 2023

All rights reserved. No part of this publication may be reproduced or transmitted in any form or by any means, electronic or mechanical, including photocopy, recording, or any information storage and retrieval system, without permission in writing from the publishers.

British Library Cataloguing-in-Publication Data
A catalogue record for this book is available from the British Library.

ISBN 978 0 7198 4297 9

Ray Newell has asserted his right under the Copyright, Designs and Patents Act 1988 to be identified as the author of this work.

Acknowledgements
An undertaking on the scale described and illustrated in this publication would not have been possible without the invaluable assistance of a substantial number of people familiar with different facets of the restoration of classic cars and Morris Minors in particular. First and foremost are the principal volunteers from the Morris Minor Owners Club responsible for much of the work involved in stripping down, assessing, refurbishing and reassembling various components and in reassembling the restored bodyshell. In this regard thanks go to Michael Radford, Kevin Dickerson and Tom Morris, who at various stages were ably supported by other club members. Professional assistance and technical advice was willingly supplied by a wide range of specialists including Mark Boothman (bodywork repairs), Alan Scott (engine rebuild), Geoff Taylor (gearbox rebuild), Brian Wood (fuel system), Graham Ryder (electrical), Robert Ingram (paintwork), Newton Commercial staff (interior trim), Mark Havard (convertibles), Steve Foreman (Traveller wood), Chris Nuttall, Iain Mckenzie, Alex Wills (commercials) and Dave Lomax (polishing). A major element of this book is the photographic content and grateful thanks are extended to all those mentioned above who have contributed images along with Cameron Shaw, Andrew Stone, Dennis Saupe, Mark Watkins, Louis Clayton and Steven Parker. Special thanks are due to John Carroll, who undertook several photoshoots to provide images for specific chapters and the book cover and to Dee Hopkinson who assisted with the preparation of the manuscript.

Typeset by Simon and Sons
Cover design by Blue Sunflower Creative
Printed and bound in India by Replika Press Pvt Ltd

Contents

1	Introducing the Morris Minor	6
2	Bodywork Repairs	18
3	Paintwork	38
4	Engine Rebuild	47
5	Gearbox Rebuild	61
6	Suspension	81
7	Steering, Wheels and Tyres	88
8	Back Axle and Differential	93
9	Braking System	96
10	Electrical System	101
11	Fuel System	108
12	Interior Trim	128
13	Reassembly	145
14	Tourers and Convertibles	160
15	Light Commercials 1953–1971	168
16	Traveller Restoration	179
17	Return to the Road	189
18	Specifications	196
	Appendix: Specialist Directory	200
	Index	206

1
Introducing the Morris Minor

The post-war Morris Minor is regarded by many as the quintessential British car, much-loved and a firm favourite amongst classic car enthusiasts. It has been voted the nation's favourite classic car on numerous occasions and has a dedicated following in Britain as well as in many countries around the world, where it was either exported as a complete vehicle or assembled from completely knocked down (CKD) components. In total 1.6 million Morris Minors of all variants were produced from 1948 to 1971. It is a testimony to the durability of the original Alec Issigonis design and the care lavished upon them by generations of owners that so many survive 70-plus years after the first models left the production lines in Cowley, Oxfordshire, in 1948.

Inevitably, the ravages of time and the elements have taken their toll and many surviving vehicles need partial or complete restoration. The good news is that due to the enduring popularity of the model range and the large number of surviving vehicles, there is a thriving network of parts suppliers and specialist restorers and a dedicated club in the UK committed to ensuring the continued use and preservation of the Morris Minor. Clubs for enthusiasts of the cars exist throughout the world, and in specific countries parts are still being manufactured.

The aim of this book is to provide helpful advice and guidance for anyone undertaking the restoration of a Morris Minor. With the specific expertise of specialists and experienced enthusiasts, all the major elements of a restoration will be reviewed and with the aid of specially commissioned photographs and diagrams, key elements will be explained, step-by-step guidance offered and helpful advice given. There will be a focus on specific vehicles that have undergone restoration. One will feature prominently. It is an historically significant vehicle, being the last Morris Minor saloon to leave the production line. Its provenance is well documented. Over a period of four years FMT 265 J was painstakingly restored to original specification by enthusiasts from the Morris Minor Owners Club, supported at key points by specialist companies and individuals skilled in the restoration of classic cars. Many thought the car to be beyond repair when it was rediscovered in 2016. Its restoration proves that, however bad the condition of a Morris Minor, it is still possible with the will, the help of specialist knowledge and expertise plus adequate finance, to return the ultimate basket-case to roadworthy or as new condition.

The Morris Minor model range.

MODEL REVIEW

Selecting the Morris Minor to buy or restore will depend on several factors, the most pressing of which will be whether the vehicle will be used for occasional or regular use. During its 22-year production run a variety of models were produced including saloons, Tourers, convertibles, Travellers, vans and pick-ups.

THE MODEL RANGE

Morris Minor Series MM 1949–53

On introduction the Morris Minor was produced as a two-door saloon and an open topped Tourer. In its day it was a revolutionary vehicle, with many innovative design features including its monocoque body design, independent front suspension, small 14-inch wheels and a compact passenger compartment. Powered by a 918cc side-valve engine it was lauded for its driveability and roadholding. A four-door model was introduced in 1951. Early models are distinguished by the headlamps being positioned low down, but due to changes forced by American lighting regulations all models had redesigned front wings with repositioned headlamps from 1951 onwards. The Series MM remained in production until February 1953.

The Series MM models are sought after by collectors. This is particularly true in the case of the rarer Tourer models. However, in original specification and with a top speed of just 62mph (100km/h) these vehicles fall into the category of being more suited to occasional use rather than a daily driver.

Morris Minor Series II 1952–56

In 1952 the merger of Morris Motors Ltd and the Austin Motor Company Ltd to form the British Motor Corporation heralded a significant change for the Morris Minor range. Series II models were introduced and were fitted with the overhead-valve 803cc engine and corresponding gearbox used in the Austin A30. Apart from the mechanical changes and a distinguishing bonnet motif, early models retained all the rest of the Series MM specification until 1954, when a new-style dash with central speedometer and a revised front grille with slatted horizontal bars was introduced. Commercial variants in the form of vans and pick-ups were introduced in May 1953 and a Traveller's Car followed in October 1953. Production of Series II models ceased in 1956.

Morris Minor Series II models fall into the rare and collectable category. This is particularly true of the convertible, Traveller, and commercial variants. In original specification they are more suited to occasional use rather than everyday transport.

Morris Minor 1000 1956–62

The new Morris Minor models introduced at the 1956 Earl's Court Motor Show heralded a significant change from the earlier Series MM and Series II models. The new Morris Minor 1000 models differed significantly in appearance and in performance. Gone was the split front windscreen so reminiscent of pre-war cars. In its place was a revised roof pressing that incorporated a full-sized one-piece windscreen and a larger rear screen. Visibility was greatly improved. Other body changes included a change to the profile of the rear wings. Mechanical changes included a new 949cc engine and a much-improved gearbox. Elsewhere revisions to the interior specifications added to the general impression that this was a big step forward for the already successful Morris Minor. All the model variants were upgraded to

Series MM Tourer.

Early Morris Minor Series II van.

Introducing the Morris Minor

Late Morris Minor Series II Traveller.

Morris Minor 1000 two-door saloon.

Morris Minor 1000 four-door saloon.

the new specifications. Performance was significantly improved, with the 948cc engine producing 37bhp, greater acceleration between the gears and a respectable top speed of 74mph (119km/h). There were numerous changes to the interior trim specifications during the period 1957–61 for saloon, convertible and Traveller models.

The Morris 1000 models are more prolific and survive in greater numbers. The combination of improved performance and driveability makes them more useable as everyday transport. As such they are popular choices as restoration projects.

Morris 1000 1962–71

In 1962 all Morris Minor models were fitted with a larger 1098cc version of the A Series engine coupled with a gearbox with baulk ring synchromesh on second, third and top gears and larger front brakes. New light units including combined side/flasher lamps at the front, and larger combined tail, brake and indicator rear lamps on saloon and convertible models were introduced in 1963. However, the last major specification change occurred in 1964, when there was a complete revamp of the interior. A revised facia, improved instrumentation and a new style of interior trim transformed the saloon, convertible and Traveller models. Commercial variants incorporated the new style facia and in 1968 8cwt models with an increased payload were added to the range. The vehicles remained in production until 1969, when convertible models were discontinued. Saloons ceased production in 1970. Traveller and commercial models continued until 1971, by which time production had switched from Cowley in Oxfordshire to Adderley Park in Birmingham. The later Morris 1000 variants are the best of the range when it comes to selecting a Morris Minor suited to everyday use in standard specification. They are also the most prolific of the surviving models in the UK and tend to be the models for which there is a more plentiful supply of replacement parts as well as equipment for upgrading and modifying from original specification.

Introducing the Morris Minor

Morris Minor 1000 pick-up.

Morris Minor 1000 four-door saloon.

Morris Minor 1000 convertible.

BUYER'S CHECKLIST

Anyone contemplating buying a Morris Minor who is unfamiliar with the various models would be well advised to seek assistance beforehand either in the form of a knowledgeable mechanic, a club official or someone experienced in owning and running a Morris Minor or other classic car. The adage 'Buy in haste repent at leisure' is one worth bearing in mind. Appearances can be deceptive and, in the case of the Morris Minor, many prospective buyers have been taken in by pleasing external appearances and what at first glance looks like a sound vehicle. The reputation of the Morris Minor as a sound, reliable and economical vehicle much loved by generations needs to be tempered with the reality that all Morris Minors are now over half a century old and that the ravages of time will have taken their toll on many components and in particular on parts of the bodyshell, which may have undergone a multitude of repairs in the past.

The following guide is included as a prelude to the detailed restoration information contained in the rest of this publication. Further detailed information for specific models including convertibles, Travellers and commercial variants is contained within the relevant chapters for those models.

External Panels

External panels including front and rear wings, doors, boot (trunk) lid, bonnet (hood), plus front and rear valances should be carefully examined for signs of rust, previous repairs, accident damage, metal distortion and overuse of body filler.

Front Wings

Front wings are prone to rusting around the headlamp unit and on the vertical back edge. This is due to dirt and traffic grime being trapped above the headlamp bowls and between the back edge of the wing, pressing on high headlamp models. Repairs are possible, but in most cases for later cars replacement wings, which are readily available, are the easiest option. For early low headlamp models where

Introducing the Morris Minor

Morris Minor 1000 Traveller.

Morris Minor 1000 6cwt van.

occur. Genuine metal replacements are difficult to source, repairs can be difficult due to the thinness of the metal and the tendency for distortion to occur when welding. Glass-fibre replacements are an option for later models.

Doors

Doors on all models are prone to rusting out on the bottom edge. Tell-tale signs of unseen problems are bubbling paintwork on the outer surface of the bottom edge of the door. Visual checks of the underside of the door bottom are advised as these tend to rot out. The absence of a metal runner to locate a rubber strip on the bottom edge of the door could indicate that previous repairs have been carried out. New old stock replacement doors do still come to light and replacement door bottom repair panels are available if the door is in serious need of repair. Metal fatigue in the form of a split is sometimes evident on the inside top edge of the door adjacent to the quarter light.

Boot Lid (Trunk)

Though similar in profile, boot lids differ between split windscreen models and later Morris 1000 models, particularly with regard to the locating points for badging. Differences also exist between early and later cars in relation to the locking boot handles, the types of seals used, as well as the types of stay used to keep the lid in the open position. Later Morris 1000 models have a self-locking mechanism in the boot stay. The main problem associated with the boot lid is the tendency for it to rot out on the bottom edge. Tell-tale signs are bubbling paintwork. A bottom edge repair panel is available.

Underside

Detailed examination of the underside of the car is strongly advised, provided of course it is safe to do so. An examination of the vehicle while it is on a ramp at a local garage or workshop would be the ideal scenario, but if this is not an option then preliminary examination while the car is still on four wheels on the ground should focus on the following areas.

replacements are well-nigh impossible to find, repairs will almost certainly be required.

Rear Wings

On rear wings the common places for rust damage are on the top edge, where the wing is bolted to the body and on the outer bottom edge. The bottom edge is also prone to splitting. Early Series MM and Series II saloon and convertible models have a different, higher cut profile to later Morris 1000 models. Later replacement Morris 1000 wings for all models are readily available.

Front and Rear Valances

The front and rear valances differ in profile between early Series MM model, two-piece valances, later Series MM and Series II valances and Morris 1000 valances. All are prone to damage and distortion and with water ingress between the chrome bumper blades and the metal valance, rusting does

Introducing the Morris Minor

Austin 8cwt pick-up.

Front Chassis Members

These run either side of the engine and should be examined for metal damage caused by inappropriate jacking up of the vehicle as well as evidence of previous repairs. In addition, care must be taken not to be deceived by concealment of rust and or body filler with the generous use of underseal. The presence of sound metal can be detected by tapping the length of the chassis member with a light hammer. A sharp pinging sound denotes sound metal while a dull thudding sound should set alarms bells ringing. Full and half-length chassis members are available as replacement items.

Central Crossmember

When viewed from the underside it is advisable to examine the bottom edge of the crossmember that runs side to side across the centre of the vehicle. Take note of any signs of delamination on the bottom edge and on later Morris 1000 models check for the presence of the jacking points, which should be present on the outer edge of the crossmembers on each side of the vehicle. Note if any previous repairs have been carried out and pay particular attention to the upper edge of the crossmember where it meets the floor. Full- and half-sized replacement parts are available to repair or replace the crossmember. Such work should be viewed as a major undertaking requiring structural bracing to avoid body flexing and distortion.

Outer Sills

The outer sills that run either side of the car should be checked for signs of metal fatigue and/or rust on the underside. A visual inspection should be followed by gently applying pressure, initially by hand, to test for signs of weakness. In an ideal world inspection of the inner box section would reveal the strength or otherwise of the sill areas. However, as this requires the removal of the cover kick panels, this would not normally be practicable on a general inspection prior to purchase.

Rear Spring Hanger Mounting Points

The front and rear spring hanger mounting points on either side of the vehicle should be examined for signs of previous repairs as well as any indication of metal fatigue, particularly where the mounting points attach to the floor area. Replacement spring hanger mounting units are available.

Inner Boot Floor

The inner boot floor area is prone to rusting due to the ingress of water.

Areas to check for signs of rust or weakness

1 Inner boot floor
2 Outer sills
3 Spring hangers (front and rear)
4 Central crossmember
5 Front chassis legs

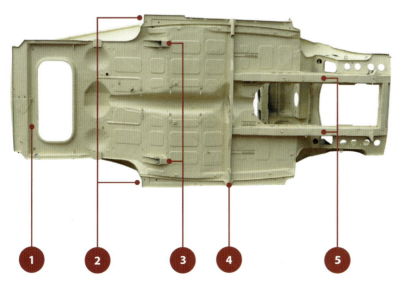

Key areas to examine for evidence of weakness and/or previous repair work. Image is of a 'new old stock' two-door saloon bodyshell.

11

Introducing the Morris Minor

Area prone to rusting

1 Rear spring hanger mounting point
2 Rear inner wheel arch, top edge
3 Rear quarter panel, bottom edge
4 Inner sill strengthening panel
5 Inner sill to inner floor area
6 A-post area
7 Chassis leg

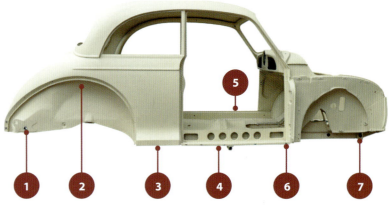

Image of side view of bodyshell with important areas to check identified.

A key area to check for damage, weakness and or rust.

If there is evidence of weakness and previous repairs around the top edge of either end of the crossmember on the floor area inside the car, further investigation may be needed on the underside.

Problems may be apparent in the rear corners and it is worth checking for signs of weakness. Beware of copious amounts of underseal having been applied as this may simply be concealing underlying problems.

Rear Inner Wings

Examination of the top edge of the rear inner wings is advisable, particularly where the cages for the captive nuts are located. Repair panels are available.

Inner Floor Area

Time spent examining the inner floor of the car is time well spent. Initial checks should include checking whether, regardless of condition, the carpets and underfelt are dry. It is advisable to lift the carpets and check the outer edges where the floor meets the inner sills and the front inner wheel arches. Look for signs of rusting as well as previous repairs and check the rigidity of the inner sills by pressing firmly on the lower area where they meet the floor. Also check the seat belt anchorage points and assess how secure they are. Any signs of weakness should be carefully noted. Next tilt the front seats forward and lift the carpet to expose the floor area above the central crossmember.

Check for signs of rusting as well as indications of previous repairs and, if present, assess how well they have been carried out. Finally lift the rear carpets. Examine the back edge of the floor area for signs of rusting as well as any indication of weakness above the front rear spring hanger mounting points.

Engine Bay

The engine bay area is sometimes overlooked when it comes to finding structural weaknesses. However, it is worth checking the condition of the inner wings, particularly the back corner where they meet the bulkhead and where the joints are on the upper part of the flat side panels. The condition of the lower tie plates that sit above the chassis legs should be noted, along with the front crossmember, which runs beneath the radiator. The good news is that replacement repair panels are available.

Interior Trim

A wide range of interiors were fitted to the Morris Minor range throughout its 22-year production run. If vehicle originality is a priority for any potential purchaser, then it is imperative that some preliminary work is undertaken to ascertain the exact specification of the interior fitments before viewing any potential purchase. Replacement interiors made to original specification are available for all models. This includes seats, door cards, side trims, carpets and all necessary fittings. New headlinings are available for all models between 1954 and 1971. The material for the rexine-covered wooden headlinings fitted to pre-1954 saloons, Travellers and commercial vehicles is no longer available.

Mechanical Condition – Engine

The range of engines fitted to the Morris Minor during its 22-year production run are renowned for their durability. Nevertheless, it is worth carrying out some basic checks before purchase. Given that the last Morris Minors were manufactured in 1971 and that some that survive fall into the 'barn find' category, the advice that follows

Inner box section. Cover plates need to be removed to expose this critical structural part of all Morris Minors.

Checks for previous repairs should be made around the area shown here.

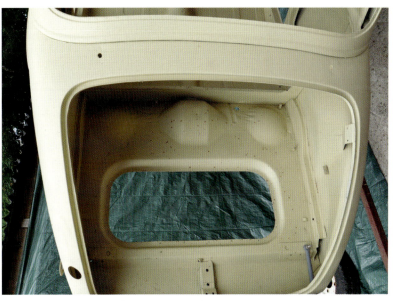

This area of the car is worthy of close examination, for the reasons stated.

Introducing the Morris Minor

Inner floor area showing original pressings, inner sills and front wheel arches.

Original engine bay and bulkhead pressings.

should be tempered with the knowledge that the cars might not have been in use for many years. As such, checks on the engine might be limited to checking the oil level and determining if the engine is turning freely by using a starting handle. For cars that are in regular use, then more extensive mechanical checks are advisable. These include removing the oil filler cap and looking for signs of a white 'mayonnaise'-type deposit on the inside of it. This may be an indication of a leaking head gasket. Uneven running when the engine is idling is worthy of further investigation, as this could be linked to a number of possible causes including incorrect carburettor setting, timing issues or, more seriously, burnt-out exhaust valves.

A typical failing on the 'A' series engines is a noisy timing chain. The sound of this is concentrated at the front of the engine and is caused by the timing chain becoming stretched and worn over time. Though annoying, it is not usually detrimental to the engine. Other noises to listen out for are deep rumbling noises, which could indicate main bearing problems, repetitive tapping coming from the top end of the engine, which could indicate worn valve gear, and excessive exhaust noise, which could be caused by loose manifold fittings or a broken seal on the exhaust down-pipe. Checks should also be made for oil leaks as well as signs of excessive blue or black smoke from the exhaust. Blue is likely to be caused by worn piston rings or valve guides, while black is likely to be linked to incorrect fuel mixture settings.

Suspension

With each of the front wheels turned outwards it is advisable to check the rubber bushes fitted to the suspension and the tie rods. Look for signs of splitting, excessive wear or perishing. Whilst in the vicinity look for any tell-tale signs on the top links that might indicate if the suspension has been greased recently, as long-term lack of maintenance can result in the suspension collapsing. Check the shock absorbers front and rear for signs of fluid leakage and efficient working. A quick check is possible by applying firm downward pressure on the top of each wing and seeing how much resistance there is before the suspension returns to its 'at rest' position. As a rough guide any more than one and a half bounces and the shock absorbers will need to be replaced.

Other Mechanical Checks

If the vehicle is capable of being taken for a test drive then the operation of the gearbox, the ease of using the clutch, the directness of the steering and the efficiency of the brakes will become apparent. Usual failings with the gearbox relate to jumping out of second gear and difficulty engaging first gear (which does not have synchromesh). Brakes should be checked for excessive travel on the pedal before engagement and whether the vehicle pulls up in a straight line when the brakes are applied. The efficiency of the handbrake and its operation should be assessed. Any more than five clicks to engage fully will need further investigation and adjustment.

Final External Checks

Assessing the paintwork and external brightwork on the car is a major consideration in any purchase. Given the age of the vehicles it is likely that the paintwork will not be original, so it is imperative to examine the quality of the respray and to look for imperfections including signs of overspray, unevenness on specific panels and variations in colour if only a partial respray has been undertaken. Check too, for the quality of replacement panels, including the use of glass-fibre panels, signs of previous repairs and the degree to which body filler has been used (the use of a small magnet is useful in this regard as adhesion will be less where filler has been used). Finally, assess the condition of the chrome fittings and brightwork. Re-chroming is expensive and, although replacement parts are available, costs can mount up.

The last Morris Minor saloon in November 1970.

FMT 265 J: THE LAST MORRIS MINOR SALOON

Morris Minor saloon production ended on 12 November 1970. The occasion was marked both by management and assembly line workers when the obligatory photographs were taken as the last two-door saloon rolled off the production line at the Cowley works in Oxfordshire. The event was widely reported in the press at the time, but no effort was made to preserve the vehicle that signalled the end of saloon production after a run of 22 years. Instead, like its predecessors, it was despatched into the dealer network and, although officially authenticated as the last saloon, it entered private ownership. That may well have been that, but in 1994 after almost a quarter of a century of use it re-emerged in Wales and was offered for sale.

Despite the best efforts of the vendors, the opportunity to save and preserve the vehicle as a part of British motoring history was spurned. Eventually the vehicle returned to private ownership where it remained until 2016. Sadly, due to unforeseen circumstances, the car remained unused for almost twenty years and in that time succumbed to the elements and deteriorated dramatically. When it was eventually acquired by new owner John Ashmore in 2016, it soon became evident that restoring the vehicle would be too much of a challenge for him personally. In an attempt to see the vehicle preserved and at least returned to roadworthy condition, he offered to sell the vehicle to the UK-based Morris Minor Owners Club, on the understanding that every effort would be made to secure its future.

Decisions, Decisions…!

With any restoration a multitude of decisions need to be made in determining how far to go, how many of the original components to retain, how much of the work to outsource and ultimately how much to spend. Ordinarily, this will be at the discretion of an individual vehicle owner. In the case of FMT 265 J the situation was much more complicated. Given the historical significance of the vehicle and the fact that its ownership did not rest with an individual owner but with an organisation serviced by a committee responsible to a wider membership, decision-making was set to be a challenge.

From the outset there was a divergence of views about what to do with the car. These ranged from keeping it in its 'as found' condition with only essential repairs being undertaken. This would be in order to return the car to a serviceable condition in order for it to be utilised as an exhibition vehicle for the benefit of club members and the general public. An alternative view was to restore the vehicle to 'as new' condition, while retaining and refurbishing as many of the original components as possible.

In the event, circumstances conspired to allow a combination of both viewpoints to be accommodated. As will be seen in the pages that follow, an extensive restoration was undertaken

As found in 2016 in need of complete restoration.

and comprehensively documented. However, in the first eighteen months of ownership, limited recommissioning was undertaken with priority being given to essential welding to stabilise the structure of the vehicle sufficient for it to be moved freely and exhibited safely. In 2018 the project was subject to major review due to the availability of substantial funding courtesy of a generous bequest from a former member of the Morris Minor Owners Club. Plan 'B' was now a feasible option and, using a combination of the skills of suitably experienced volunteer members and recognised specialists, work commenced to totally restore the vehicle to a condition similar to that when it left the production line in 1970.

In large part what followed is illustrated and explained in this manual with specific aspects of the restoration being subject to in-depth review and analysis sufficient to be an aid to would-be restorers. Where appropriate references have been made to other Morris Minor models pre-dating FMT 265 J and separate chapters highlighting aspects of restoration applicable to Traveller, convertible and commercial models have been included. It is hoped that the shared knowledge, as well as providing an opportunity to benefit from the experience of others, will provide a renewed confidence to would-be restorers and that as a result many more Morris Minors will be preserved and continue in use for many years to come.

BRITISH LEYLAND (AUSTIN-MORRIS) LIMITED
Sales Division

LONGBRIDGE BIRMINGHAM ENGLAND B31 2TB · TELEPHONE 021-475 2101 · TELEGRAMS SPEEDILY BIRMINGHAM TELEX · TELEX 33491

your ref
our ref

26 January 1971

Morris Minor 1000 2 door Saloon
Colour: Trafalgar Blue
Chassis number: 1288377
Engine number: 65314
To Invoice: 1671405

This is to Certify that the above was the last Minor 1000 Saloon produced for Sale at Cowley on 12th November, 1970.

C N EDMUNDS
MANAGER FLEET OPERATIONS

A SUBSIDIARY OF BRITISH LEYLAND MOTOR CORPORATION LIMITED

Contemporary official authentication added to the provenance of the vehicle.

2
Bodywork Repairs

INITIAL ASSESSMENT

Detailed examination of the last saloon revealed some positive aspects that added to the provenance of the vehicle. Despite 46 years having elapsed since the vehicle left the production line, most of the original mechanical components remained intact. Checks with factory records via a Heritage Certificate obtained from the British Motor Industry Heritage Trust revealed matching numbers for the engine and back axle. Alas, the same could not be said for the gearbox, as at some stage a replacement gold seal unit had been fitted. Closer examination showed that although in a poor state of repair the outer panels and all interior fitments were as they would have been when the vehicle left the factory. No modifications or significant additions had been made to the original specification for a late Morris Minor 1000 two-door saloon, except for a Smith's period rear window demister.

On later Morris Minor 1000 models the chassis number, apart from appearing on the chassis plate attached to the bulkhead, was also stamped into the floor pan on the driver's side on right-hand-drive models. As this area is prone to rusting out, it is frequently the case that the floor panel has either been replaced or repaired with the subsequent loss of the stamped number. Remarkably, in the case of the last saloon the floor area was one of the strongest parts of the car and, although repairs were needed to adjacent panels, the stamped number had survived intact and was clearly visible for all to see. This proved to be a real bonus and, as well as adding to the provenance of the vehicle, it provided further encouragement to ensure its survival and eventual restoration.

At certain stages the viability of restoring the original bodyshell was called into question due to the extent of the rust and corrosion present throughout the metal structure. Words alone cannot convey the severity of the rust damage on key structural parts of the bodyshell and on some of the outer panels. The adage 'A picture is worth a thousand words' was never more apt than at this stage in the assessment process. The images (opposite) give a better impression of the enormity of the task that lay ahead to return the vehicle to a structurally sound condition.

Initial assessment begins.

Bodywork Repairs

The structural integrity of the car was compromised by the extent of the rot on the front chassis leg.

Central crossmember. Not entirely a lost cause!

Engine bay tie plate. Detached!

Jacking point and outer sill area. Cause for concern.

Front suspension. In imminent danger of total collapse.

Rear quarter panel. Serious corrosion fully exposed when viewed from the underside.

Rear spring hanger. Little room for optimism when the extent of the damage shown here was revealed.

PLAN OF ACTION

The severity of the corrosion throughout the whole of the bodyshell and the outer panels and the extent of the repairs required far exceeded initial expectations. Clearly the knowledge and expertise of an experienced welder and classic car restorer would be needed, not only to assess the true extent of the work required and the feasibility of retaining the structural integrity of the original bodyshell, but to carry out the work.

The task was entrusted to Mark Boothman, who, after an initial assessment, agreed a phased approach to complete repairs necessary to stabilise the bodyshell sufficient for it to be moved as a rolling shell without causing any further structural damage.

Bodywork Repairs

WORKSHOP FACILITIES

As an experienced restorer of vintage and classic vehicles, Mark not only possessed the knowledge of how best to set about the various tasks that would be involved in all phases of the restoration of the Morris Minor bodyshell and associated panels but had the equipment and tools to hand in a fully equipped workshop complete with a two-post lift.

Ever-conscious of health and safety in the workshop, particularly when welding, Mark endorsed the following helpful guidelines.

ABOUT WELDING

In the modern era the type of welding favoured for welding steel in automotive repairs is Metal Inert Gas (MIG) welding. MIG welding requires a high degree of skill and a considerable deal of practice to become competent in creating effective, strong and neat welds. It is beyond the scope of this publication to provide detailed guidelines, or to provide advice for the enthusiastic novice wanting to tackle MIG welding as part of a home restoration.

For anyone wishing to develop welding skills, lots of opportunities exist at Adult Learning Centres and Colleges specialising in vocational courses where, under the guidance and tuition offered by skilled and experienced tutors, adult students of differing levels of competence are catered for. Courses ranging from familiarisation courses of twelve hours' duration over a six-week period to those of longer duration leading to nationally approved awards are offered. These longer courses tend to have broader-based course content covering the whole spectrum of welding techniques including MIG, TIG, gas welding, brazing and spot welding.

MIG welding involves a technique that utilises electrical current in conjunction with a welding torch into which a continuous reel of steel wire is fed to a shrouded tip. Before being operated the item being welded must be earthed via the welding machine. This creates a circuit and

Specialist Tools and Equipment

- 250 amp MIG welder
- 0.8mm MIG welding wire
- Plasma cutter
- Reciprocating air saw
- 4½-inch grinder
- 1mm slitting discs
- 5mm grinding discs
- G clamps
- Mole grips
- Spot weld removal tool
- Joggling tool
- Punch and flange tool
- Door aperture bracing jig

Welding-related Health and Safety Issues

- Always disconnect the vehicle battery prior to commencing welding.
- Never weld in an area where there are flammable materials, such as petrol.
- Empty and remove the fuel tank and/or fuel lines prior to undertaking welding repairs.
- Always remove carpets, underlay coverings, adhesive sound-deadening coverings and interior upholstery before commencing welding repairs.
- Always weld in dry conditions and keep trailing leads off damp floors.
- Always wear protective clothing. Wear leather welding gloves and ensure arms are fully covered. Wear a hat or cap.
- Always use an approved type of welding mask.
- Have safety glasses/goggles available for use when using grinding equipment.
- Always work in a well-ventilated but draught-free area and avoid breathing in fumes created by the welding process.
- Be aware of the potential dangers of both welding and grinding sparks and the damage they can cause to paintwork and glass either on the vehicle being worked on or to adjacent vehicles.
- Always have an appropriate type of fire extinguisher close at hand.

Small and compact Snap-On Spot Weld removal tool.

Bodywork Repairs

> **Tip:** Where welds need to be ground back, care needs to be exercised so as not to inadvertently weaken the metal in the immediate vicinity of the weld by being too enthusiastic with whatever grinding materials are being used.

BODYWORK REPAIRS

From the outset it was obvious that a serious amount of fabrication and the fitting of numerous repair panels would be required to return the bodyshell and some of the body panels to a sound condition. In fact, at one point the idea of sourcing one of the known surviving 'new' unused bodyshells (*see* Chapter 1) was considered but quickly rejected, due to the historical nature of the vehicle in question. While recognising that large parts of the bodyshell would need replacing, the priority remained to salvage as much of the original metalwork as possible.

As outlined in Chapter 1, would-be restorers of Morris Minors are in the fortunate position of having ready access to an extensive range of repair panels, many of which are referred to elsewhere in the text. Where specific panels are not available, as in the case of some parts for commercial vehicles for example, specialist companies and individuals are available to provide a bespoke service to fabricate small batches of specific parts.

It is worth noting that just because a replacement panel is available for a particular model it should not be assumed that it will be a tailor-made fit. In many cases the panel will have to be modified or customised to meet the requirements of the repair being undertaken. This proved to be the case during the restoration of the last saloon. There were a limited number of occasions when the use of ill-fitting repair panels was declined in favour of fabricated purpose-built replacements.

Methodology

Each restorer will have their own preference for the type of welding best suited to their skill set and for the techniques to use when completing specific repairs. Understandably, certain

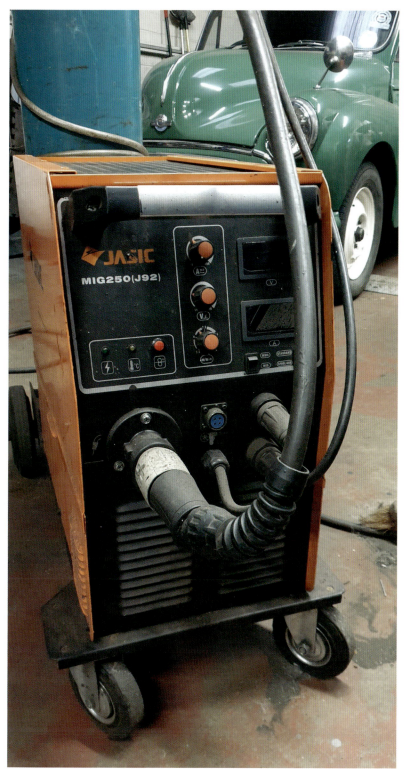

Jasic MIG 250 J92 welding machine.

allows an arc to be created when the trigger is operated. The arc is shrouded in an inert gas, usually a mixture of argon and CO_2, which prevents the molten metal from oxidising and aids the extent of penetration in the weld.

MIG welding has the advantage of providing a degree of flexibility in temperature control with heat being directed in a more localised way. This has the advantage of reducing the risk of panel distortion. MIG welding is also useful for plug welding, which can act as an alternative to spot welding. Its main advantage is the potential for strong, neat welds. In the case of the last saloon MIG welding was used extensively to fit both manufactured and fabricated replacement panels and metalwork.

Bodywork Repairs

techniques will be repeated on many occasions during a full restoration.

In illustrating the extent of the repairs undertaken and describing some of the techniques adopted for this restoration there will inevitably be some repetition, but it is hoped that the approach adopted to completing some very challenging restoration tasks will provide an insight into the art of the possible, while at the same time giving encouragement to would-be restorers wishing to tackle individual repairs or to take on a more extensive restoration.

Work Begins

In order for the most essential structural repairs to stabilise the very weak bodyshell to take place, the engine and gearbox were removed, and the front suspension partially dismantled to allow full access to both front chassis legs. Prior to any structural work taking place, the tie-rod bars were disconnected from the chassis leg mounting point and the torsion bars removed completely but with the splines retained 'in situ' at both the front and rear.

Tip: If disconnecting the torsion bars fully, clearly mark each one as being from the left or right of the vehicle. If being refitted, they **must not** be interchanged. It is also useful to mark the position of the splines for realignment purposes if they are subsequently separated.

The doors were left in position to assist with the rigidity of the bodyshell and, once positioned on the two post lift, the underside of the vehicle was supported by adjustable 'underhoist' stands.

Front Chassis Leg Replacement

Before any structural components were removed, time was taken to identify, measure and record details of specific reference points for alignment and fitting purposes. Apart from establishing whether part, or all, of each of the chassis legs would need to be replaced, measurements were taken from key points including the position of the engine mounting tower bolts and the eye-bolt mounting point. Options available included replacing the front sections of each chassis leg or fitting a full-sized replacement. Half- and full-sized chassis legs were readily available. Even though the front sections of both chassis legs were in a terrible state, the rear sections, which had gained some protection from the elements by being covered in oil, were intrinsically strong. As removing both chassis legs in their entirety may have further compromised the structure of the bodyshell, it was decided that replacing half of each chassis leg would be sufficient.

Tip: Caution needs to be exercised when removing panels not to remove too many at the same time, as doing so may cause the bodyshell to flex.

Under normal circumstances removing a chassis leg would entail drilling out a substantial number of spot welds located along the top edge and where it comes into contact with other body pressings. Due to the amount of corrosion this task was made easier as the effectiveness of many of the spot welds had been considerably reduced.

Having first identified the extent of the half chassis leg and clearly marked the maximum length on what was left of the original, a slitting disc was used to cut along the top edge on both sides initially until sound metal was encountered. After checking twice, the vertical cut was made where the join would occur when the new chassis leg section was fitted. However, there was much work to do before that could occur, as the rest of the metalwork immediately above where the new chassis leg would fit was intrinsically weak. Repair panels had to be fabricated and fitted and all remaining fragments of metal where the previous cutting had occurred had to be removed to provide a clean flat surface for the new panel to fit against.

A considerable amount of measuring and alignment checking was undertaken before the replacement chassis leg section was offered up, clamped in position and tacked using the MIG welder before being seam welded. The whole process was repeated on the other side before attention turned to installing replacement tie plates in the engine bay.

New old stock half chassis leg required some refurbishment before fitting.

Replacement chassis leg aligned and clamped in position.

Bodywork Repairs

Additional fabrication was required in the area above the chassis leg.

The front half of both chassis legs was replaced along with the tie plates.

and G clamps were then deployed to hold all the panels in the required position. With the bolts in the engine mounting apertures tightened, the panels were tacked, prior to seam welds being made on both sides of each crossmember to secure the tie plates in position. Due to other repairs being needed to the front inner wing panels and the 'turrets' beneath the bulkhead, the task of attaching the tie plates to the inner wings was temporarily put on hold.

Inner Floor and Crossmember Repairs

One of the positive aspects of the bodyshell was the strength of the inner floors. Some minor reinforcement was required at the edges where the floor meets the inner sills, and in the area adjacent to the front inner wheel arch on the driver's side. Due to the inherent strength of the rest of the floor area, the localised weak metal was cut out and a replacement panel made using specialist tools, including joggling and punch and flange tools. It was then fitted in place by the favoured method of using self-tapping screws before being seam welded in position.

Despite extensive corrosion at either end of the crossmember on the underside, the central part remained unaffected. Close examination of the floor area above the crossmember along with the central section on the underside prompted the decision to limit replacement to the end sections. The corroded parts were separated from the underside of the floor by using a

Tie Plates

With the chassis legs correctly aligned and welded in place, attention switched to accurately locating the tie plates and the front crossmember in position. As a starting point the apertures for the engine mounting towers were used to temporarily locate each of the tie plates. Further alignment checks were made to ensure accuracy where they fitted on top of each of the chassis legs, where they butted up to the respective inner wheel arch panel and their proximity to the front crossmember panel. Mole grips

Regular spirit level measurements provided reassurance that things were properly aligned.

Bodywork Repairs

A variety of clamps were used to secure panels in position prior to welding.

Significant progress in restoring the structural integrity of the car was achieved by having new chassis legs, tie plates and a front crossmember in place.

Fabricated panel for floor repair.

slitting disc. Any remaining metal fragments were removed using a 5mm grinding disc to create a smooth clean surface on the underside of the floor in readiness for the replacement sections to be attached. Care was taken to use the measurements taken previously using the apertures on the crossmember as reference points before locating the exact position where the diagonal cuts were to be made on the original crossmember prior to the new sections being butt welded in place. The relevant measurements were checked at least twice before holes were drilled in the top edges of the replacement crossmember end sections and self-tapping screws inserted in the floor from the underside to secure them in position prior to seam welding on the top edge and butt welding at the diagonal join. With welding complete the screws were removed, the holes plug welded and the edges ground back. At this stage the jacking points were not fitted, as further work was required on the sill areas and this needed to be completed before they were aligned and attached to the crossmember. It is worth noting that the jacking point ends of the crossmember must be positioned beneath the bottom of the sills in order for them to be supported.

Sill and Underfloor Areas

In spite of all the rust and corrosion and the fact that even the kick plates covering the front inner sills had rotted through in parts, the inner boxing plates had remained intact and proved to be in very sound condition. The same proved to be the case with the inner sills, which, apart from the occasional sign of weakness where they joined the inner floor and more serious rot at the base of the A posts, remained structurally sound, thus providing a solid base to work from. Some reinforcement was added to the base of the boxing plates and with plenty of sound metal to work to, new sill extensions were fitted and new panels were added to the underfloor area on both sides.

Rear Quarter Panels

The rear quarter panel area on the driver's side was in a very distressed state, particularly when viewed from the underside. Major reconstruction was required using a combination of fabricated sections and readily available repair panels, including an inner sill repair panel, an undersill panel and an outer bottom half repair panel. Given the severity of the corrosion, the original outer curved panel was cut out to allow sufficient access to the inner sill panel, which had become detached at the bottom

Bodywork Repairs

Areas of the inner floor and sill were in sound condition.

Diagonal butt weld option was adopted to provide additional strength.

Rigidity restored. Jacking points to be added later.

Boxing plate showing repairs.

Boxing plate with new under-sill panel fitted.

Outer edge of floor repair.

Front under-floor repair.

edge. Repairs were made sufficient to restore sound metal to which the inner sill repair panel was welded. Attention also had to be paid to the bottom of the 'B' post where it joins the sill. A fabricated repair section was welded in place, with careful checks made subsequently to ensure that when fitted, alignment of the outer repair panel was not compromised. Due to the proximity of the front spring hanger mounting point to the area being worked on, it was decided to fit a replacement item in conjunction with the rear quarter panel repairs.

Important note: *Extra care needs to be taken when locating the spring hanger mounting point. There is no margin*

Bodywork Repairs

for error in positioning the repair panel and in locating it in relation to its counterpart. Precise alignment is critical for the refitting of the rear springs.

Critical to the success of fitting the rear quarter repair panel was its alignment with the profile of the front edge of the rear wing and the back edge of the door. Mole grips were used to secure the bottom edge in position, while four self-tapping screws were deployed to hold the flat edges of the upper part of the panel and the new section in position in readiness for the MIG welder to be deployed to weld them together. Special care had to be taken to avoid any distortion on the panels. This was definitely a task for an experienced welder well versed in temperature control when MIG welding. With the screws removed and the holes plug welded, the area was carefully ground back using a grinding disc to begin with and a flat disc to finish off in order to leave a smooth, even finish.

The extent of the repairs required to the inner rear quarter panel revealed.

Rear quarter panel underside panel in position.

Panel alignment with underside repair panel.

Rear quarter panel secured in place in preparation for welding.

Rear quarter repair panel aligned with the base of the repaired B post.

CHEMICAL TREATMENT

Following the essential repairs necessary to provide structural rigidity to the bodyshell, the decision was made to have the car and all associated body panels chemically treated to remove the rust in readiness for further repairs and painting. Various options including bead or sand blasting were considered but rejected due to the extent of the rust present in all areas of the bodyshell, the risk of causing further panel damage and the anticipated difficulty of adequately accessing the hidden areas of the vehicle.

SPL (Surfacing Processing Limited) was consulted and engaged to undertake the work. Comprehensive advice relating to the options available as well as their specific requirements prior to the vehicle and panels being delivered to their premises in Dudley, West Midlands, was greatly appreciated.

With the new front chassis legs, tie plates and front crossmember fitted to the engine bay along with repairs to the central crossmember and outer sill areas completed, it was felt that no additional bracing or strengthening was necessary. To minimise the risk of damage in transit, the bonnet, boot lid and front panel were fitted to the bodyshell while the front and rear wings and both doors were transported separately. On arrival at SPL the bodyshell was manually lifted by hand and placed on a wooden pallet before being placed in a specially manufactured, protected process cradle in readiness for the various treatments to be undertaken. The panels were treated separately.

SPL pride themselves on having developed a unique four-stage process to thoroughly clean and chemically

Bodywork Repairs

Last saloon en route to SPL for chemical dipping.

Bodyshell devoid of rust and ready for further repairs.

Weaknesses in the engine bay area were exposed...

The extent of the rust removed fully exposed in the inner rear wing areas.

... and in the 'A' post.

... as well as the inner boot floor.

treat automotive bodyshells and their associated components. The process begins by using an advanced dehydration technique in which organic coatings such as underseal, filler, mastic sealants, adhesives and anti-vibration or sound deadening materials are broken down and denatured. This is followed by an immersion process using an alkaline hydrocarbon solution, which removes any remnants from the dehydration process as well as paint, grease, oil or carbon. This stage is completed by rinsing using a high-pressure jet.

Bodywork Repairs

With all contaminants removed the serious business of rust removal commences by immersing the bodyshell in a dilute solution of inhibited phosphoric acid. The inhibitors prevent the acid from attacking the mild steel while allowing the solution to tackle whatever corrosion is present. The process is aided by tilting the cradle that secures the bodyshell backwards and forwards within the solution to ensure that all areas are successfully treated.

The last stage in the process is termed the 'passivation rinse'. This involves subjecting the shell to an advanced agitated alkaline neutralisation and passivation process, which leaves the bodyshell in a bright preserved condition. This is followed by the application of a high-pressure manual wash containing a neutralising preservative. Care is taken at this stage to make sure that it is directed towards any folds, seams, or recesses in the bodyshell. The same process is applied to other body panels or components.

With the process complete, the bodyshell was ready for further repairs to be undertaken. The effectiveness of the treatment was evident and, as SPL staff had advised at the outset, while the process will not damage the steel it will show up evidence of previous repairs and expose the areas that have been subject to corrosion. While this was plain to see, the extent of the areas affected was alarming. On the positive side of things, the process did at least expose the areas of sound metal where welding repairs could be undertaken.

SPL offers an additional service in regard to protecting treated bodyshells and panels. With the cleaning process complete, the option of applying E Coat protection (electrophoretic paint) is available to all customers. Bodyshell and/or additional components are subjected to an eleven-stage cleaning and pre-treatment process that deposits a corrosion-resistant layer of Zn/Mn/Ni phosphate before being immersed into PPG Electrophoretic Epoxy Primer, which is electrically bonded to the surface prior to being cured in an oven set at 185°C for 45 minutes. The result is an impermeable, durable primer finish compatible with all brands of automotive-approved refinishing paint systems.

In the case of the last saloon, this option was not taken up due to the extensive welding repairs that still needed to be undertaken.

Additional Problems Revealed

On return from SPL the effects of the chemical treatment and derusting process were plain to see. The advance information that indicated the aggressive nature of the chemical and derusting process proved to be entirely accurate. Fortunately, with the repairs already completed and lots of new metal introduced, the basic structure of the bodyshell remained unaffected. However, as anticipated any remaining areas of weakness were exposed, particularly at the rear of the vehicle. Further work and yet another reappraisal were required.

Rear Inner Wing and Boot Area

If the extent of the corrosion in the rear inner wing area and around the rear spring hanger mounting points looked ominous before the bodyshell went for chemical dipping, it looked even more challenging afterwards. A measure of just how challenging, was that twenty hours would be spent reconstructing both inner wings and the surrounding area including the inner boot floor.

In the event there were four elements to the repairs needed: replacing the rear section of both inner wings; installing upper flange panels; fitting rear spring hanger repair kits; and reinstating a replacement inner boot floor panel and an outer aperture panel. The reconstruction and alignment of the new metalwork needed in this area of the bodyshell was a complicated undertaking and required a significant amount of forward planning and careful sequencing of tasks involved.

As the images below illustrate, work commenced by adding structural rigidity to the inner sections on both sides of the vehicle by inserting rear spring hanger repair panels using what remained of the original metalwork as a reference point. Careful measurement and alignment once again became a priority, not only for the positioning of the inner wing repair panels but for the rear spring hanger mounting points.

So far as the inner wing panels were concerned, sufficient sound metal remained in the front sections on both sides, although as the images illustrate, fabricated repairs were needed on the front outer edge and at the base where it joins the end of the sill panel. Retaining what structural strength there was and supplementing it with the fitting of a rear inner wing repair panel was the preferred option. This had the added advantage of providing a reference point for the upper flange, which was carefully aligned with the retained portion of the inner wing. The residual part of the inner spring hanger mounting was also used as a reference point before the rear panel was positioned, clamped and tacked before being welded in place. Time, effort and patience were required to grind back the welds and neatly dress the areas where new metal had been introduced. Also key to the success of this complicated operation was accurate alignment of the outer boot floor aperture panel, not only at either end where it joined the inner repair panels but also where the bumper iron mounting supports passed through.

The sequencing of the repairs to this part of the vehicle was critical to the success of the operation.

'A' POST AND FRONT INNER WING REPAIRS

Ordinarily repairs to the 'A' posts and the front inner wings is a relatively straightforward task requiring, in most cases, fabricated repairs to the bottom area of the hinge pillar where it meets the inner sill and in the area at the base of the inner wing next to the bulkhead. In the case of the last saloon, following the chemical treatment process, close examination of the A posts and the area immediately adjacent to the back edge of the inner wing panels suggested that further investigation would be necessary to establish the extent of the corrosion behind the outer panels. The initial concerns proved to be justified, prompting the decision to cut away substantial areas of metalwork to gain access to the inner panels. Once revealed, it became apparent that fabricated panels would

Bodywork Repairs

The chemical treatment process confirmed the extent of the work that needed to be done to reintroduce strength to the rear of the vehicle.

The spring hanger repair panels were fitted and carefully aligned using the remnants of the original fitting as reference points.

Rear inner wheel arch repair panel trial fit.

Rear inner wheel arch panel tacked in position.

Shipping plate added.

Additional welding of fabricated parts was required to add new metal in key areas where original panels were retained.

Repairs were replicated on the nearside inner wheel arch.

Alignment with the outer boot floor aperture panel was critical to the success of the operation.

Bodywork Repairs

Completed repairs with welds ground back and metal coated with rust inhibitor.

be required to repair certain areas to reintroduce strength to the inner sections before attempting to repair or replace some or all of the component parts of the 'A' posts.

The inner face and base of the 'A' posts on both sides of the car showed serious signs of corrosion and were deemed incapable of providing sufficient support for the doors, a fact previously confirmed by the flexing of the panel when the doors were lifted. Repairs involved removing the front portion of the hinge pillar by using a slitting disc in order to expose the inner section and determine how much fabrication would be required to reinstate damaged areas before fitting replacement panels. The extent of the work is shown below. Reassured by the strengthening work undertaken on the inner panels and the introduction of new hinge support brackets in the 'A' posts, new outer panels were first tacked before being seam welded in place. In conjunction with the work on the 'A' posts, work progressed on fitting new upper inner wing panels with the original lower curved inner wing panels being retained and repaired where necessary. Having this fixed position assisted with alignment of the new panels, a process that was further aided at a later stage by the fitting of the front panel. New panels included front inner wing extension panels and inner wing support brackets. Once welded in position, preliminary checks on door and outer wing fitment were undertaken to provide reassurance regarding door and front wing fitment and accuracy in terms of door shut lines, wing bolt positions and the back edge alignment of the front wings. Fortunately, no major issues were encountered.

ROOF PANEL

Following the chemical dipping process, the full extent of corrosion in the roof area and in adjacent inner rear panels became apparent. It proved to be more extensive than anticipated and prompted a major rethink about how to deal with the complexity of some of the repairs needed around the rear window aperture, the outer swage line and the inner area next to the rear parcel shelf. The corrosion here was so severe that it was deemed to be compromising the structural integrity of the car. Gaining sufficient access to the area affected to carry out the essential repairs proved to be well-nigh impossible. This prompted a great deal of discussion and debate and a radical approach to solve the problem.

Serious corrosion was exposed when outer panels were cut away to allow essential structural repairs to be undertaken.

Bodywork Repairs

Repairs underway, as viewed from inside the car.

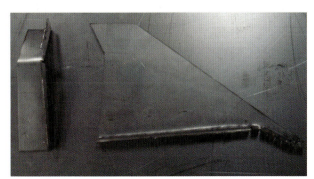
Fabricated repair panels for the bulkhead area.

New inner panel welded in position.

Inner area left unpainted, as welding still to be completed in this area.

Bodywork Repairs

'A' post repairs. Replacement hinge plates fitted.

New hinge pillar welded in place.

Alignment of full inner wing extension panel using front panel to ensure accuracy.

A new inner wing strengthening bracket was fitted. Note alignment with lower inner wing panel.

Inner wing panel and 'A' post repairs complete and in protective primer.

A replacement roof section and inner rail was sourced from an already scrapped Morris Minor. The rationale behind this decision was that with the damaged parts removed from the original roof, better access would be available to complete repairs to the critical inner panels. It was also thought that adopting this option would be less labour intensive and more cost effective than attempting to fabricate and fit replacement parts that might not replicate the original outer swage line.

The spot welds around the lower part of the rear window aperture were removed using a spot weld removal tool. The lower section of the roof panel was removed using a slitting disc. All surrounding metalwork was then cleaned back to bare metal using a grinder in preparation for the replacement panel to be fitted. Attention then switched to

Bodywork Repairs

repairing the severely corroded inner panel, which was now accessible with the roof section removed. Sections were fabricated and welded in place to replace the structural integrity of this part of the vehicle, which had been compromised by the severity of the corrosion. With the inner repairs complete the replacement outer roof section was cleaned and cut to size in preparation for fitting to the car. The bottom edge was screwed in place before being spot welded in position. To ensure that sufficient strength was re-introduced to this area of the vehicle, the area around the window aperture was clamped, spot welded and then seam welded for good measure.

Considerable weakness in different areas was exposed due to the chemical treatment process.

Drastic action was needed to ascertain the true extent of the damage.

Inner support rails had suffered badly and were very weak and in some areas non-existent.

Donor roof 'repair' section clamped in position.

Roof repair area was planished on both sides.

Bodywork Repairs

Roof repairs complete. Strength restored.

ROOF GUTTERING

The chemical treatment highlighted areas of weakness in the roof panel, particularly in the area next to the guttering. To repair the affected area the guttering was removed using the spot weld removal tool. This was done to allow better access to the curved part of the roof panel, which needed to be replaced. Specialist equipment including a joggling tool, rollers and a swaging machine were utilised to fabricate repair panels with the same profile and curvature of the roof. After being spot welded in place, and ground back to recreate the original profile, the guttering previously removed was spot welded back in position to replicate the original specification.

Though it was painstakingly slow to complete this part of the restoration, with particular care having to be taken to measure and align the replacement panels and constantly check that they remained accurately positioned while welding was taking place, the decision to adopt this course of action was justified in the end, not just because of the end result and the standard of workmanship, but the knowledge and peace of mind that the strength of the vehicle had been enhanced as a result of the efforts made.

BODYWORK STRIP-DOWN

The construction of the Morris Minor saloon models differed from that of their convertible, Traveller and light commercial counterparts, a fact noted in later chapters devoted to these specific models.

While removing most of the body panels including front and rear bumpers, valances, the bonnet, boot lid, doors, wings and front panel is a relatively uncomplicated process, it is one that requires a patient, methodical approach to removing and undoing the various-sized nuts, bolts and screws. It is worth remembering that over the lifetime of any vehicle being restored that when parts have been removed in the past there is no guarantee that original factory-fitted nuts, bolts and screws have been replaced with ones that match the original specification. Where references have been made to the size and thread of specific items in this section, they refer to original specification items.

Front and Rear Bumpers and Valances

The front and rear bumpers, valances and sprung supporting irons are easily removed as complete assemblies by undoing the two ½ inch BSF nuts from the threaded mounting bars.

Another area requiring attention fully exposed following the chemical dipping process.

Guttering replaced having been removed to allow for other repairs to the roof.

Bodywork Repairs

Front and Rear Wings

The front and rear wings are secured in place by $5/16$ BSF hexagonal-headed screws utilising large washers. These are screwed into threaded metal housings. There are six for each of the rear wings and eight for each of the front wings. Two smaller bolts that fasten each of the front wings to the inner panel need to be undone, along with the three 2BA nuts that hold each of the front hockey sticks in place.

As the screws are fastened in place from the underside, with each one passing through a large washer and the aperture in the wing before being tightened, added to the fact that over time they may have rusted into the metal housing given the exposure to road grime and the elements, they may prove difficult to remove. Liberal use of penetrating fluid may help along with a $5/16$ ring spanner. In extreme cases of corrosion, such as in the case of the project car, the metal housings may just break away from the inner flange.

Before removing the wings from the vehicle, all electrical connections from the wiring loom to the headlamps, front and rear indicators, rear lights and brake lights will need to be disconnected.

Bonnet and Boot Lid

The inner bonnet stay will need to be disconnected prior to removing the bonnet by undoing the hinges on either side. It is useful to retain the nuts for the hinges along with the felt gaskets, either as a pattern for replacement purposes or reuse. The same applies to the boot lid, where the first task should be to release the wiring loom from the retaining clips on the underside and disconnecting the cables from the number-plate lamp. With the adjustable boot lid stay fitted to later models removed and both hinges undone the boot lid can be lifted clear, either with the hinges attached or removed.

Front Panel and Grille

Sequencing the tasks involved in releasing and removing the front panel as a stand-alone, even if it is just to assist with the removal of the engine rather than part of a full restoration,

Repaired front panel after chemical treatment.

The bonnet required substantial repairs due to panel damage as well as extensive areas of rust.

Original front and rear valances were discarded due to rust and distortion.

Bodywork Repairs

will ease the task and minimise the risk of unintended damage.

- Remove the front bumper, valance and support irons.
- Remove the three 2BA nuts from the threaded studs on each of the hockey sticks either side of the panel, noting that these tend to shear off.
- Remove the split pin and washer from the bonnet pull stay.
- Drain the radiator before releasing the four retaining bolts that secure it to the inner mounting panel. Disconnect the top and bottom radiator hoses.
- Disconnect the air intake duct connected to the front panel (later car only).
- Release the four nuts and bolts that secure the front panel to the front inner edge of the front wings.
- Release the eight nuts and bolts on the bottom edge to free the panel from the front crossmember.
- With these tasks complete it should be possible to remove the front panel with the grille panel, its surround and the top chrome bar intact.

Panels

A thorough assessment of all the panels was undertaken once they had been removed. While mindful of the agreed principle of retaining as many of the original parts as possible, the severity of the corrosion in many of the panels meant that the economic viability of repairing them was far outweighed by the cost of simply replacing them with new old stock items where possible. For this reason, all but one of the wings were replaced with genuine new old stock items rather than pattern replacements. These items needed little attention other than removing surface rust, an objective that was achieved by chemical treatment later in the restoration process. One rear wing fitted to the car was salvaged, stripped to bare metal, subjected to minor refurbishment and primed and reused. The original bonnet, which had sustained some damage, was retained and subsequently repaired. However, the boot lid, which could have been restored using an off-the-shelf bottom edge repair panel, was deemed uneconomical to repair and was replaced by a second-hand item in excellent condition.

The doors presented something of a challenge due to the severity of the rust damage present, particularly on one of them. A replacement door was sourced and, although sound, it required further work to meet the exacting standards being set for the rest of the vehicle. This proved to be a more cost-effective option. Considerable work was carried out on the other door, which had been subjected to previous repairs – a fact that became visible after it was subjected to chemical treatment.

The front panel was retained, with repairs being carried out on the bottom edge. Although attempts were made to salvage and repair the front and rear valances, the extent of the rust and the absence of metal in much of the area that sits behind the bumpers meant that there was little original sound metal to work with. Replacements were sought, refurbished and fitted.

Door Repairs

Prior to any repairs being undertaken on each of the doors, the door frames, door handles and windows including the quarter lights all had to be removed along with the window winding mechanism. This proved to be a time-consuming and at times frustrating process, due to the proximity of all the internal components. The following sequence was followed.

- The removal of the interior door and window winding handles by undoing the Phillips-headed screws in each.
- The removal of the door card by prising it away from the door frame and releasing the triangular-shaped spring clips.
- The removal of three rubber grommets located on the outer edge of the door that conceal three bolts that secure the door glass channel in place.
- The removal of the three bolts along with the single bolt that secures the bottom edge of the door glass channel in place.
- The release of two nuts situated under the quarter light. Particular care needed to be taken when releasing these, as they have a tendency to snap.

Releasing the window winding mechanism

If the window is still fitted it needs to be fully closed before the window winding mechanism that is attached to the door frame can be removed. This is achieved by removing four bolts and spring washers. With the window winder disengaged from the lift channel at the bottom of the window glass, the process of extracting it from the door can be attempted. Some careful manoeuvring may be required to ease the mechanism through the aperture at the bottom of the door. With the window winding mechanism disengaged and all nuts and bolts released, attempts can be made to extract the frame and the window glass clear of the door, although it should be noted that this task is easier said than done.

Removal of the door handle

With the door frame and window glass removed, attention can then focus on removing the door handle and locking mechanism. It is worth noting that later door handles were slightly modified, with the inclusion of a split pin to secure the locking bolt in place. The removal process is fairly straightforward, requiring the removal of the split pin, spring and flat washer that hold the lock plunger in place followed by the removal of the three Phillips-headed screws that hold the door handle and lock in place. The handle can then be freed from the door.

Other Door Repairs

Morris Minor doors tend to rot out at the bottom due to the accumulation of water inside the door. Tell-tale signs include the rust bubbling through on the bottom curved edge and weakness on the underside. Replacement panels in the form of

Bodywork Repairs

full-length bottom repair panels shaped to the correct profile as well as underside repair panels are available. For the last saloon an underside repair panel was fitted on the replacement door, which, although far from perfect, was in much better condition than the original door, which had completely rotted through. A slitting disc was used to cut out the rusted area on the underside of the door. With the interior of the door exposed, the opportunity was taken to check on the internal structure and to clean back and rust-proof the inner edges before welding the replacement under panel in place.

Replacement door still in need of repair.

New under panel fitted and 'spot'/MIG welded in place.

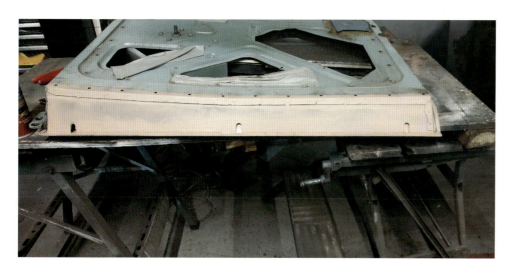

Temporary rust preventative primer added in advance of chemical treatment.

Fortunately the lower outer edge was sound and free of rust 'bubbling'.

3
Paintwork

HISTORICAL BACKGROUND

In the early years of Morris Minor production, the preparation of the bodyshell prior to painting was time consuming and labour intensive. On the early models two main paint finishes were used. These were Synthetic and Synobel. The type of paint used on an individual vehicle was identified on the chassis plate, which was mounted on the bulkhead. The letter 'S' indicated Synthetic while 'SYN' denoted the use of Synobel. These were preceded by the letters MNR, which indicated the make of vehicle – 'Morris Minor'. Sequential chassis numbers were stamped underneath. From April 1952 a more detailed system of identification was used on a revised chassis plate attached to the bulkhead. Paint type was identified by the second of two numbers that were included. 1 represented Synthetic, 2 Synobel and 3 Cellulose. A code for the generic paint colour was also added. A Black, B Grey, C Red, D Blue and E Green.

Consequently, the identification code FBA 11 as illustrated would indicate the vehicle was a Morris Minor (F), two-door saloon (B), painted in Black (A) in right-hand drive for the home market (1) and painted using Synthetic paint (1).

This system continued in use up to January 1958, when the second number identifying the paint type was dropped. This preceded the introduction of a smaller type of chassis plate, with changed model identification codes. Throughout the 1960s Cellulose paint was the dominant paint type used by the British Motor Corporation Ltd and British Leyland Ltd on home-produced models. CKD (Completely Knocked Down) models exported to overseas assembly plants for final assembly were painted in primer and then finished in colours and paint types specific to the individual plants.

ADVANCED TECHNOLOGY

In the early 1950s Morris Motors Ltd established a new rustproofing and paint facility at the Cowley works in Oxford. It was heralded as one of the best of its kind in Europe. It incorporated a new rustproofing element named 'Rotodip'. Each bodyshell, complete with wings, bonnet, doors and boot lid, was mounted on a revolving spit that travelled on a chain-driven conveyor through a 300ft (91.44m) Rotodip plant. The process involved each bodyshell being immersed and rotated in six tanks to chemically clean, rustproof, bonderise and prime the shell and accompanying panels before being stoved (heat treated) prior to entering the paint spraying area. After further quality control checks, the rustproofed painted shells were then moved to the assembly lines.

This highly acclaimed system certainly boosted Morris Motors Ltd 'Quality First' advertising claims and no doubt helped in the longevity of the Morris Minor.

REPAINTING OPTIONS

For anyone undertaking a major restoration project, serious consideration

Paintwork preparations 1950s style.

1957 Chassis plate indicating model, body type, colour, RHD home market and paint type.

needs to be given to determining how far to go with the repainting process and what type of paint to use. If, as in the case of the featured project car, the vehicle is completely stripped and the bodyshell and associated body panels subjected to a chemical dipping process, then it is a matter of deciding which materials to use in the repainting process and whether to employ the services of a professional paint sprayer, with facilities such as a spray bake oven. For the home-based restorer, undertaking the repainting process is not a task to be undertaken lightly. There are a number of things to consider, such as having suitable space in which to work, environmental considerations including temperature control, as well as personal health and safety issues, not to mention having access to the correct equipment including a suitable spray gun, a compressor and adequate respiratory safeguards.

PAINT CHOICES

Cellulose Paint

Cellulose paint is the option of choice for those seeking authenticity in replicating the original paint finish for the majority of surviving Morris Minors. Regulations relating to the use of cellulose-based paints changed in 2004, though it is still available and permissible for use in the restoration and repainting of 'classic and vintage vehicles'. For the home restorer wishing to prime, repaint localised repairs, or complete panels, aerosol cans can be purchased and a wide range of colours can be mixed. For those repainting a complete vehicle, cellulose paints and associated thinners can be acquired from specialist paint suppliers. Colours are available in RAL, BS (British Standard) and Classic Car shades.

The main advantages of using cellulose-based paint for the home restorer is its ease of use, the opportunity to get a high gloss finish straight from the gun and the resulting durable finish it provides. Since it is a solvent-based paint, it will be necessary to wear a breathing mask and to work in a well-ventilated area.

Two-Pack Paint

Two-pack paint became the mainstay of automotive finishing in the early 1970s. Unlike cellulose paints, which are solvent based, two-pack paints rely on a chemical process initiated by the application of an isocyanate hardener. The base coat requires clear lacquer finish. The application of this type of paint requires specialised equipment and ideally the use of a temperature-controlled spray booth. The use of an air-fed mask, painters overalls and gloves are strongly recommended. Since the application of two-pack paint and clear lacquer coats causes the build-up of static that can cause bits being drawn from clothing and hair, the use of painters' hooded overalls is another consideration to be borne in mind.

The main advantage of using two-pack paint is the high shine that can be produced on a durable resistant surface, which is less likely to fade due to the effect of ultraviolet rays.

Water-Based Paints

The emergence of more environmentally friendly water-based paints in the automotive industry has added a further option to be considered. While widely used for the repainting of modern vehicles, it is not a realistic option

BMC colour swatches 1961–69.

Paintwork

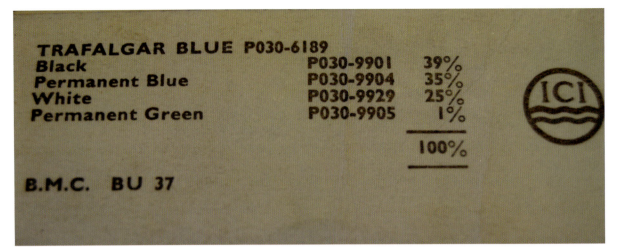

Trafalgar Blue paint details and ICI Code BU 37.

for the home restorer undertaking a one-off repaint due to the equipment required and the processes involved in its application. Water-based paints require more precise control of the environment where they are being applied. This includes temperature control, moisture levels and the regulation of the compressed air available both for the application of the paint and for the drying process. In addition, successful application requires practice as well as in-depth knowledge of the air-drying process and the acquisition of specialised equipment, including a spray gun used exclusively for the application of water-based paint.

PANEL PREPARATION

It is often stated that the time and care taken in the repair and preparation of metalwork prior to the application of paint will pay dividends in the long term. There are many factors to be borne in mind when considering the repainting of individual panels or a complete vehicle. These range from deciding whether to paint over existing paintwork or to strip the paintwork off completely and return the panel or complete vehicle to bare metal. In cases where the vehicle is stripped to bare metal, an etch primer or oxide primer should be applied. This will act as a rust inhibitor whilst repairs are ongoing. Where the vehicle is not being stripped back completely to bare metal and some of the original paint is being retained whilst localised repairs are undertaken, it is important to take note of the possibility of there being an adverse reaction if a different type of paint or primer is used.

It is useful to check a small, localised area, first by sanding back and then wiping the panel with a suitable panel wipe such as Upol Anti-Silicone Panel Wipe before applying a primer coat to see if a reaction occurs. Some aerosol primers will react with old cellulose paint and two-pack paints. If a reaction does occur, it will be necessary to apply an Isolator coat such as Promatic Isolator Sealer or Bar Coats, both of which come in a variety of colours. This will act as a barrier and should reduce the risk of any further problems.

CASE STUDY

The preparation and final paint of FMT 265 J was outsourced to a company with the facilities and skilled staff experienced in the application of 2K (Two-Pack) paints. The bodyshell and most repaired panels had previously undergone a chemical stripping process prior to extensive repairs being carried out. Consequently, when the bodyshell and associated panels arrived at the paint shop, they had a combination of etch primer and a light protective coating of 'Cure rust' applied as a preventative measure to stop the build-up of surface rust.

On arrival at the paint shop, an extensive assessment was made to ascertain the extent of the previous repairs and to determine how much filler work would be required. This was in the knowledge that as the work progressed it would be necessary to remove the protective coating applied, as well as any lingering traces of rust that might still be present following the repairs that had been undertaken. Cleaning back to bare metal with the use of rotary wire brushes and abrasive pads was deemed essential if the surfaces were to have a good key for the application of primer coats.

The Underside

With all outer panels removed the bodyshell was turned on its side to provide easy access to the underside. With the previously applied etch primer and protective coating removed, the bare metal was cleaned and degreased using panel wipes to remove any grease, oil, or other contaminants in readiness for initial priming. Epoxy primer was used due to it being water resistant, having excellent adhesion properties and the fact that it provides a sound base for carrying out any reshaping following the application of filler. Two coats of epoxy primer were applied and left to dry for 24/48 hours. Close examination of the underside then followed, with any areas requiring filler work being identified, filled and left to dry. Once dry, the filled areas were sanded down using 320 grade grit paper, cleaned and then re-primed. Further cleaning and degreasing occurred before the outer bodywork was masked off up to the sills.

With the vehicle and the spray booth brought up to temperature, 22–24°C, the whole of the underside was then coated with 3M sprayable sealer to provide additional protection. This sealer is similar in appearance to stone

Paintwork

Orbital sander being used with 320 grit to clean the metal prior to priming.

3M sprayable sealer.

chip applications. Using it involved a 'wet on wet' process with the sprayable sealer being applied then left to 'flash off' for approximately 30 minutes before being painted over in body colour using 2K Helios direct gloss. It was then left to fully harden for 48 hours.

Filling, Priming and Profiling

With the car back on its wheels, work commenced on identifying the other parts of the bodyshell requiring filling. All areas requiring such work were keyed with 120 grit prior to the application of filler. Works Pro Ace filler was the preferred choice. Some areas that had been subject to major repair required more than one application to restore the correct profile. The sanding of these areas required the use of 80 grit paper at the outset with 120 grit being used as a finisher. Various sanding blocks were used to ensure that the correct profile was achieved, an aspect that in the case of the Morris Minor required special attention, especially when dealing with the curvature on particular panels.

Due to the fact that the bodyshell had been subject to chemical dipping, the areas that originally would have been lead loaded when the bodyshell had been manufactured had been adversely affected due to the lead being removed. To retain this original feature, a specialist was engaged to fill and profile the seams either side of the boot aperture before they were primed using epoxy primer.

Close attention was also paid to specific areas in the engine bay, the boot area and the cabin, where it was deemed necessary to apply seam sealer. White Sikaflex sealer was applied to areas such as the inner wings and the chassis rail that runs across the bulkhead below the battery tray in the engine bay.

With the filler work satisfactorily completed, the bodyshell was moved to the spray booth where it was cleaned and degreased. Once the booth was up to temperature (22–24°C) three coats of Dupont Cromax spray putty were applied and then left to cure. The Cromax application was applied over the whole of the car and on individual panels. Its use was favoured due to its qualities as a fine finishing tool and the benefit it provides in filling and covering small imperfections.

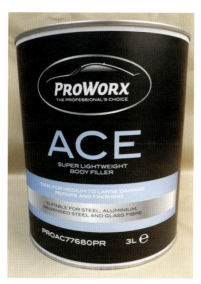

ProWorx Ace Filler.

Panel Fit and Alignment Checks

At this stage, all detachable panels including wings, doors, bonnet and boot lid were fitted to the bodyshell and checks made on the panel fit and alignment as well as the curved profiles, particularly on the front wing and door area and on the boot lid and adjacent panel. Priority was given to adjusting the panel fit, to ensure that even gaps could be achieved and that adjacent panels aligned properly with

Paintwork

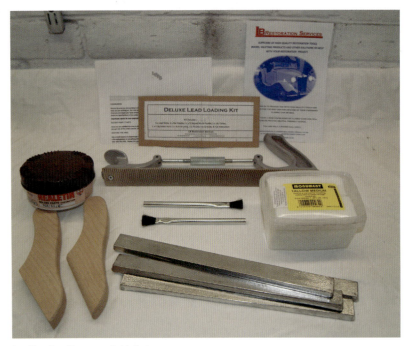
Lead loading kits are available for home use.

Rear seam lead loaded, filed and rubbed down ready for priming.

Cromax spray putty.

the curved areas flowing evenly from one panel to the next. Over the space of a few days individual panels were prepped, primed and filled where necessary using the same techniques as described previously. The process began by using 120 grit to begin with followed by 240 grit to finish. Particular care was exercised on curved areas, including the front and rear wings and the doors where the curvature is quite pronounced.

Inside Cabin

Back in the spray booth the inside of the cabin was cleaned, degreased and prepared for the application of a coat of etch primer. Once up to temperature (22–24°C) a coat of Lesonal 1K CF etch primer was applied followed by two coats of MIPA 4+1HS primer. This was then left to cure for 24 hours. Further remedial work was completed where necessary in preparation for the application of the colour coat to the interior surfaces. Particular attention was paid to areas such as the dashboard, windscreen pillars and cant rails in preparation for the high gloss finish, as all of these areas would remain visible painted in body colour when all interior fitments were eventually added.

Final Pre-Gloss Finish Preparations

With the interior painted and fully dried, exterior panels were refitted and properly aligned in readiness for further sanding and fine detailing prior to the application of top coat finishes. Finer 320 and 400 grade sanding papers were used at this stage, with regular checks being made for consistency in the finish being achieved over the whole of each individual panel. With a satisfactory finish present and no blemishes evident, the car was returned to the booth to again be cleaned and degreased. With the panels removed the interior cabin and the underside were masked off. Attention then focused in applying the spray sealer to the front and rear inner wing panels and to the inside of the front and rear wings, with adequate time being allowed for this to cure in advance of further work being undertaken.

Paintwork

Bodyshell masked and in primer.

600 preparations completed, attention switched to the use of an orbital sander with a 500-disc interface pad with the aim of removing any remaining flat edges on the curved surfaces and any imperfections missed during the 600 flatting process.

Final Topcoat

With all panels removed from the bodyshell final preparations were made to move the car into the booth in readiness for the final paint. Individual panels were placed on racks and painted separately. All surfaces were cleaned and degreased and the necessary areas on the bodyshell masked off. With the spray booth at optimum temperature, the bodyshell and all panels were left inside for fifteen to twenty minutes to get all metalwork up to temperature prior to any spraying being undertaken. This was done to avoid any potential problems with micro-blistering. With the booth, all panels and the car up to temperature (22–24°C), a light coat of Helios 2K direct gloss, mixed 2:1 with medium hardener and 10 per cent 2K thinners was applied followed by three wet coats. With final coats applied the booth temperature was increased to 70°C for 35 minutes to assist with drying and then all parts were left to harden off for two days before attention switched to final finishing and the fitting of the painted panels. Final checks were made to see if there were any imperfections in the paint such as 'orange peel' effect or areas that may have been affected by the paint being applied 'dry' due to a momentary drop in pressure in the spray gun. After 48 hours to allow the freshly applied paint to harden, the bodyshell and all panels were given a light 'nib' using fine 1500 wet and dry. After a further 24 hours the process was repeated using 2000 grade in advance of machine polishing using 3M fast-cut polishing compound to ensure that any flatting marks were successfully removed. Care was then taken to remove any compound residue before the final stage in the polishing process was undertaken using 3M ultrafine compound in conjunction with a waffle pad to achieve a swirl-free, high-glaze finish.

The next stage involved the application of a 2K black gloss guide coat. This served a dual purpose in that it gave a good indication of how the final finish would look as well as providing a sound base for further work to be done, including identifying any low or high spots on the panels requiring flatting back prior to the application of the final colour coats. This process was applied to every individual panel and the rest of the bodyshell and then left to cure for several days before any further work was undertaken. With the black gloss guide coat finish cured, work began to flat the surfaces using 600 wet and dry paper. Imperfections in awkward areas were rectified with the use of a very fine red Scotch abrasive pad and elsewhere rubbed down using a variety of rubber blocks. This process was applied across the whole bodyshell and each individual panel. With the

Paintwork

Body panels were re-fitted at various stages to ensure proper alignment and to check panel gaps.

Three wet coats of direct gloss were applied to the bodyshell and all panels.

Prior to polishing, the paintwork was subjected to final treatment using fine 1500 and 2000 grade wet and dry to remove any imperfections.

For the final stage, 3M ultrafine compound was used to achieve a high gloss finish.

Paintwork

Painted in readiness for final assembly.

4
Engine Rebuild

INTRODUCTION

For anyone considering undertaking the strip-down and rebuild of an A Series engine, certain considerations need to be borne in mind. While the engine configuration is straightforward, access to the correct tools, equipment and replacement parts as well as engineering expertise are prerequisites for a successful rebuild. It was for these reasons that in the case of the project vehicle, Alan Scott, an experienced engineer in the rebuilding of A Series engines, was engaged to rebuild the original engine fitted to FMT 265 J. The information that follows is based on his invaluable experience in rebuilding hundreds of 'A' Series engines.

A rebuild to purely standard specification was an option to maintain originality. However, given the introduction of unleaded fuel and other mechanical improvements not available in 1970, the decision was made to allow some departures from originality to improve performance and ensure the longevity of the engine. Reference will be made to these in the rebuild section.

ENGINE REMOVAL

The tasks outlined here are necessary if removing the engine on its own. It is not necessary to follow the exact sequence outlined here, but it is recommended to first disconnect the battery before draining the cooling system, removing the radiator and associated hoses, as well as disconnecting any heater hoses and undoing the four bolts that hold the single fan blade in place. Drain the oil from the engine and allow time for as much oil as possible to drain from the sump. Dispose of the used oil responsibly. The exhaust should be separated from the manifold, the carburettor and air cleaner removed and the flexible pipe from the fuel pump disconnected. Remove the starter motor and dynamo after disconnecting all wires from the coil. To avoid potential damage

Cutaway engine showing the main features of the A series engine as fitted to the Morris Minor. This preserved example was created by BMC apprentices in the 1960s.

Engine Rebuild

on removal of the engine, remove the distributor by releasing the single bolt that secures it.

Before releasing the engine from the engine mounting brackets and disconnecting it from the gearbox, support the engine with suitable lifting equipment such as an engine hoist. Turn attention to releasing four nuts, bolts and washers that secure the left-hand front mounting bracket (tower) to the tie plate before removing the nuts and lock washers that secure the two engine mounting brackets to the rubbers. Return to the top of the engine and remove the engine steady bar, which is fixed to the engine by the rear cylinder-head stud. Next, disconnect the clutch retracting spring from the plate at the rear of the engine before turning attention to releasing all the bolts that secure the gearbox to the engine. With all bolts removed and the front of the gearbox supported by a jack, the process of separating the engine can begin. Care needs to be taken when moving the engine forward not to damage the main gearbox drive shaft when separation occurs. Once free, the engine hoist can be utilised to manoeuvre and lift the engine clear.

ENGINE STRIP-DOWN

Before undertaking the strip-down of the engine, it is advisable to ensure that adequate space is available either on a bench or at floor level in which to work, and that the external parts of the engine are free of oil and dirt. Before commencing work thought should be given to having suitable sized storage containers on hand in which to store and label parts as they are removed.

Removing the Cylinder Head

With the rocker cover removed locate the nine head bolts, four of which go through the rocker pedestals and five of which go through the block. Using the diagram opposite, loosen the nine head bolts half a turn at a time in the reverse order to that shown. This is essential to avoid the head warping as a result of the nuts being released unevenly.

> **Tip:** Leave the four pedestal rocker nuts in place at this stage as this will make the separation of the head from the block easier.

If the head proves difficult to separate from the block, do not use excessive force or implements such as screw drivers or chisels to dislodge the head from the block, as this will inevitably cause damage to one or both faces.

If the water pump has not been removed at this point, disconnect or simply cut off the short hose between the head and the water pump. Before attempting to lift the head from the block, place a piece of wood between the head and the block before removing the four rocker nuts and taking out the rockers. Remove the pushrods and place them through a pre-prepared piece of cardboard with the holes appropriately numbered and positioned. This will enable them to be reinstated correctly when the head is reassembled after refurbishment.

Well-used engine in need of restoration. Note oil leaks.

Engine Rebuild

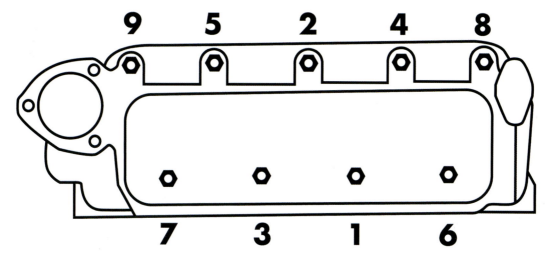

Sequence diagram for releasing cylinder head bolts.

First steps. Rocker cover removed.

With the cylinder head removed, the true state of the engine can be assessed.

Stripping the Block

A complete overhaul of the engine requires most components to be removed from the block before being assessed for wear and prepared for refurbishment. The block itself can then be chemically cleaned at an engineering company prior to any further work deemed necessary being undertaken.

With the engine in an upright position, remove the oil filter canister before taking off the valve chest covers. This will allow access to the cam followers, which are easily removed by placing a finger in the cam follower and pulling each one forward.

Next turn the engine upside down and rest it on the bench with the block face facing downwards on a clean surface. Remove the sump by undoing the $7/16$ AF bolts, ensuring that the oval-shaped washers that sit underneath the nuts are retained for reinstallation. With the sump removed it should then be possible to remove the oil strainer.

Moving to the rear of the engine, remove the flywheel by knocking back the lock tabs before undoing the four $9/16$ bolts. Remove the engine back plate and then turn attention to removing the oil pump by knocking back the lock tabs and undoing three $7/16$ nuts.

Tip: Replace the oil pump with a new unit.

Returning to the front of the engine, focus on the task of removing the crankshaft pulley bolt. Prior to attempting this task it will be necessary to lock the crankshaft in position by placing a block of wood between the inside of the block and the crankshaft. Pressure can then be applied by using a spanner on the pulley nut, which is often notoriously difficult to release. Prior use of penetrating fluid is a useful option. With the nut removed the pulley can be gently levered off, but care must be taken not to cause damage to the pulley by using excessive force.

With the pulley released, attention should then switch to removing the timing chain cover to reveal the crankshaft and camshaft sprockets. Before these can be removed along with the timing chain, the locking tab must be knocked back and the camshaft securing nut released. It should then be possible to gently lever off the timing gears.

Tip: It is important to note the timing marks on both sprockets, as these will be used as reference points when rebuilding the engine.

Access to the engine front plate and the triangular camshaft thrust plate is now possible and these can be easily removed by the knocking back the lock tabs and then undoing the two $7/16$ bolts on the front plate and the three $7/16$ bolts and starred washers on the thrust plate. Before removing the camshaft, the distributor drive has to be removed. The sleeve is held in place on the block with a single $7/16$ bolt. The sleeve itself holds in the distributor drive, which needs to be removed. This can be accomplished by use of a long $5/16$ stud, which can be screwed into the end of the drive. Once twisted to the right it can be released and withdrawn.

Engine Rebuild

Removing the Crankshaft

With the engine standing on the flywheel end, the process of removing the conrods and pistons can be undertaken.

Begin by releasing the big-end bearings by knocking back the eight locking tabs and undoing each of the retaining nuts, before turning attention to releasing and extracting each conrod and piston in turn through the top of the block. It is important that the two halves of each conrod are kept together after the bearing shells have been removed. The conrods are normally numbered 1–4. Parts should not be mixed from one to another.

With the engine positioned on the head face, the next phase, which involves knocking back the locking tabs and unbolting the six bolts that hold the three main bearing caps in place followed by the two 7/16 bolts that secure the main bearing cap, can be completed. With the main bearing caps removed it will then be possible to inspect the bottom half of the bearing shell. With these tasks completed the crankshaft can be removed from the crankcase with a sight rotation to release it.

Important note: Do not under any circumstances remove the wired bolts at the flywheel end of the block that secure the half-moon-shaped scroll, as these are a factory-set installation.

Crankshaft in used condition.

Crankshaft with main bearing shells removed.

FORWARD PLANNING

With the engine stripped, the process of assessing the condition of internal components can begin. Damage or excessive wear on some components may be immediately apparent, while others may need the expertise of an engineer with access to specialised equipment to precisely measure and determine the extent of the wear and the serviceability of individual parts. For the home-based restorer, it is advisable to seek advice and engage the services of a local engineering company to properly assess the condition of the block, the crankshaft, the big end and main bearings in order to gauge the extent of the work required and the costs involved.

CHECKLIST

Bores

Any assessment of the bores should take account of ovality as well as excessive internal wear. A quick and easy check is to feel for a ridge at the top of each bore. If present, it will be necessary to bore and hone the cylinders and fit oversized pistons. These are available in four sizes for the 1098cc engine (plus 20, 30, 40 and 60 thou).

Cylinder Head and Engine Block Faces

The faces of the engine block and the cylinder head need checking to determine whether one or both need to be skimmed. In most cases it will be the cylinder head that needs skimming. This requires the use of specialist equipment and the services of an engineering company.

Tip: Always have the cylinder head skimmed if rebuilding the engine.

Main Bearing Shells

Lead indium bearings should be matt grey in colour. However, if they are badly worn there will be traces of copper where the lead has been worn away. If this is the case replacement is the only option and the crankshaft will need to be reground.

It is important to note that while main bearing shells are the same for 803cc and 948cc engines, they differ from those used in 1098cc engines. They are not interchangeable.

The Camshaft Thrust Plate

The thrust plate that fits behind the large timing wheel should be checked for signs of wear. If wear is evident, it should be replaced. Replacements are available.

Other Associated Components

As a matter of course a new oil pump and a new water pump should be sourced and fitted.

Conrods and Pistons

In normal circumstances the conrods should be capable of being reused. However, with the pistons normally being replaced with an oversized set, it is important to check before attempting reassembly that all the ancillary components are present. In the case of 1098cc pistons, eight circlips – two per piston – should be present.

ENGAGING PROFESSIONAL ASSISTANCE

As previously mentioned, completely rebuilding an engine will inevitably mean engaging the services of a specialist engineering company to undertake tasks that require the use of specialised equipment. In normal circumstances this will involve boring the block, honing the bores, regrinding the crankshaft and cleaning all components to remove swarf and any carboned oil deposits. In exceptional cases it may be necessary to have the block skimmed.

CYLINDER HEAD: CONVERSION FOR USE WITH UNLEADED FUEL

In the case of an A Series engine being rebuilt in the modern era, it is unlikely that the cylinder head will be restored to original specification due to the need to modify the valve sets to take account of the use of unleaded fuel. Though fitting new components may be within the capabilities of an experienced mechanic, specialist equipment will be required to skim the cylinder head. The conversion process involves fitting new valve guides and reaming them out to valve stem size. New hardened steel valves capable of being used with unleaded fuel that burns at a higher temperature should be fitted along with hardened seats on the exhaust valves. All eight valve seats need to be cut in preparation for lapping in using fine carborundum paste. The cylinder head can then be skimmed in readiness for refitting once the engine block has been reassembled.

REASSEMBLY OF ENGINE BLOCK

While the block is with the engine specialist, it is advisable to request that they undertake the fitting of the four core plugs, as this requires a degree of force to be used to ensure proper alignment and a secure seal. It

Well-worn main bearing shells indicating that a crankshaft regrind will be required.

Engine Rebuild

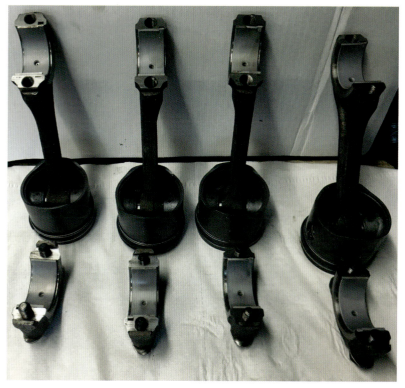

Pistons and conrods with new bearing shells ready for refitting.

Fitting a new water pump is highly recommended.

is also helpful if they fit the camshaft bearings. With the block mounted on an engine stand for ease of working, begin the reassembly process by putting the crankshaft bearings back in, provided the engineering company has not already done so. Refit the reground crankshaft and then fit new bearing shells and thrust bearings, making sure there is a 2 to 3 thou gap between the faces of the thrust bearings. Working on a bench, fit the pistons to the conrods in readiness for final assembly and, if they have not already been fitted, insert the piston rings. Returning to the engine and with it turned on its side, separate the big-end bearings numbered 1–4 before fitting the conrods in sequence. Torque down the big-end bolts and rotate the crankshaft by hand to test for smooth operation. Once complete, place a wood chock in the crankshaft before torquing it to the required specification. Complete the operation by fitting the oil pump strainer.

Tip: Fit a magnetic sump plug, as this will help protect the engine. Any residual material can be removed when the oil is next changed.

DUPLEX TIMING CHAIN

Once it becomes worn, the original style timing chain used on the A series engine can become very noisy. A more permanent solution to overcome this problem is to fit a stronger and more durable duplex timing chain kit. Some adjustments need to be made to accommodate duplex fittings. These include ensuring that the bottom two $7/16$ bolts originally fitted to the face of the front plate are replaced by two countersunk allen bolts to prevent the chain being fouled in operation.

With the camshaft fitted to the block along with the cam keep plate, align the two gears utilising the dots on each face before checking with a straight-edged ruler to double-check that they are sitting parallel. At this stage loosely position the chain on the gears. Focus should then switch to refitting the distributor drive as per instruction in the

Engine Rebuild

Boring the block.

Honing the bores.

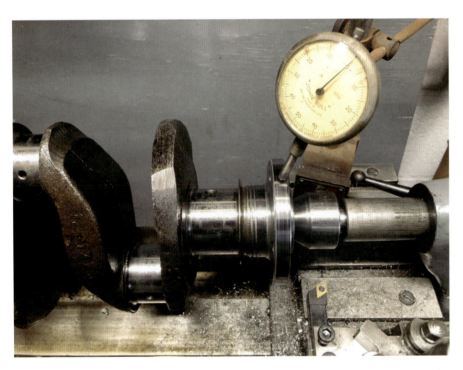

Checking tolerances on the crankshaft.

Cylinder head cleaned and blasted in preparation for further work.

Engine Rebuild

New valve guides fitted and reamed out and hardened valve seats installed.

Cutting three angled valve seats using specialised equipment.

workshop manual. The drive sleeve and the securing $^7/_{16}$ bolt and cam lock washer need to be fitted and torqued to the required level before the oil thrower is fitted to the crankshaft. Returning to the timing chain cover: with the chain located on the sprockets attention should focus on installing a new oil seal on the timing chain cover before temporarily placing the front pulley in position to help with aligning the cover and securing it in the correct position, initially with two bolts. With the front pulley removed, the remaining securing bolts on the timing cover can be fitted and tightened. The pulley can then be reinstalled, and the large starter dog bolt torqued down.

Tip: If possible fit a magnetic sump plug when completing the engine rebuild.

REAR OIL SEAL CONVERSION

A common problem associated with the A series engine is the persistent oil leak that occurs when the rear crankshaft oil scroll becomes worn. A recent solution in the form of a rear oil seal repair kit has been devised to resolve this problem. It is available from specialist suppliers.

Engine Rebuild

Completed modified cylinder head ready for use with unleaded fuel.

New core plugs fitted.

Camshaft bearings (arrowed) installed.

Components including the engine front plate cleaned and blasted in readiness for re assembly. Note arrows denoting position of countersunk fixing points.

Duplex timing chain in position. Note arrowed countersunk bolts.

Engine Rebuild

Timing chain cover in position along with sump.

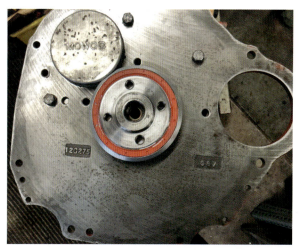

Critical to the success of the conversion is the installation of the seal. This is inserted into an aluminium carrier, which fits round the end of the crankshaft.

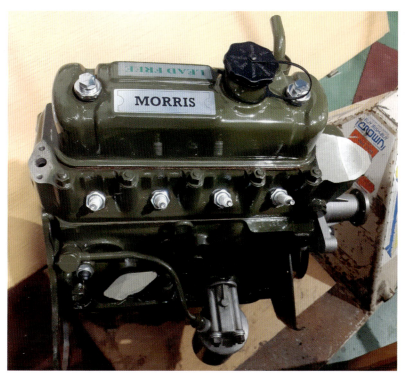

Engine reassembled and painted in specially mixed Land Rover bronze green enamel engine paint.

COOLING AND HEATING SYSTEM

The components associated with the cooling and heating system used in Morris Minors changed significantly over the course of production. They tended to be model specific and linked to one of the four designated engines. Heaters did not become part of the general specification for standard models until late on in production and if required, had to be purchased as an optional extra on new cars.

Series MM models that were powered by a 918cc side-valve engine utilised a pressurised thermosyphon system in conjunction with a radiator with a large capacity header tank. It was not until 1950 at engine number 77001 that the engine was redesignated USHM 3 and modified to accommodate the fitting of a front-mounted external water pump. At this point it became feasible to fit a heater. The type adopted was a Smith's recirculatory heater. A kit incorporating the heater and water pump was available as an optional extra for retrospective fitting to models that had the necessary modification to the bulkhead to accommodate the routing of the heater hoses.

Series II models fitted with the 803cc OHV engine adopted a different style of radiator characterised by a slimmer profile domed header tank. A more compact water pump was introduced. The inclusion of a heater as part of the specification for new vehicles remained as an optional extra on standard models. However, the Smith's recirculatory heater kit was available for purchase as an aftermarket accessory if required.

The domed type radiator remained in use until 1960, when it was superseded by a revised design with a more rectangular-shaped header tank. When the Morris 1000 948cc models were introduced in 1956 the water pump was modified for use with the new engine block. This revised water pump is not interchangeable with the earlier Series II type. During 948cc production, at car number 654750 provision was made for the fitting of a fresh-air heater. The system adopted required a blanking plate to be fitted beneath the parcel shelf for the fresh-air intake. Available in kit form, when the fresh-air heater was fitted, the blanking plate that was affixed using screws could be removed and ducting fitted around the existing recirculatory heater.

The Smith's recirculatory heater was upgraded on 948cc models but

57

Engine Rebuild

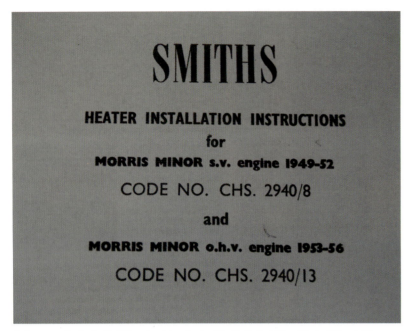

Reference codes for the Smith's recirculatory heater fitted to Series MM and Series II Morris Minor models.

Series MM water pump.

Series II water pump.

remained as an optional extra on standard models and as an aftermarket accessory. The full kit is illustrated opposite.

With the introduction of the 1098cc Morris 1000 models in 1962, the use of the previously available Smith's recirculatory heater continued with Deluxe models having this unit supplied as part of the specification. However, during 1963/1964 there was a transitional arrangement where the type of heater supplied was either the Smith's recirculatory type with rheostat control or a new style 2.8kw heater with a three-position vent control with an on/off switch. At this time a further change was made to allow the water control valve to be operated from inside the car. Previously the tap positioned to the rear of the engine block had to be operated manually to control the flow of water to the heater. This later type first introduced in September 1963 was fitted as standard from October 1964. A similarly styled but more powerful 3.8kw heater became available as an option in March 1964. Additional changes included the addition of fresh-air ducting, which necessitated changes to the bulkhead and the radiator cowling. This was effective from car number 1039564.

PROJECT CAR

This later style arrangement was present on the last saloon. The original heater unit, which had been inoperative for well over twenty years, was removed, the matrix flushed out and the overall condition fully assessed. When stripped down it became immediately apparent that it would not be in keeping with the rest of the restoration to ignore the amount of surface rust on the inside panels. Consequently, they were cleaned down, treated with a rust inhibitor, primed and painted before being reassembled ready for installation. Full checks were made on the motor, which reassuringly still worked perfectly. Additional checks were made on the condition of the foam rubber blanking plates before they were refitted as part of the reassembly.

Radiator

The original radiator was sent to a specialist company and was re-cored,

Engine Rebuild

Early type Smith's recirculatory unit as fitted to Series MM and Series II models.

Later reference for Smith's recirculatory heater.

Heater unit with rheostat control.

Ducting and hoses as supplied.

Component parts for fitting.

Later style water pump.

pressure-tested and repainted in readiness for reinstallation. When refitted, new hoses with replacement jubilee clips, a new 82°C thermostat and a new radiator cap were used.

Useful Technical Information

Cooling system capacities
Series MM 13.5 pints
Series II 9.75 pints
Morris 1000 948cc Without heater 9.75 pints
With heater 10.75 pints
Morris 1000 1098cc Without heater 8.75 pints
With heater 9.95 pints

Engine Rebuild

Heater unit as removed.

Strip-down revealed substantial rust on inner panels.

Disassembled parts in primer…

The main case required major refurbishment.

… and painted.

Heater unit reassembled and ready for reinstallation.

5
Gearbox Rebuild

GEARBOX

Gearbox Identification

Three different gearboxes were used with each of the 803cc, 948cc and 1098cc A series engines fitted to the Morris Minor. They are easily identified by their external appearance. The smooth case APHM 803cc gearbox was also used in the Austin A30. While the internal components are the same, the A30 main shaft is approximately 2.5 inches shorter to accommodate a different prop-shaft length. The 9M 948cc smooth case gearbox was also used in the Austin A35 and the Austin A40 and featured a remote-control gear change. It is easily distinguished from the later 1098cc gearbox, which had additional strength courtesy of a distinctive ribbed outer casing.

Since it is not uncommon for A-series gearboxes to have been swapped around between models and other manufacturers, including Austin and MG, an additional check may be needed to ensure authenticity and accuracy when ordering replacement parts. The lay gear tooth count chart overleaf, supplied by Andrew Bywater, is a useful reference guide.

Gearbox Removal

Removing the gearbox from the vehicle can be done by taking out the engine and gearbox together or by separating the gearbox from the engine while leaving the engine in situ. Both methods will require the battery to be disconnected, the cooling system to be drained and the heater tap at the rear of the engine and the engine steady bar to be removed. If the engine and gearbox are being removed together, the radiator will need taking out and the exhaust will need to be disconnected from the engine. With these items removed there will be greater scope for downward engine movement when removing the gearbox separately. Alternatively, the removal of the front bumper assembly and the front panel will allow for the removal of the engine and gearbox together, with the aid of an engine hoist.

With the front carpets removed and working from the inside of the vehicle undo the brass screws that

Gearbox repair kit.

Gearbox Rebuild

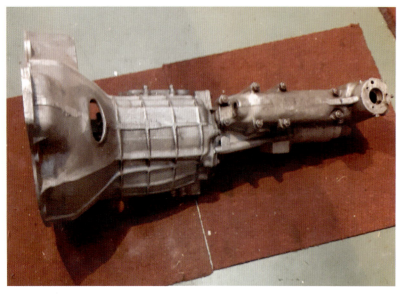

1098cc ribbed case gearbox.

BMC part no.	Tooth count	Original application
22A288	13;18;23;29	APHM smooth case – 803cc Minor, Austin A30
22A287	13;18;24;28	9M smooth case – 948cc Minor, Austin A35, A40, and 9C smooth case – Healey 'Frogeye' Sprite
22A207	13;19;23;26	9CG smooth case – 948cc MG Midget Mk I, Austin Healey Sprite Mk I – *note 1*
22G083	13;19;24;28	10MA and 10MC ribbed case – 1098cc Minor, Austin A35, A40
22G76	13;19;23;26	10CG ribbed case – Early 1098cc MG Midget – *note 1*
22G232 or 22G1100	13;19;23;26	10CC ribbed case – Late 1098cc MG Midget and 12CC, 12CD, 12CE ribbed case – 1275cc MG Midget – *note 1*

Note 1. Although the MG Midget lay gears have the same tooth counts, they are not interchangeable as the tooth angles can vary and the overall length of the lay gear varies by approximately 0.5mm depending on whether it is a smooth or ribbed case.

hold the metal gearbox cover plate in place noting the position of the four longer screws that fit in the gearbox support. Remove the curved oil filler cover plate. Next, remove the anti-rattle spring and plunger from the side of the gear lever housing before undoing the screws that hold the gear lever in position. Carefully extract the gear lever, noting the 'O' ring at the base on 948cc and 1098cc gearboxes.

Moving to the exterior of the vehicle, jack the vehicle up and securely position it on axle stands at a convenient height to allow access to the underside. Disconnect the gearbox earth lead attached to the crossmember. Next, drain the gearbox oil via the drain plug on the underside before turning attention to removing the propeller shaft. Before doing so, carefully mark the propeller shaft flange and the pinion drive flange. Disconnecting the propeller shaft from the gearbox is best done by removing the four bolts that secure the propeller shaft to the differential and easing it out of the back of the gearbox.

Before disconnecting the gearbox from the engine, the clutch adjuster return springs should be removed along with the clutch adjuster rod. Removal of the clutch relay lever should follow next, before the removal of the two bolts either side of the shaft to gearbox and chassis member along with the split pin and clevis pin.

With the engine and gearbox still supported, attention should focus on removing the four bolts securing the gearbox crossmember to the chassis rails either side of the vehicle along with the two nuts securing the rear rubber mountings. The engine should then be lowered as far as it will go before removing the bolts that secure the gearbox to the engine. Two of the bolts secure the starter in position, and with these removed the starter can be extracted.

Separation and removal are achieved by pulling the gearbox rearwards while rotating the unit through 30 degrees in order to clear the steering rack. It is essential that the gearbox is supported during this process and that it is not allowed to hang on the main drive shaft, as this could potentially cause distortion to the main drive gear shaft.

REPLACEMENT OR REBUILD?

Replacement Options

For the home restorer with a faulty, noisy or damaged gearbox there are several replacement and repair options to consider. These are simply replacing the unit with a used known item that is working perfectly, acquiring and fitting a replacement reconditioned unit or stripping and rebuilding an existing unit. The information that follows relates principally to the stripping down and rebuild of a later 1098cc ribbed case gearbox, though the principles outlined are applicable to earlier 803cc and 948cc gearboxes. It is worth noting though that the earlier gearboxes had synchromesh cones while the later 1098cc units had baulk rings fitted.

Preparation

It is essential that the gearbox strip down is undertaken in a clean, dust-free working environment. Before commencing the dismantling process, any residue of oil and dirt on the exterior casing should be removed using a proprietary cleaner for the removal of oil and grease. The previously drained gearbox oil should be disposed of with environmental considerations in mind.

Removal of the Remote-Control Housing and Rear Cover/Extension

With the gear lever already removed and the gears in neutral, attention should now focus on the remote-control housing at the rear of the gearbox. With the eight retaining nuts undone it can be lifted off. The speedo drive should then be unscrewed, and the pinion removed.

Gearbox Rebuild

To remove the rear extension part, it is advisable to stand the gearbox upright on the bell housing, making sure it is sufficiently supported to allow clearance for the input shaft and avoid any potential damage. With the nine screws that secure the extension in place removed, it should then be possible to lift the extension slightly before twisting it in an anti-clockwise direction to enable the control rod to be disengaged from the selector rod end. It can then be lifted clear.

Side Cover Plate

Attention should now focus on the side cover plate. Care needs to be exercised when releasing this, as two detent springs and plungers are held in place by the plate, and these can come out at pace. With the plate removed an initial assessment of the condition of the gear teeth can be made. This may determine the extent of the work required, particularly if the gears are badly worn or chipped. It may also assist in deciding which of the options outlined above are best suited to the budget available. In this regard, it is useful to inspect any residue in the oil drain plug, which has a concave 'cup' shape that tends to collect broken teeth and other metal fragments.

Clutch Release Bearing and Lever

The clutch release bearing is removed by prising off two retaining springs that attach it to the clutch lever fork. The clutch lever can be removed after the nut and locking washer on the clutch lever bolt have been removed and the bolt has been unscrewed. Note that the pedestal has an internal thread to assist the locking action.

Front Cover Removal

The front cover should be removed next by undoing the seven retaining nuts with a 7/16" socket spanner. Gently prise the cover away using an old bolt from the clutch lever pedestals as a reaction.

Removal of Selector Rods

With the gearbox placed on its side with the bell housing furthest away, locate and remove the two plugs at the front along with the spring and plunger on the lower one. Using a slim line 7/16 inch socket via the gearbox drain hole, remove the reverse fork locating bolt locknut and the bolt. Attention should then focus on the removal of the selector rods. The following sequence should be adopted.

Removing the remote-control housing.

Disengaging the control rod from the selector rod end.

Gearbox Rebuild

The seven nuts securing the front cover are easily accessed.

Normally the lay shaft can be easily tapped out.

Third/fourth, first/second, reverse. As the rods are drawn out the two interlock balls should be removed. These should be visible through the holes in the rear of the casing. It may be necessary to use a piece of welding wire to assist with the removal.

Tip: A small, pen-sized magnet is useful to retrieve balls and plungers when they are released.

At the end of this process there should be a collection of springs and plungers, including three single-ended plungers with springs, two ball bearings and a single double-ended plunger. In operation the spring-assisted plungers provide the 'detent' effect when a gear is selected, and the double-ended plunger and two balls provide the 'interlock', which prevents more than one gear being selected at once.

Tip: With the selector rods removed, the selector forks can be reattached to help keep everything together until reassembly.

Removal of Key Components

For the next stage in the strip-down, specialist tools or home-sourced equivalents will be required to assist in the removal of the layshaft, main shaft and first motion shaft.

Layshaft Removal

Tap out the layshaft using a small diameter drift, if it does not slide out on its own. When the drift is removed, the laygear and two shims should drop into the case. It will not be possible to remove the laygear just yet. It should be noted that there is a locating peg on the main shaft-bearing carrier. As this will need to be in the same position when reassembly occurs, a useful tip is to mark the alloy casing as a reference point.

Main Shaft and First Motion Shaft Removal

The application of moderate heat using a small blowtorch or a hot air gun to help expand the aluminium casing can prove useful when attempting to remove and separate some of the key internal components. Heating the rear of the casing prior to removing the main shaft assembly through the rear of the gearbox is a useful strategy. The laygear should be kept out of the way whilst removing the shafts. To remove the first motion shaft, first heat the front of the casing before tapping the first motion shaft forwards by about a quarter of an inch. Next remove the large circlip, re-heat again before pressing the shaft back into the box and removing it from the inside (1098cc) or from the outside (948 or 803cc).

The reverse-fork locating bolt is accessed via the gearbox drain hole.

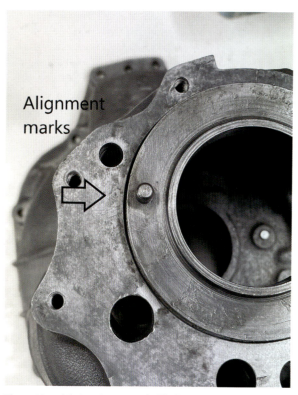
The position of the locating peg marked for future reference.

The laygear can now be extracted along with the two thrust washers. The larger thrust washer is located at the front of the case. The reverse gear assembly can be removed by releasing the securing bolt underneath and tapping the short shaft into the gearbox. The main shaft should be scrutinised for signs of wear and assessed for further attention. Undo the large nut. It is common for this nut to work loose on its own, resulting in the worm drive not being held tight enough. A consequence is that the speedometer will not work.

The bearing and housing should be tapped off along the rear of the shaft. The third and fourth gear synchronizer will slide off the other end. The third speed main shaft gear is removed by pushing in a spring-loaded pin in the hole on the shaft and rotating the splined thrust washer so that the plunger is held down. This will allow the gear and the washer to slide off. Make sure the tiny plunger and spring are retained.

The second and third speed gear bronze bushes should be removed next. As these are quite a tight fit, they may need to be heated gently with a plumber's blowlamp to expand the bronze. The three-piece assembly is designed to be locked in place by the splines on the end and there is also an interlock ring that joins the two together. This ensures that the bushes do not rotate with the gears.

The first-gear synchronizer assembly will now slide off the back of the shaft. However, care needs to be taken not to lose a tiny 'slug' (1098cc only), which may fall out from inside the assembly when it is off the shaft. If the gearbox has been previously

The application of heat to the outer casing, prior to removing the main shaft assembly.

On the 1098cc gearbox, the main shaft assembly is removed from inside the casing.

Gearbox Rebuild

rebuilt, it will have a small spacer washer between the bearing and the first gear synchronizer (1098cc only). A new one will be supplied with the new third motion bearing – but it is important to remember to discard it if an earlier smooth-case gearbox is being rebuilt. The shaft should now be inspected for damage.

Helpful Tips

- It is always worth replacing the synchronizer springs in the $1/2$ and $3/4$ assemblies. The ball bearings are usually reusable. If in doubt check them with a micrometer.
- It is worth having some replacement springs and balls available, as it is very easy to lose these during re-assembly.
- When disassembling the synchronizer hubs, place them inside a large, strong plastic bag. When the outer rings are separated, three springs and balls will fly out at speed. If the task is completed inside a plastic bag, the risk of

Removing the reverse gear assembly.

The third speed main shaft gear with the hole for the release mechanism visible.

Bronze bushes being gently heated to aid release.

losing any components will be reduced.
- If the gearbox has not been rebuilt before the laygear roller bearings will need to be removed (aftermarket ones will just drop out). The roller bearings are not held in a cage but will come out individually with separate channels that hold them in place. The channels are held in place by circlips front and back. These are quite difficult to remove, as there are no holes allowing circlip pliers to be used. It is usually necessary to bend the circlips inwards slightly with a fine punch or similar implement. They can then be teased out by using a thin screwdriver.
- When the main casing has been relieved of all its parts, it is necessary to make sure it is as clean as possible before reassembly begins. A selection of bottle brushes of different diameters and some white spirit is recommended. If available, the use of compressed air is useful in making sure the inside of the gearbox is free of any debris. Particular attention should be paid to the plunger holes.

Before starting the actual rebuild, it is advisable to read through the process outlined in the pages that follow. The information that follows has been compiled using the experience of people familiar with the processes involved in rebuilding gearboxes. It highlights the recommended sequencing of the work involved and includes step-by-step illustrations of the reassembly process, as well as providing helpful practical hints and tips and advice on some of the pitfalls that can be encountered.

Before commencing the rebuild of the gearbox it is worth considering what tools and equipment will be required to do the job effectively. Key to the operation is having all the necessary replacement parts to hand at the commencement of the work. During the strip-down, worn or damaged parts should have been identified. It is prudent to replace all the wearing parts. Better to incur the expense of acquiring new superior quality parts at this stage than to risk previously installed parts failing and the entire process having to be repeated. The parts listed below (or on the side panel) should be regarded as 'consumable' and be replaced as a matter of course.

RECOMMENDED REPLACEMENT PARTS

- 1st motion shaft bearing
- 3rd motion shaft bearing
- Laygear bearings (x2)
- Layshaft
- 3rd motion shaft nose bearing (1098: Needle roller, 948: Phosphor bronze)
- 1st motion and 3rd motion shaft bearing shims (as found necessary)
- Baulk or synchro rings as required
- Locking washers
- Laygear thrust washer (if required)
- Gasket set
- Speedo drive oil seal
- Clutch fork
- Clutch fork close tolerance pivot bolt
- Locking washer for pivot bolt
- Tail shaft oil seal
- Fibre washers 9.5mm $^3/_8$" (x 2)
- Clutch fork rubber gaiter and two bell housing dust covers
- Nuts, bolts and spring washers as necessary

Parts availability is good.

ASSESSMENT GUIDE

Key components that will need checking for signs of wear or damage include the following.

- Baulk rings and gears
  The baulk rings may be reused if they still have internal grooves that have not been worn completely away. These can be tested on the bench by attempting to 'twist' the rings when pressed against the conical surfaces on the 2nd/3rd/4th gears. It should be possible to assess the remaining 'grip' available. Check the condition of the corresponding conical surfaces on the gears. They are normally smooth black in appearance. If they are shiny or have damaged surfaces, the synchro will not work properly, and the gears will 'crunch' when engaged. The small 'dog teeth' on the gears should also be checked for excessive 'rounding'.
- Laygear and reverse gear
  The parts that usually take the most wear are the first-gear ring and the corresponding teeth on the laygear. The reverse idler also takes its share of the wear. If the teeth on either the first-gear ring or the reverse idler are badly damaged, the gearbox will be excessively noisy in these gears and in the worst-case scenario will jump out of gear. Good second-hand or new parts are available.
- Selector rods
  Selector rods can be found to have longitudinal wear ridges from the action of the detent plungers, but replacement of these will be a judgement call. If found to be excessively worn, better second-hand items will need to be found as new ones are not available.
- Synchro hub springs
  It is not always necessary to strip the synchro hub assemblies, but it is worth considering doing so, as the springs tend to weaken.

Helpful Hints

- Always aim to work in a clean area and regularly check the inside of the gearbox casing and all components for signs of unwanted grit, dirt or debris.
- Have a small oil dispenser filled with 20w50 engine oil to hand to lubricate various components as and when required.
- Have a plentiful supply of different-sized shims and thrust washers to select from, as these tend to be measure and select at the point of usage.
- Ensure access is available to heat sources such as an oven or a plumber's blowtorch for the heating of various components and the gearbox casing as required.
- Exercise patience throughout the rebuilding process and resist the temptation to force components into position.

GEARBOX REASSEMBLY

A useful starting point in the process of reassembling the gearbox is to concentrate on three sub-assemblies relating to the gears. These include the first motion shaft (input shaft), the third motion shaft (output shaft) and the layshaft and laygear assembly. Pre-assembly of these components is recommended in readiness for fitting into the casing. Key elements of the various assembly processes undertaken by Geoff Taylor are illustrated and explained in the pages that follow.

The recommended order of rebuild is:

- Test-fit lay gear and set end float
- 1st motion shaft
- 3rd motion shaft
- Reassembly of gearbox
  - Reverse idler
  - Laygear
  - 1st motion shaft
  - 3rd motion shaft
  - Layshaft
  - Selectors and detents
  - Tail housing
  - Remote housing
  - Front cover

Laygear End Float Measurement Check

The laygear when fitted has a specified end float of 0.003 inches. In order to achieve this when refitting, it may be necessary to use different-sized thrust washers. In exceptional cases the use of an oilstone may be needed to take a fraction off the washer to achieve the desired result. Prior to checking, fit new bearings into each end of the laygear. Replacement bearings are caged, so do not need clips to hold them in place. Once fitted, lower the laygear into the gearbox with the large end and the accompanying large thrust washer at the front. Once the small thrust washer has been fitted at the rear, use a feeler gauge to measure the gap. Adjust accordingly to achieve the 0.003 inches end float and then remove the laygear and washers from the case.

1st Motion Shaft

Reassembling the first motion shaft is quite straightforward. It requires the bearing to be fitted along with the lock tab and nut. The images in the following sequence show the process of rebuilding the first motion shaft (see Figs 1 to 3 opposite).

3rd Motion Shaft

The third motion shaft is the most complex assembly of the gearbox. Setting out all the components on a clean surface prior to commencing the assembly process is strongly recommended. If the synchro hubs have been taken apart the first step is to reassemble them so that they are ready to fit to the shaft. The outer ring slides on the hub with detent balls and springs located within the hub. These must be held in as the ring is slid on and correctly positioned. There are various methods to hold the balls/springs down while fitting. Whatever method is selected, it is essential that the assembly is placed inside a plastic bag, so that in the event of the balls flying out they are safely contained.

A special BMC tool makes this job easier. In the absence of the tool a sturdy cable tie or jubilee clip can be used to hold all the balls and springs in position (see Fig. 4 opposite).

Main components of the 1098cc gearbox.

Gearbox Rebuild

Fig. 1 Slide the bearing on to the first motion shaft noting the position of the groove. Do not fit the clip yet.

Fig. 2 Fit the lock washer noting the position of the tab.

Fig. 3 Fit the lock nut and tighten it up firmly. Bend the lock tab up against one of the flat surfaces on the lock nut.

Fig. 4 Special BMC tools. 18G471 dummy layshaft and hub synchroniser assembly ring 18G144, with a modern nylon version of the hub tool.

Putting the Hubs and Selectors Back Together

The third and fourth hub and ring assembly should be attempted first. It is important to line up the three indents in the ring with the matching indents in the hub. These are intended to give clearance to the 'ears' of the baulk rings. As both sides of the ring are identical, it does not matter which way round the hub is fitted as long as the indents match. However, the way the assembly fits on the shaft does matter. In the case of 803cc or 948 gearboxes, there are no indents on the hub due to the different synchro system used.

Fitting the first and second hub is more complicated. Several things need to be borne in mind. It is important to note that the position for first gear is to slide the ring away from the synchro ring indents and that the wider plainer edge of the gear ring faces away from the indents. Before proceeding any further note the position of the three identical holes on the inside of the ring that contains the synchro springs. Note also that there is a larger fourth hole, which houses a tiny 'slug'.

With the two components facing the correct way they need to be oriented radially. Close examination of the ring teeth will show that one of the teeth is 'relieved', that is reduced in height. Key to completing the operation is the rotation of the outer ring, so that the relieved tooth lines up with the hole for the slug. The slug can be installed at this point. It is important to double-check the alignment before proceeding.

Fitting Bearings: Tips

- Before attempting to fit bearings, make sure the bearing surfaces on the shaft are clean and polished up as any small burrs will make it more difficult to fit the bearing.
- Any operation involving fitting a bearing needs to be completed swiftly and in one motion.
- Never use force or hit the bearing to transfer pressure from the inner to outer race (or vice-versa).
- Applying moderate heat to the bearing prior to assembly makes the task easier.

Gearbox Rebuild

There are two types of third-motion shaft bearings. The original third motion shaft bearing had a longer inner race than the outer. Replacement bearings have a spacer fitted to compensate for this. It is important to note that this spacer is only necessary on the 1098 assembly. It must not be fitted to earlier gearboxes. Like the input shaft bearing the outer has a groove in for a clip and this must be positioned correctly facing backwards towards the prop shaft. As with the input shaft bearing, once heated it should fit on easily. First position the spacer before fitting the warmed bearing, remembering to pay attention to the groove.

The images in the following section (Figs 5-16) show the process of rebuilding the third motion shaft.

Tip: Use a bag tie to hold the pin in place.

Fig. 5 Check that the shaft is clean before fitting the bearing to the shaft. Note the position of the groove.

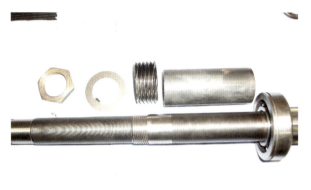

Fig. 6 Fit the spacer and speedometer drive gear. It is worth putting a dab of Loctite or Bearing Fit under the scroll to stop it coming loose.

Fig. 7 Fit the lock washer ensuring the tab faces outermost in the groove followed by the nut. Tighten it up firmly.

Fig. 8 Fit the rear-bearing carrier and clip onto the bearing. It is easier to fit the clip first and then bring the carrier up to it.

Fig. 9 Make sure the slug is fitted (circled) to the 1st and 2nd gear hub. Be careful fitting the hub as the outer gear ring will move quite easily causing the detent balls and springs to fly out never to be found again.

Fig. 10 1st and 2nd gear fitted along with the thrust washer. It is important to ensure that it is replaced the same way that it was removed from the shaft. The outline of the splines on the washer on the side that faces the hub can be clearly seen.

Gearbox Rebuild

Fig. 11 Fit the bronze 2nd gear bush making sure the castellated part is as shown before fitting the baulk ring into 2nd gear. Make sure the point on the three nibs face innermost. Imagine them as pointing the way in.

Fig. 12 Fit 2nd gear onto the bush followed by the coupling washer.

Fig. 13 Fit the 3rd gear bush onto the shaft ensuring the castellated part mates into the coupling washer fitted previously.

Fig. 14 Fit 3rd gear onto the bush as shown.

Fig. 15 This part is fiddly. The locking pin and spring must be fitted to the hole in the shaft. The pin must be held in while the locking ring is fitted over and turned until it clicks into place.

Fig. 16 The lock ring fitted. The pin can clearly be seen in the topmost groove holding the ring in place. The 3rd motion shaft is now complete and can be placed aside.

71

Gearbox Rebuild

Rebuild of the Sub-assemblies into the Casing

With a completed 1st and 3rd motion shaft and the laygear end float set, final checks should be made to ensure that the casing is clean and ready for the installation of various components.

> **Tip:** Before starting this process put the completed 1st motion shaft in a bag and put it in the freezer.

Reverse Gear Idler and Laygear

Figs 17–20 illustrate the fitting of the reverse gear idler and laygear.

1st Motion Shaft

The previously assembled 1st motion shaft can now be fitted. On 1098cc gearboxes it is fitted from the inside. Having been in the freezer, fitting it will be easier. Warming up the area of the box where it is to be fitted with a hot air gun will aid installation.

3rd Motion Shaft

Refitting the 3rd motion shaft into the box requires quite a few things to happen simultaneously to ensure that new parts being fitted line up and parts that have already been fitted do not fall out or get damaged. It may be useful to examine the illustrations that follow (Figs 23–28) before completing this task. Key to the operation is an awareness that there is a relieved section of the bearing housing to clear the reverse gear idler and a hole with a corresponding dowel in the tail housing that must line up when the shaft and housing is fully in position.

Final Fitting of the 3rd Motion Shaft, Rear Bearing Housing and Layshaft

This step (Figs 29–33) requires the gearbox to be placed in an upright position on the bell housing with a couple of pieces of wood underneath to protect the 1st motion shaft. It is worth remembering that the laygear is not retained at this point and that the rod suspending it may fall out.

Fig. 17 Oil the reverse idler shaft and fit it to the casing, noting the end with the hole goes innermost.

Fig. 18 Fit reverse gear and push the shaft fully home. Line the hole in the shaft up with the hole in the casing. (Note that a screwdriver slot in the shaft allows it to be turned).

Fig. 19 Fit the locating pin in from outside the casing with a spring washer and nip it up.

Fig. 20 Fit the bearing into each end of the laygear before fitting the laygear into the casing along with the thrust washers. It helps to suspend the laygear on a slim rod temporarily.

Gearbox Rebuild

Fig. 21 Fit the 1st motion shaft into the box allowing access to the groove in the bearing to fit the clip. On this 1098 gearbox tap it through further than needed at this stage.

Fig. 22 Carefully fit the clip into the groove and then tap the assembly back so the clip sits in the recess.

Fig. 23 Place the 3rd gear baulk ring into the plain side of the 3rd/4th hub.

Fig. 24 Fit the hub to the shaft and place the 4th gear synchro ring in.

Fig. 25 Place some grease onto the nose of the shaft and fit the small roller bearing.

Fig. 26 When fitting the 3rd motion shaft the cut-out in the bearing housing must line up with the reverse gear idler (inset) so it does not foul the gear.

Gearbox Rebuild

Fig. 27 The peg on the case and the hole in the bearing housing. These and the tail housing all have to line up. Resist the temptation to push the bearing housing fully home when fitting it.

Fig. 28 Feed the 3rd motion shaft in at an angle so as to clear reverse gear. As it clears, lower it down to line the nose bearing up with the 1st motion shaft and push it in only as far as required to keep the nose located. Try to get the cut-out in the bearing housing in the right place to clear reverse gear. Do not push it fully home yet. Take care not to knock the hubs when fitting, otherwise the balls and springs may fly out.

With care, it should be possible to select each of the gears by sliding the respective hub in the direction of the gear intended. The hub should slide over with a good 'snick' sound as it engages the gear. Make sure the box turns freely and smoothly for each gear. Reverse gear is selected by leaving the box in the neutral position and sliding the idler into mesh. Another gear has now been introduced to the train between the laygear and first gear. This is what causes the output shaft to rotate in the other direction. Having checked the operation of the gearbox, return everything to neutral (*see* Fig. 34).

TESTING THE ASSEMBLY

Having reached this stage it is a good opportunity to check for free movement in the gearbox and to check that the gears can be selected. If something is not right, now is the best time to identify and rectify. First, give everything a shot of oil including the actual gears themselves. Leave the box lying on its side as the layshaft at this point is floating and not retained. The gear hubs are in the neutral position meaning the input and output shafts should be free to turn independently of each other. The laygear will rotate with the input shaft, but the gears should just spin freely. Ensure there is no roughness or tight spots and that everything feels good.

SELECTOR MECHANISM

With the above checks satisfactorily completed, work to refit the selectors and interlocks can commence. A patient approach to completing this task is strongly recommended.

Fitting Selector Forks and Rods

With these tasks completed, check that all the selector fork screws are tightened up along with the locknuts. While they need fastening tightly it is worth remembering that they are threaded into brass. Consequently, it is important that they are not over-tightened (*see* Figs 35–48).

Final Check

At this stage it is worth checking again that all the gears can still be selected. With the interlocks fitted it should only be possible to select one gear at a time with the others becoming locked out until the one selected is returned to the neutral position.

FRONT COVER AND TAIL HOUSING

Prior to fitting the tail housing and front cover measurements need to be taken to determine the size of the shims required. These are select on assembly shims for use between the cover/housing and the bearings. The BMC workshop manual recommends the use of 0.006-inch shims and suggests measuring to check. A digital Vernier caliper is a useful tool for this task.

Gearbox Rebuild

Fig. 29 The rear bearing housing sitting proud.

Fig. 30 Lower the rear tail casing on so the peg locates in the hole in the housing. Twist the casing as appropriate to line the holes up where it screws to the main casing. Lift the tail case off and check the location of the bearing carrier.

Fig. 31 Using a soft drift carefully and evenly tap the bearing housing home.

Fig. 32 With the box back on its side, the laygear can be brought into mesh and the layshaft fitted.

Fig. 33 The end of the layshaft that has the cut-out section needs to end up in the bell housing and be oriented as shown where it will locate into the front cover.

Fig. 34 Internal view of gearbox with gears refitted.

Gearbox Rebuild

FITTING SELECTOR FORKS AND RODS

Fig. 35 Fit the reverse selector fork in position with the screw towards the oil drain hole.

Fig. 36 Fit the 3rd/4th selector fork.

Fig. 37 Fit the 1st/2nd selector fork.

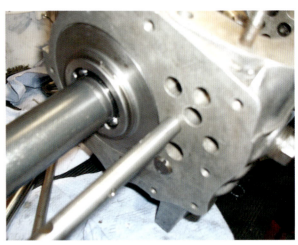

Fig. 38 Fit the reverse selector rod into this hole.

Fig. 39 Fit the rod through the reverse selector fork and pass it through the hole in the 3rd/4th selector and finally into the front of the casing, making sure the screw in the reverse fork locates into the indent.

Fig. 40 Fit a double-ended slug into this hole and make sure it goes all the way home. They sometimes need to pass through a hole further down to get to where they need to be.

Gearbox Rebuild

Fig. 41 A rod can be seen here making sure the slug is where it needs to be (arrowed). Note that it has had to pass through another hole in the casing.

Fig. 42 Next fit the 1st/2nd selector rod, feed it through the fork and right the way in. As with reverse gear, make sure the indent in the rod lines up with the screw in the fork and nip it up.

Fig. 43 The 3rd/4th selector rod goes here. Position it and pass it through the fork, but do not position it all the way home just yet.

Fig. 44 Drop an interlock ball into this hole and using a thin rod make sure it is fully home.

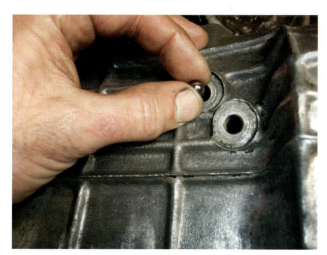

Fig. 45 Roll the box over and drop an interlock ball into this hole (the rear of the box is to the left).

Fig. 46 Push the 3rd/4th selector rod home and nip the screw up making sure it fits to the indent in the rod.

Gearbox Rebuild

Fig. 47 Fit the slug and retainer shown here into this hole. Rounded end first, followed by the spring and then the cap with a new ³⁄₈ fibre washer fitted. Nip it up.

Fig. 48 The plain pin goes into this hole, along with a new fibre washer before being nipped up.

MEASURING FOR SHIMS

Fig. 49 Measuring how far the bearing protrudes.

Fig. 50 Measuring the depth of the recess in the cover or housing.

78

FITTING THE SIDE COVER

Fig. 51 There are two spring loaded detent plungers that must be fitted before the side cover is fitted. Fitting the side cover requires the detent plungers and springs to be fitted along with the gasket and cover, as illustrated in Figs 51 and 52.

Fig. 52 Fit them into the hole shown here. Do not be concerned about the different heights. Carefully fit the gasket followed by the cover. Secure it with the nuts and washers, nipping them up evenly.

Fig. 53 Spacer shown fitted to 1st and 2nd selector rod between selector fork and casing. Spacer shown fitted to 1st and 2nd selector rod between selector fork and casing in order to prevent the selector for first gear travelling too far.

Gearbox Rebuild

In simple terms you need to:

- Measure how much the bearing protrudes from the face of the box (not the clip).
- Measure the thickness of the gasket when it has been compressed by fitting.
- Measure the depth of the recess in the cover.

Add the figure obtained for the depth of the cover recess to the thickness of the gasket. From this, subtract the amount the bearing protrudes, and this will provide the measurement for shimming.

Figs 49–50 illustrate measuring the front cover for shims. The procedure is exactly the same for the tail housing.

Fitting the Front Cover

Make sure the face is clean and the layshaft is oriented correctly. It will be obvious when fitting the gasket if it is not. Carefully fit the gasket over the studs, grease the shims lightly and fit them into the recess in the front cover. Place the front cover on followed by the spring washers and nuts. Make sure the cover is sitting flush and not riding high. Resist the temptation to pull it into position by tightening the nuts. Once correctly and evenly aligned tighten the nuts (47in/lb is recommended).

Fitting the Tail Housing

To complete this task it is best if the gearbox is in an upright position. Prior to fitting the tail housing make sure all the faces are clean before placing the gasket on the gearbox end. Coat the shims with grease before placing them into the bearing recess in the housing. The housing has to be lowered on to the casing so as to allow the selector finger to engage in the rods. This may need some wiggling in order to make it fit. As a guide when looking down, imagine that the drain plug is at 6 o'clock. Lower the housing so that the bottom is at 5 o'clock. In this position it should be possible to engage the finger in the selectors while rotating the housing clockwise and into position. Resist the temptation to force or hit the housing to get it in position. As with the front cover, make sure it is accurately located and not riding high. The screws should not be used to pull the housing into position.

Finally, fit the triangular steady bracket.

REMOTE HOUSING

The remote housing mounts on top of the tail housing and transmits movement from the gear lever to the selector rods. Place the gaskets over the studs. Lubricate the remote control rod and grease the cup in the tail housing. Check that the nylon selector bush is intact and fitted to the ball that protrudes from the bottom of the remote control unit. Align the selector bush with the cup in the tail housing so that it will just drop straight in as it is lowered. Ensure that the bush does not get pushed up the shaft because it is not correctly aligned. Lower the remote housing on, fit the spring washers and nuts and nip them up.

At this stage it is well worthwhile fitting the gear lever to the housing to ensure everything operates as expected and checking that all gears can be selected, everything turns freely and nothing has fallen into the gearbox unnoticed. In effect this is the last opportunity to rectify any faults before the gearbox is fitted to the car. Provided all is well, fit the side cover.

OUTPUT OIL SEAL

Where the prop-shaft yoke enters the gearbox, there is an oil seal housed in a metal housing that is tapped onto the end of the tail housing. Clean the seal housing and end of the tail housing, wipe some silicone gasket compound around the inside of the housing and tap it on up to the shoulder in the casting.

> **Tip:** Use the old oil seal to protect the top of the new one whilst tapping in on to the shoulder. Make sure it is installed evenly by tapping gently around the circumference.

STARTER PINION COVER

The very last part to be fitted is the domed cover located by three screws that covers the starter pinion. It is possible to do this when the box is in the car, but it is extremely awkward getting at the screws. Place the cover on and tighten the three screws.

TIPS AND MODIFICATIONS

There are a couple of useful modifications that can be done to the gearbox while it is apart. One is to prevent first gear overthrowing and effectively jamming and the other is to fit larger diameter screws for the steady cable bracket.

1. *First gear overthrowing*

    In normal use, it is possible to overthrow first gear either by simply being too enthusiastic when selecting the gear or by selecting the gear when the car is rolling. The result is that the selector moves too far and this allows the balls to start escaping in the hub, jamming the gear and preventing it coming out of gear. With luck some careful 'jarring' of the gear lever will be sufficient to push them back in. If this fails internal inspection will be required.

    In order to prevent the selector for first gear travelling too far, adding a 1.9mm-thick brass spacer to the selector rod is one solution. This addition prevents the selector from travelling too far while allowing sufficient clearance for when selecting the gear and for the gear to find its correct position (*see* Fig. 53).

2. *Steady cable bracket*

    The steady cable bracket can have quite a pull on it and over time it is fairly common for the threads to become weak or stripped in the gearbox. The holes are blind, so putting a nut behind is not an option. It is possible with care to enlarge these to $5/16$ UNF. This task is best undertaken when the casing is empty, as it will be easier to get a drill in and to clear out any resulting swarf or debris. A 6.9mm tapping drill plus the taps will be required. If available, a pedestal drill should be used, utilising the depth stop to avoid drilling through.

6

Suspension

INTRODUCTION

The Morris Minor suspension design remained unchanged throughout production from 1948 to 1971. It was heralded as being innovative and successful when introduced and attracted plaudits for its comfortable ride and excellent roadholding. Using independent front suspension and torsion bar springing at the front and semi-elliptic leaf springs at the rear in conjunction with double-acting lever arm hydraulic dampers on saloon, convertible and Traveller models, the system proved dependable and problem free when maintained well. Commercial variants introduced in 1953 adopted the same arrangement but used telescopic shock absorbers on the rear and on later 8cwt models stronger steering arms on the front.

FRONT SUSPENSION

Torsion Bars

The torsion bars fitted to both sides of the vehicle are critical in determining the ride height. Should adjustment be required there is an adjustment plate at the rear end of each torsion bar. The recommended ride height for an unladen vehicle is determined by the difference between the inner and outer fulcrum points on the suspension arm. If this is set at $1^5/_8$ inches (41.27mm) then the ride height will be correct. When making height adjustments using the adjustment plate located at the rear of the torsion bar it is important to note that if the car needs to be raised from its original position a lower hole needs to be selected while a higher hole needs to be selected if the car is being lowered. Movement of ¼" (6.35mm) is achieved by selecting a higher or lower hole. Adjustment is also possible using the splines on the torsion bar. Movement of one spline will result in a height difference of 1½ inches (38.1mm).

Torsion Bar Removal

With the front wheel removed and a jack placed under the rear section of the lower suspension arm, disconnect the bolt and nut holding the tie bar from the fork on the suspension arm along with the nuts and bolts that hold the two sections together. Remove the front half. Disconnect the fulcrum pin from the suspension arm before lowering the jack sufficiently to take the load off the torsion bar. Move to the centre of the car and remove the nut from the rear end of the torsion bar as well as the stepped washer and the nut and bolt that secures the torsion bar lever to the crossmember. Remove the bolt, nut bolt washers and vernier plate. Remove the nut and washer from the eye bolt. It should then be possible to pull the torsion bar out of the chassis and remove it.

Replacing or Refitting Torsion Bars

In the case of the project car, the torsion bars along with the rest of the

The Morris Minor suspension remained largely unchanged throughout 22 years of production (1949 Morris Minor Series MM set-up pictured).

Suspension

The vernier plate showing adjustment positions.

front suspension were removed prior to the bodyshell going for chemical stripping. Due to an oversight, the torsion bars were not marked up to identify which side of the car they came from. Consequently, replacement torsion bars had to be found and fitted. For the purposes of making the vehicle mobile, the torsion bars were fitted without main components such as the engine and gearbox fitted. This necessitated resetting the torsion bars after final assembly of the vehicle.

Fitting Torsion Bars

Start the process of refitting a torsion bar by fitting the rear arm lever to the splines on the torsion bar before fitting the rear part of the lower suspension arm onto the splines at the front end of the bar. Identify the horseshoe washer that fits in the recess of the rear arm lever and ensure that the chamfered side is fitted facing the front of the car. Put the threaded stud at the end of the torsion bar through the hole in the crossmember. Returning to the rear section, loosely fit the stepped washer and nut onto the end of the torsion bar. Then working from the rear of the crossmember, pass a bolt with a flat washer through the slot to align with the correct hole in the vernier plate located on the other side. Ensure that the flat washer that acts as a spacer is fitted between the vernier plate and the arm before placing a spring washer and nut loosely on the end of the bolt.

Returning to the front of the torsion bar, fit new rubbers into the eye bolt before putting the eye bolt rubber through on to the fulcrum pin. Then put the eye bolt into the chassis and loosely fix the washer and nut on the other side. Return to the crossmember and fit the stepped washer into the hole and tighten up. Do not tighten any of the other screws or nuts yet.

Switch attention to the front half of the suspension arm. With the front half of the suspension arm refitted and checks made on the seating of other suspension seals and rubbers, the road wheels should be refitted prior to the car being gently lowered and allowed to settle before further checks on the ride height are carried out. Ideally both sides should sit evenly with a distance of $1\frac{5}{8}$ inches between the inner and outer fulcrum pins on the suspension arm on an unladen car.

Torsion bar showing front locating point.

Torsion Bars: Important Considerations

- Torsion bars are not interchangeable, except when new.
- A torsion bar that has been in use on one side of a vehicle must not be used on the opposite side.
- When removing torsion bars with the intention of reusing them, mark them left and right to assist in replacing them correctly.
- Torsion bar settings and adjustments are best done when the engine and gearbox are in place due to the additional weight at the front of the vehicle.
- If originality is a priority, torsion bars should be painted silver. The rear lever arm and the rest of the suspension components should be painted black.

FRONT SUSPENSION

Kingpin Assembly

The main component in the front suspension is usually referred to as the kingpin or suspension upright. It includes threaded areas for the fitting of top and bottom trunnions, as well as a steering arm, and incorporates the stub axle.

Removal of the Front Suspension Upright

With the vehicle securely supported on axle stands or positioned on a hydraulic lift, begin the removal process by locating the lower suspension arm and removing the bolt that holds the two parts together. Undo the nut that secures the tie rod to the lower arm before turning attention to releasing the bottom trunnion, which is secured by two nuts. Remove the front nut first. An additional nut, which secures the torsion bar to the lower arm, should then be removed along with one on the tie bar fixing bracket and a bolt that secures the tie bar to the forked locator and another on the tie bar. Remove the tie bar from the forked locator before removing the nut from the back of the locator. At this point it should be possible to remove the front part of the lower arm.

Remove the split pin if one is fitted and then loosen the nut that secures the track-rod end to the steering arm. Using a ball joint splitter, split the track-rod end. With this accomplished, remove the previously loosened nut and separate the steering ball joint from the steering arm.

Remove the nut and washer from the fulcrum pin. With a jack placed under the suspension arm pressure can be relieved on the bottom trunnion. The fulcrum pin can then be pulled out from the arm. This should allow for the base of the upright to be removed from the suspension arm. Undoing the nut that secures the top trunnion to the shock absorber will allow for the suspension leg to be removed from the vehicle, provided of course that all brake components have been disconnected.

CHECKING FOR WEAR

With the key suspension components removed from the vehicle, an in-depth assessment should be undertaken to check for general condition and signs of wear. Most important is the amount of wear on the threaded area and the amount of play in the top and bottom trunnions. Excessive wear will mean the sourcing of a new unit. In the past, it was possible to machine-cut the threads and fit oversized trunnions, but this is no longer an option. The key indicator of excessive wear is the amount of sideways movement on the top and bottom trunnions. Assessing the condition of all the rubber components fitted is advisable and replacement recommended. The fulcrum pins need to be assessed for wear on the threads as well as the pin itself.

Replacing Rubber Bushes

If a major overhaul of the front suspension is being undertaken, it is advisable to replace all the rubber bushes. These are available as complete kits. An alternative to the original-style rubber bushes is available in the form of polyurethane bushes. Opinions vary on the relative merits of polyurethane bushes. While favoured by restorers for their hard-wearing, durable qualities as well as their resistance to contaminants such as oil, it is accepted that they are not as good as their rubber counterparts in absorbing vibrations and road noise generated through the suspension, due to the solid nature of the compound. For restorers seeking originality as well as a softer quieter ride, rubber bushes will always have the advantage.

Routine Maintenance

Most components on the front suspension are quite durable, but failure to lubricate both the top and bottom trunnions can result in catastrophic failure, resulting in the suspension collapsing and the road wheel tucking under the front wing. It is recommended that the trunnions are greased every 3,000 miles (4,800km).

REASSEMBLY OF THE FRONT SUSPENSION

Attach the top and bottom trunnions to the threaded parts of the kingpin

New old stock suspension uprights often referred to as kingpins.

Polyurethane suspension bushes are an option favoured by some restorers … but not all!

Suspension

screwing them down to within half or three-quarters of a turn of the bottom thread. It is important to note that the left-hand kingpin has left-hand thread at each end. Ensure that new rubber bushes are carefully positioned within the trunnions. If using new kingpins, remove the steering arm from the old unit and fit to the new one ensuring that the woodruff key is in position. Tighten down. Moving to the vehicle, start at the top of the suspension unit and put the new bush on the damper arm unit before pushing it through the top trunnion. Fit the other bush along with the spacer, tab washer and nut, but do not fully tighten at this stage.

Move to the bottom and put the lower link fulcrum pin through the bottom trunnion, fitting the chamfered washers with the chamfer next to the trunnion on both sides before fitting the rubber rings over the washers. Align the fulcrum pin with the hole in the suspension arm by jacking the arm up to the same level as the pin. Push the pin through and then fit the spring washer and nut to secure it. Then fit the front section of the lower suspension arm and join the two parts together, but do not fully tighten at this stage. Next turn attention to refitting the tie bar, complete with new rubbers, by first fastening it to the chassis location point before attempting to fit the vertical bolt at the other end, which must be aligned with three holes before being secured in place with a spring washer and nut.

Shock Absorbers

The Armstrong double-acting lever-arm shock absorbers fitted to the front and rear of all Morris Minor models (except for vans and pickups, which used telescopic shock absorbers on the rear) are renowned for providing reliable and prolonged service provided they are regularly maintained. Regular checking of fluid levels within the individual units is recommended every 3,000 miles (4,800km) and in the case of the front assemblies this is a straightforward exercise. With care taken to avoid the ingress of dirt or contaminants, the filler screw can easily be removed to allow for topping up using light hydraulic fluid. It is important not to overfill. The recommended level is $3/8$ inch (9.525mm) from the top of the cover. In the case of the rear units the process is more complicated, because the units need to be removed from the vehicle for the topping-up process to be carried out. This entails removing the split pin and nut from the damper-arm link and the nuts, bolts and spring washers, which secure the unit to the spring bracket. Units usually only need replacing if the internal seals fail. Excessive or persistent fluid leakage is a good indicator. New, later-style replacements are available as is an exchange service. Earlier style units as fitted to Series MM cars that are much rarer can be re-commissioned.

REAR SUSPENSION

The rear suspension on Morris Minors consists of a leaf spring arrangement in conjunction with lever arm hydraulic shock absorbers on saloon, convertible and Traveller models and telescopic shock absorbers on vans and pick-ups.

Tie bar ready to be fitted to the suspension arm and chassis.

Suspension arm fitted in readiness for assembly on the bottom of the kingpin.

Suspension

Complete kingpin assembly. Accurate adjustments can only be made with the engine and gearbox fitted and the vehicle standing on all four road wheels.

Throughout production four different leaf spring arrangements were used.

Up to car number 680463 seven-leaf $7/32$ inch (5.5mm) springs were used. In December 1958, the number of leafs was reduced from seven to five and the thickness changed to ¼ inch for saloons and convertibles. Traveller models retained the use of the seven ¼ inch leaf arrangement (6.35mm). Later Traveller models were fitted with seven-leaf $5/16$ inch (7.93mm) springs. Commercial vehicles had a different arrangement. Series II vans and pick-ups had seven leaf springs fitted up to van number 6043, but thereafter eight $5/16$ inch (7.93mm) leaf springs were fitted. When 8cwt models were introduced in April 1968, the number of leafs was reduced to seven but the size of the individual leafs was increased. 6cwt models retained the eight-leaf arrangement. It is important to note that the rear leaf springs as fitted to commercial variants are not interchangeable with those used on saloons, convertibles or Travellers due to the fact that the rear eye is larger.

Rear Spring Removal

Replacing the rear springs is a straightforward task that can be undertaken by the home restorer. Removing rusted-in or corroded nuts and bolts tends to be the main difficulty. Soaking these items in penetrating fluid such as WD

Armstrong double-acting front lever arm suspension unit.

Suspension

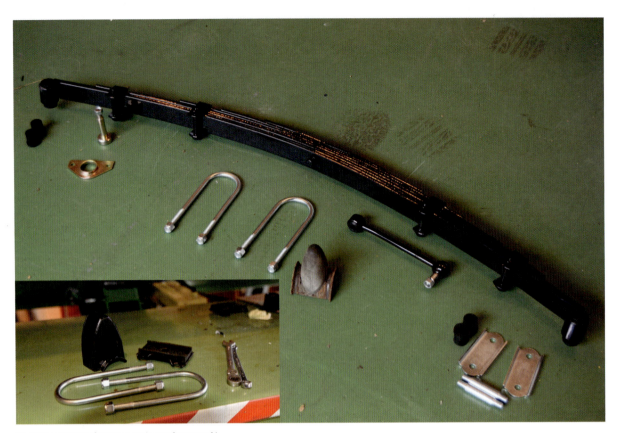

Component parts of rear suspension replacement kit.

40 prior to tackling the job may help, but often it is easier to remove the nuts by cutting them off with an angle grinder. All necessary replacement parts are readily available. Once the vehicle has been jacked up, the body should be supported on axle stands and the following suggested sequence followed.

Start by loosening but not removing the rear shackle nuts before turning attention to removing the large U bolts and bump stops that fit over the axle. It may be necessary and easier to cut the U bolts off. With the axle supported, ideally with a trolley jack, remove the nut from the front bolt before attempting to tap the bolt out. This is likely to prove difficult. With the two small bolts already removed, tap the bolt through along with the retaining plate into which the central bolt fits. With the bolts removed the plate and the bolt will come out together. At this point it will be necessary to use the jack to take the weight of the spring before turning attention to removing the already loosened rear shackle nuts. Remove the inner and outer shackle plate and, using a drift, attempt to push the top pin out. It should then be possible to detach the spring and lower it using the jack.

Rear spring fitment with lower central pin fitted and fastened to the rear shackle.

Suspension

Rear spring front fixing. It is important to fit the locating plate before pushing the central pin through.

Work in progress showing the position of components including U bolts, rubbers, plates and the rear shock absorber unit and fixings.

Fitting a New Spring

With new components available, the fitting of replacement springs is quite straightforward. However, it is a task made easier if there is an extra pair of hands available to help. The use of one or more jacks to support the axle and the weight of the spring is advisable. It is also helpful to note that on each spring there are three clamps. The end which has two clamps positioned closer together is the front of the spring. The single clamp faces the rear.

Begin the process by working on the front end of the spring by first inserting a new rubber bush into the outer end of the spring. Put the front end of the spring in position and then insert the front bolt complete with the second bush on the shaft before loosely fitting the nut. Next fit new bump stops onto the axle casing making sure they are centralised before turning attention to installing the U bolts. Ensure that the top and bottom plates are located on the pads before sliding the U bolts through the shock absorber base plate and tensioning all four nuts equally.

Offer up the rear end of the spring. Before attempting to fit the pins through the rubber bushes, a useful tip is to have hot water on hand to soak the rubber bushes in before fitting. This helps make them more pliable. Using a jack to assist with alignment, the first step is to fit the bushes and centralise the pins before attempting to push the top pin through the chassis. Repeat the process for the bottom pin where it goes through the spring. With both pins in position the challenging task of fitting the rear shackle plates can be attempted. A 'G' clamp is a useful aid in compressing the shackle plates together sufficiently to allow for the fitting and tightening of the four nuts. It is recommended that when changing the rear springs that both springs are changed at the same time. With new springs in position, all jacks removed, and the full weight of the vehicle placed on the springs, all nuts and bolts should be checked and fully tightened.

7
Steering, Wheels and Tyres

14-inch wheels were used on all Morris Minors throughout production. However, during the period 1948–1971 the design of the wheels changed several times. When the Series MM models were introduced in 1948 the use of 14-inch wheels was quite innovative. Pre-war cars tended to use much larger diameter wheels. In the case of the post-war Morris Minor, the wheels were fixed using four bolts. They are easily distinguished from later wheels by a three-pin fixing for the hubcap and an aperture to allow for brake adjustment while the wheel was in place.

This type of wheel continued in use on early Series II saloon and convertible models. The introduction of the Traveller model in October 1953 brought with it several mechanical changes. A new one-piece three-quarter floating rear axle arrangement was accompanied by a stud type fixing for the wheels, revised spacing between the stud holes and a repositioning of the pins to accommodate larger hubcaps. These changes were extended

Morris Minor Series MM wheels used four bolts to secure them in place.

New wheel rims painted in dark silver. (RAL 9007)

to the rest of the model range from January 1954. Towards the end of Series II production, a revised stronger wheel pressing was introduced, which incorporated contoured pressings for locating the hubcaps. Later Series II wheels are not interchangeable with those used on Series MM models.

Continuity was maintained when the Morris 1000 models were introduced in 1956 and continued in 1962, when the final major upgrades were applied to the 1098cc models. The only significant change relating to wheels was the introduction of stronger, wider 4½ J wheels for use on 8cwt commercial vehicles in 1968.

Tip: On earlier cars with the bolt-type fixing, several different threaded bolts were used during production. Exercise care if replacing bolts to ensure consistency of the thread pattern on all bolts used to avoid stripping the threads on the wheel hub.

COLOUR SCHEMES

When it comes to frequently asked questions in relation to wheels fitted to Morris Minors, determining the correct colour when it left the factory is top of the list. For those wishing to retain a degree of authenticity when completing a restoration, the following summary compiled using factory records should prove useful.

TYRES

From the outset, Dunlop 5.00 × 14 crossply tyres were fitted to all Morris Minors and this continued to be the case until the larger engine 1098cc models entered production in 1962. At this point 5.20 × 14 tyres were fitted and this remained the case until 1968, when radial tyres were made available as an optional extra with Dunlop SP 145 × 14 being the type most frequently used. The Dunlop C41 crossply tyre was eventually replaced by the Dunlop D75 tyre during the final years of Morris Minor production. Recommended tyre pressure on crossply tyres for normal use is 22lb sq/in front 24lb sq/in rear and for radials 24lb sq/in front and 26lb sq/in rear.

Modern Equivalent Tyres

In most circumstances the preferred tyre for modern-day usage is the radial tyre. Circumstances in which crossply tyres are used include owner preference or when vehicles are being displayed in Concours competitions, where originality is a key consideration. This rarely happens due to the difficulty in obtaining suitable-sized crossply tyres and the fact that competitors using radial tyres are not usually subjected to penalties. Crossply tyres currently available include Excelsior 500/520 × 14. Several manufacturers produce radial tyres suitable for use with Morris Minor wheels, including brands such as Michelin, Bridgestone, Pirelli Cinturato and Hankook. In the case of the project vehicle, Pirelli Cinturato 145 × 14 CA 67 tyres were fitted on new wheels, which were painted in the correct dark silver colour.

Stronger wider wheels were introduced for use on 8cwt commercial vehicles.

Model	Date	Description
Series MM	1948–1953	Wheels painted in body colour.
Series II	1953–1956	Wheels painted in body colour.
Morris 1000	1956–February 1959	Wheels painted in body colour. With the exception of the following body colours, Black, Dark Green and Turquoise all of which had wheels painted Birch Grey.
Morris 1000	February 1959–July 1960	Wheels painted Pearl Grey.
Morris 1000	July 1960–1962	Wheels painted Old English White.
Morris 1000	1962–September 1967	Wheels painted Old English White.
Morris 1000	October 1967–June 1969	Convertible. Wheels painted Dark Silver.
Morris 1000	October 1967–November 1970	Saloons. Wheels painted Dark Silver.
Morris 1000	June 1970–April 1971	Traveller. Wheels painted Light Silver.

Steering, Wheels and Tyres

Morris 1000 wheel with revised pressing finished in Old English White.

Original Dunlop D75 tyre. (Fitted for demonstration purposes not road use.)

Modern Excelsior 500/520 × 14 Crossply tyres as fitted to Series II wheel with three-pin hubcap fixing.

Modern Pirelli Cinturato 145 × 14 CA 67 radial tyres are well suited for Morris Minor motoring.

STEERING

From the outset the Morris Minor utilised rack and pinion steering. It remained in use throughout production on all models and became widely recognised as a reliable and effective system. Central to it is the steering rack, which is secured to the base of the steering column by a pinch bolt and fixed by two brackets to the toe board area that is visible beneath the crossmember, which runs across the bulkhead underneath the battery tray. The outer ends of the rack are

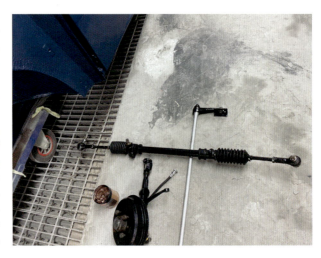

Refurbished components, including the steering rack.

Steering, Wheels and Tyres

connected to the steering arms on the suspension uprights by short tie rods with a ball joint at each end. Synthetic rubber bellows, which are resistant to oil contamination, seal each end of the rack. They are filled with Hypoid oil and, as part of routine maintenance, it is recommended that every 12,000 miles (19,300km) they should be topped up via the rack housing oil nipple, which is accessed from inside the car and located on the toe board.

With regular maintenance the steering rack presents few problems. In the event of excessive play being encountered it is possible to acquire a replacement rack. Similarly, if there is excessive movement in the ball joint assembly, replacement items are readily available.

In the case of the project car, new ball joints were fitted to the original steering rack, which was in sound condition with no apparent deterioration in the condition of the rubber bellows. Care was exercised in the fitting of the rack to ensure proper alignment, particularly with the steering column splines and the oil lubrication aperture. With the car having been completely stripped and repainted, particular attention was paid to refitting the steering rack brackets. At first the rack and the associated brackets were loosely fitted. Final tightening only occurred after all the rest of the steering assembly was attached.

Tip: When connecting the steering rack to the steering column, make sure that both the flat part of the pinion shaft and the steering column pinch clamp slot are facing upwards.

Aligning the Steering Rack

With the steering column attached and the fixing brackets for the steering rack sufficiently loosened off to allow for sideways movement when pressure is applied, turn the steering wheel one turn to the left and then to the right. Check for any movement in the rack. Repeat the process until there is no detectable movement at which point the rack will be correctly aligned.

Wheel Alignment

In the straight-ahead position, the front wheels should toe in towards each other by $3/32$in (2.5mm).

Steering Wheel Alignment

In instances where the steering wheel and steering column have been removed from the vehicle as part of a major restoration, it is critical that they are properly aligned when refitted. In the case of later models, it is crucially important to ensure that the steering column is properly centred and aligned with the front wheels in order for the indicators to properly self-cancel. To enable this to happen it is essential that the slot on the steering column clamp is in alignment with the mark on the end of the pinion. This mark is located at the bottom dead centre when the wheels are in the straight-ahead position.

It is also important to accurately align both the self-cancelling mechanism and the outer casing on the steering column on reassembly. This is best achieved with the bottom nuts and bolts on the clamp loosely

Trial fit ... ideally a two-person job.

Aligning the oil nipple with the aperture in the toe board is critical.

Steering, Wheels and Tyres

Securing brackets in position.

fastened. A locating pin needs to be identified and fitted into a small hole on the outer casing of the steering wheel. With everything in line and secure and the top and bottom clamp screws tightened, the operation of the self-cancelling unit can be checked once the steering wheel has been carefully positioned and secured in place by the large centrally positioned hexagonal nut.

Tip: When fitting the self-cancelling indicator switch, be aware that there is a locating dowel on the steering column switch that fits into a hole on the outer casing of the steering column.

Final fit.

8

Back Axle and Differential

During the time the Morris Minor was in production, different types of back axle were used in conjunction with different engine and transmission arrangements.

Commercial variants used the 4.55 : 1 ratio on later models – a departure from the saloon, convertible and Traveller models that were supplied with the 4.22 : 1 ratio as standard.

Longevity was the hallmark of the back axle, crown wheel and pinion, half shafts and associated components. However, after decades of service many units are getting to the stage of needing to be refurbished or replaced. Telltale signs, apart from a noisy or whining back axle, include problems with the back axle casing, particularly in the area at either end where the bump stop rubbers are located in position by the U bolts. Over time, accumulations of road grime can exacerbate the rusting process, resulting in weakness developing in the area between where the metal base of the rubber bump-stops fits and the casing. When such a situation arises, options are limited, as new, replacement axle casings are not available. The usual course of action is to source a better condition casing and following a complete strip down, replace or refurbish the internal components as required.

REPLACEMENT OUTER CASING

When this scenario was encountered as part of the restoration, a sound replacement axle casing with its internal components already removed was sourced, checked and sent for powder coating.

With the original rear axle removed from the car, the strip-down process began by removing the brake drums by undoing the two securing screws and pulling the drums off the studs. With the Phillips screw that secures each of the half shafts removed, the half shafts were withdrawn from the axle and checked for signs of excessive wear or damage on the splines. Fortunately, both were in good condition and deemed suitable for refitting in the replacement casing.

Attention then turned to the universal joint and the nose flange. With no visible signs of leakage from the oil seal, it was decided not to disturb the existing fittings or to attempt to release the nut, which is torqued at 140lb/ft. This decision was taken based on previous experience when this task was entrusted to a specialist engineering company with the facilities and equipment to complete the task, replace the oil seal and torque back up to the required specification.

With the eight nuts and locking washers on the central part of the axle casing released, the differential was withdrawn and the crown wheel and pinion examined for signs of wear or damage, safe in the knowledge that if required, new replacement crown wheel and pinion sets are available for 949cc and 1098cc axles. Fortunately,

Late 1098cc axle with 4.22 : 1 ratio.

Model	Axle	Ratio
Series MM	Semi-floating	4.55 : 1
Split Casing		
Series II	One-piece casing	5.375 : 1
¾ floating		
Morris 1000	One-piece casing	4.55 : 1
948cc	Changed crown wheel and pinion	
Morris 1000	One-piece casing	4.22 : 1
1098cc	Oil filler repositioned	
The 4.55 : 1 axle was available for 1098cc models as an option.		

Back Axle and Differential

there were no signs of excessive wear or damage on any of the components and so, once cleaned in preparation for reinstatement into the new casing, attention turned to reassembly.

Prior to this being undertaken, it was necessary to remove the brake shoes and rear single wheel cylinder on both sides along with the banjo, bleed nipple and the accompanying rubber seal at the rear of the back plate. It was then possible to remove both rear back plates by releasing the four bolts that secure each of them in place.

Half shafts being withdrawn, with care taken not to damage the splines.

Tip: When refitting the back plates, if new bolts, nuts and spring washers are being used as part of the reassembly process, resist the temptation to use nylon nuts, as heat generated by the braking system has the potential to melt them.

REASSEMBLY

Prior to reinstalling any of the components into the new axle casing, attention needed to be paid to the holes for the bolts for the differential. Following the powder coating process, excessive paint needed to be removed from the inner edges of each hole and the outer edge was scrupulously cleaned back to bare metal in preparation for the fitting of the paper gasket. Attention was also paid to the breather hole located on the middle part of the axle on the driver's side. The threads were checked and cleaned. The specification for this threaded hole is $1/8$th BSP (British Standard Pipe). A new breather assembly was installed at this stage.

Eight nuts need to be released from specially knurled bolts in order to separate the casing.

The following sequence was followed for the reassembly of the rear axle.

1. The differential complete with the nose flange was carefully aligned and refitted into the new casing, complete with a new paper gasket. Care was exercised to ensure that during the fitting process the paper gasket was properly seated and that it remained undamaged while parts were being aligned. Each of the eight nuts was tightened a bit at a time in a sequence that allowed for even tensioning.

Reassuringly, checks on the case-hardened surfaces revealed that they were still in pristine condition.

Back Axle and Differential

2. Both backing plates were reattached using four bolts, new spring washers and new 5/16 BSF nuts.
3. The gaskets for the bearing housings were positioned prior to the bearing housings, complete with new bearings and seals being fitted on either side. Note was taken of the fact that the threaded nuts are handed.
4. The half shafts were carefully aligned and manoeuvred into position, with care being taken to recognise that after the initial positioning there is a need for the splined end of each shaft to be lifted slightly to allow them to locate accurately with the differential. Care was also exercised to ensure that the holes in the bearing housings were aligned with the holes for the half shaft, so that the countersunk screws could be properly fitted.
5. The rear brake cylinder, rubber boot along with the banjo fitting on each side were installed, with specific attention being paid to making sure that the copper washers were properly seated and not fouling the rubber boots.
6. To complete the task the brake shoes and brake drums were refitted.

Special attention needed to be paid to removing the powder coating from all mating surfaces.

Reassembly concluded with refitting the brake assembly.

9
Braking System

INTRODUCTION

All models of the Morris Minor used Lockheed hydraulic brakes. The operating principle remained unchanged throughout production, with the most significant change in the components used being the increase in size of the front brake drums from 7 to 8 inches when the 1098cc engine was introduced in 1962. One other difference related to the master cylinder. On models using 7-inch front brakes the internal bore size was $^{13}/_{16}$ inch, but this changed to $^{7}/_{8}$ inch when the 8-inch drums were introduced. The internal seals were also changed to reflect the difference in size. Given that the master cylinders are interchangeable, this is not a crucial factor.

Key components of the braking system include a brake master cylinder, which incorporates a fluid reservoir, a total of six wheel cylinders, two each on the front and one each on the back wheels, two flexible brake hoses on the front to accommodate front wheel movement and one on the back axle casing and four sets of brake shoes. The front brake shoes operate in conjunction with two wheel cylinders, each of which operates one brake shoe. This method is commonly referred to as 'two leading shoe brakes'. In contrast a single wheel cylinder is deployed on each of the rear wheels giving rise to the description 'one leading and one trailing shoe design'. The handbrake operates in conjunction with the rear brakes by means of steel cables, one to each wheel.

HELPFUL TIPS

Before commencing work on the braking system, it is important to consider the following items.

- Make sure if working on the vehicle when it is raised from the ground that it is secure either by using axle stands or, if on a jack, that the wheels in contact with the ground are chocked to prevent movement.
- Be aware of the harmful effects of breathing in brake dust. Do not use a compressor to blow brake dust off components. Use soapy water with a cloth to remove traces of brake dust and then dispose of the cloth in a plastic bag.
- Be aware of the harmful effect of brake fluid on paintwork. Replacing fluid in the system with a modern brake fluid equivalent such as Dot 5 can alleviate this problem.
- Avoid mixing different types of brake fluid when replenishing the reservoir.
- Clean the area around the brake master cylinder before removing the cover plate to avoid debris entering the system when the filler cap is removed.

All Morris Minor Models had 7-inch rear brake drums.

Braking System

- If dismantling rubber parts that are going to be reused, always clean each item using clean brake fluid and no other liquid.
- If the brake shoes are removed from the back plate, do not depress the brake pedal. Doing so will force the wheel cylinder pistons out of the bores. As a precaution, fitting a clamp over the pistons or wiring them in position is a good preventative measure.

DISMANTLING THE FRONT BRAKES

With the vehicle jacked up and/or secured on axle stands with the handbrake applied, remove the wheel and slacken off the two adjuster screws on the brake shoes before disengaging one of the shoes from the two wheel cylinders. By releasing the tension on the springs, the other shoe can be removed. Next remove the flexible brake hose, noting that the inner end of the hose is fixed to a bracket. It is important to follow the sequence outlined to avoid causing damage to the fittings. Begin by unscrewing the union nut on the metal pipe before undoing the locknut, which secures the hose to the mounting bracket. To do this the hexagon fitting needs to be held securely. With the inner end of the hose now free, it can be unscrewed from the wheel cylinder where it passes through the back plate. At this point it is worth checking the presence and condition of the copper washer in the assembly and, if necessary, consider replacing it on reassembly. The wheel cylinders can then be removed by undoing the two securing screws. It is worth noting that on later models the flexible hose bleed screw and bridge pipe, screw directly into the back of the wheel cylinders.

DISMANTLING THE REAR BRAKES

With the usual safety considerations in mind, including chocking the front wheels if working at ground level and raising the rear of the car with a jack, the process of dismantling the rear brakes should begin by removing the road wheel and then releasing the handbrake. The brake adjustment needs to be released using the single adjuster followed by the removal of two countersunk screws before the brake drum can be released. The use of a soft mallet may be necessary to free the drum. The brake shoes can then be accessed and released in similar fashion to the front ones, as already described. Attention should then focus on the rear of the back plate where the metal brake pipe needs to be released where it meets the banjo adapter. With the adaptor unscrewed the portion that carries the bleed screw can be

Work in progress. Powder-coated back plates with 'genuine' new wheel cylinders fitted.

Assembled brake linking pipe at rear of wheel cylinders along with the new flexible brake hose.

Braking System

freed. The handbrake cable then needs to be released from the wheel cylinder lever and the rubber boot on the back plate removed before the wheel cylinder can be released from the slot in the back plate.

THE MASTER CYLINDER

The location of the brake master cylinder inside the chassis leg on the off side of the vehicle has been the subject of much debate over many years, not least because of the issue of accessibility when it becomes necessary to repair or replace the unit. If as part of

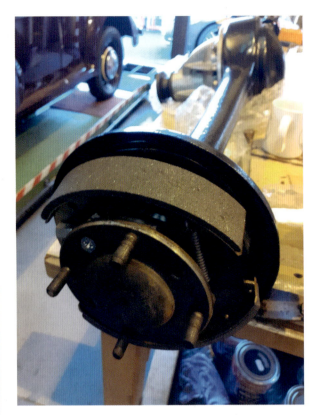

Rear brake assembly in progress. Note position of brake shoe spring.

Example of fully assembled front brake components.

7-inch rear brake drum.

Handbrake cable linkage and bleed nipple assembly.

a major restoration when a vehicle has been stripped of most components as in the case of the last saloon, this is much less of a problem. However, removing or replacing the master cylinder as a standalone operation with a fully functioning vehicle requires careful planning and knowledge, not only about the associated components linked to the master cylinder but other components in the vicinity of its location. Reference to a workshop manual containing exploded diagrams and explanatory notes is a useful back-up.

Removing the Master Cylinder

In the case of a major restoration such as the one undertaken with the last saloon, most of the components recommended for removal to provide easy access to the master cylinder had already been removed. These included seats, floor coverings, the gearbox cover and both torsion bars. While it is not strictly necessary to remove all these items, if the task is a stand-alone one, the removal of the torsion bar on the off side of the vehicle is recommended to allow unrestricted access to the two bolts with special heads that secure the master cylinder in place. Alternative methods are frequently deployed to manoeuvre the torsion bar sufficiently to gain access to the bolts without removing the bar. Such methods, though widely practised, are discouraged, due to the possibility of causing damage to the torsion bar or inadvertently putting pressure on the Vernier plate used for adjustment. The removal of the gearbox tunnel has the advantage of allowing greater access to the area surrounding the master cylinder location.

With the two bolts removed and the cover panel released by undoing the eight screws holding it in position, the master cylinder can be accessed. To extract it from the chassis leg, the front and rear brake pipes need to be disconnected from the banjo union at the rear of the master cylinder and the rod at the front disconnected from the bottom of the foot pedal. The master cylinder can then be removed.

In the case of the last saloon, due to the period of time that had elapsed since the braking system had functioned, apart from the backing plates, none of the original components were retained. The original steel brake pipes were replaced by Automec copper/nickel ones that, unlike the originals, have the advantage of not rusting. Complete sets are available for different models within the Morris Minor range. New flexible hoses were acquired, as were new wheel cylinders, brake shoes, master cylinder and other ancillary parts. Complete assembly kits are available. Care was taken in the selection of the wheel cylinders. Two options are available when it comes to purchasing replacement wheel cylinders. Replacements remanufactured to the original specification are offered as 'genuine' while 'pattern' replacements, which are a cheaper option, are made to a slightly different specification. Both do the job for which they were intended. It is a matter of personal choice. For the last saloon, genuine specification parts were acquired and fitted.

Being shoehorned into the front chassis leg makes access to the master cylinder challenging.

Braking System

Master cylinder removed.

ACTIVATING THE SYSTEM

With all components fitted and final checks made on all connections, the decision was made to fill the master cylinder using silicon-based Dot 5.1 brake fluid, due to its longer-lasting, non-hydroscopic properties. To activate the system, fluid was added to the master cylinder and the filler cap replaced before the brake pedal was depressed six times. The fluid level was then checked, replenished and the process repeated. Once satisfied with the fluid level, the process of bleeding the brakes to expel any air in the system was set in train. This was undertaken as a two-person operation, even though a specialist kit was available for single person usage.

Mindful of the fact that the master cylinder reservoir needed to remain at least half-full at all times to avoid air being drawn into the system, the filler cap was lightly replaced to prevent any fluid escaping before bleeding the brakes commenced. Armed with a suitably sized piece of 'bleeder' tubing and a glass jar, a small quantity of brake fluid was added to the jar. Starting with the wheel furthest away from the master cylinder, the left rear wheel, the bleed screw was slackened off using a $^7/_{16}$ AF spanner. One end of the tube was placed over the nipple with the other end in the jar beneath the level of the fluid. The willing assistant was instructed when to depress the brake pedal and advised to allow the brake pedal to return without assistance. This action was repeated a number of times, before the instruction was given to hold the pedal firmly to the floor at the point when there was no sign of any air being expelled into the fluid in the jar. The bleed screw was tightened before the pedal was released and the pressure on the pedal checked. The fluid level in the master cylinder was checked and replenished before the same procedure was repeated on the rear right wheel followed by the left front and finally the right front. Checks were made repeatedly on the amount of travel on the brake pedal after each session. To make doubly sure that no air was left in the system, the whole process was repeated for each wheel.

> **Tips:**
> - Do not allow the fluid in the master cylinder to fall below the half-full mark. When full the fluid should be ½ inch (13mm) from the bottom of the filler neck, with the brakes in the off position.
> - Later-type master cylinders are fitted with a dished copper washer between the piston head and the main cup to ensure that the transfer holes in the piston are kept clear. It is imperative that this washer should be fitted to all assemblies with its concave side against the main cup and its convex side in contact with the piston.

Out with the old, in with the new. Replacement master cylinders are readily available.

10
Electrical System

The electrical system used on all Morris Minor variants was 12-volt positive earth with constant voltage control for the charging system. An exception to this specification occurred with some later models when an alternator was fitted. In such cases polarity was switched to negative earth. Other departures from standard specification may have occurred if modifications have been made such as the fitting of a radio where, if a dynamo is in use, the earthing polarity may have been changed to negative.

REPLACING THE WIRING LOOM

The wiring loom fitted to the Morris Minor is of the braided type with either braided inner cables (early type) or PVC insulated cables (later type).

Replacement looms remanufactured to original specification are available for all Morris Minor models. It is essential when ordering a new loom to be specific about the model type, the year of manufacture and the types of inner cables and the connectors used in the original loom. It is also important to indicate if any ancillary cables are required for non-standard additional components that may have been fitted subsequently.

It is not normal practice for manufacturers of replacement wiring looms to provide fitting instructions or to label individual harnesses. As they are made as exact replicas of the original, it is advisable when removing the original loom to label key parts of the loom for future reference when refitting. It is also worth paying attention to the location and condition of the securing brackets for the loom, as they may need some refurbishment prior to being reused.

Given the number and variety of the coloured cables, particularly those fitted to the regulator box, a useful tip is to cut the original cables leaving part of them in position as a reference point for when the loom is connected to new or refurbished components.

Removing the Wiring Loom

Removing the wiring loom is a straightforward operation. There are three distinct areas to concentrate on. The most accessible is inside the boot area and the underside where the cable goes through the boot floor. This is a good place to start the removal process, followed by the engine bay and then the area behind the dashboard. Aim to keep the loom intact and withdraw all elements to the inside of the vehicle.

Tip: Resist the temptation to cut the loom into sections to ease removal. It is useful to have an intact loom for future reference when installing the new one.

Underside and boot area
- Release the loom from the spot-welded clips located on the inner edge of the lower floor before disconnecting the wires from the combined rear light/brake light and indicator units on either side.
- Undo the wires on the numberplate lamp. With the spare wheel removed release the split rubber grommet where the braided loom goes through the boot floor.
- Push the loom through the hole and pull through to the underside of the vehicle.
- Working from the underside of the vehicle, locate the spot-welded metal clips that secure the loom to the body. Release this part of the loom, which runs parallel to the propshaft and the gearbox and passes through the crossmember and feed through into the engine bay.

Engine Bay
- Release the metal retaining holder that secures the loom to the bulkhead by undoing the three Phillips-headed screws.
- Unclip the loom from the spot-welded retaining clips on the inner wing and the panel that runs beneath the radiator.
- Disconnect the bullet connectors to the headlamps and indicators on both sides and remove the bolted clamps securing the loom at the base of the inner wings.
- Remove wires from all components including the starter solenoid, dynamo or alternator, coil, and oil pressure and temperature sensors.
- Remove the rubber grommet on the passenger side of the bulkhead and retract the single braided branch of the loom to the inside of the vehicle, having disconnected the wires to the fuel pump and wiper motor.
- Disconnect the cables to each of the terminals on the regulator box and fuse box or for ease of reference when refitting the new loom, cut each of the cables leaving sufficient length to be able to identify the relevant colour for each terminal.

Behind the dash
- First disconnect the speedometer cable followed by the wires attached to the following items:
- Illuminating bulbs
- Oil warning light
- Main beam warning
- Ignition light

101

Electrical System

Disconnect the wiring to the following:
- Voltage stabilising unit
- Ignition switch
- Wiper switch
- Lights and panel switches

Disconnect the electrical wires connected to the following:
- Steering column, horn and indicators
- Heater
- Earthing points
- Interior light

With all wires disconnected, it should then be possible to withdraw the rest of the loom from the engine bay and from behind the dash into the car.

The original wiring loom was removed as one piece and the various clips and brackets kept for future reference.

WIRING LOOM: HELPFUL TIPS

- If possible, retain the original bulb holders at the rear of the speedometer. The originals tend to be stronger than the replacement items currently available.
- Ensure that there is a good supply of new connectors available for use when refitting the new loom.
- Retain all wiring associated with the headlamp and indicator units.
- Note that on four-door saloons the wiring harness is routed differently on models fitted with trafficators.

FITTING A REPLACEMENT LOOM

Key Points

Replacing the wiring loom requires a degree of patience, logical thinking and a basic understanding of principles associated with electrical wiring.

Reference to the appropriate wiring diagram for the year and model of the vehicle concerned is essential. With a production run spanning 22 years and a wide variety of models, there are a vast number of variations of diagrams available. The diagrams were included in the handbook originally supplied with the individual vehicle. Replacement copies are normally available at autojumbles or online.

Fitting the New Loom

A useful starting point for refitting the wiring loom is to feed the main part of the harness through the bulkhead from inside the car, carefully identifying the routing of the ancillary strands starting with the one that goes behind the dashboard and enters the engine bay through the aperture adjacent to the fuel pump. Other strands include those that are routed inside the engine bay and the one that is routed to the rear of the car. Once satisfied with the positioning of the loom on the curved edge of the inner wing and along the front edge of the front crossmember, attention should switch to correctly locating the strand that fits beneath the car along the side of the chassis leg on the driver's side before passing through the aperture in the central crossmember and entering the car through the aperture in the boot floor, which allows access to the rear lights and the inner part of the boot lid. With the loom loosely positioned, final checks should be undertaken to ensure that there is no undue tension being placed on any part of the wiring, particularly where it comes in contact with the car body. With checks complete, the loom should be secured in place using the welded metal supports. With all wiring suitably positioned, the time-consuming and methodical process of connecting the different components can begin.

Electrical System

Routing of the loom through the bulkhead.

Initial feed through the bulkhead without grommet fitted to allow for correct positioning of the loom in the engine bay.

Grommet fitted prior to metal securing ring being added.

Wiring for fuel pump through bulkhead on passenger side.

Locating point for loom on front crossmember.

Original RB106 voltage regulator reinstalled with new wiring and original-style spade connectors.

FITTING THE WIRING LOOM IN A LATE MODEL MORRIS 1000

For the inexperienced restorer wishing to undertake the refitting of a wiring loom in a late model Morris 1000, the following guidelines devised in conjunction with classic car enthusiast Graham Ryder should prove useful both in terms of sequencing the work and identifying the key components associated with each section of the wiring loom.

It is helpful when beginning the process of connecting the wires from the thickest part of the loom located in the engine bay to focus on the fusebox. Purple and brown

Electrical System

wires go to the left of the box, while green and white wires go to the right. Tidying the wires behind the fuse box is advisable before securing it to the bulkhead.

With the voltage regulator fixed in position, wires should be attached in the following sequence before the harness is once again placed firmly against the bulkhead.

A1 – 2 x Brown – Blue stripe wires.
A – 2 x Brown wires.
F – Yellow – Green stripe wire. Thin wire to field winding.
D – 2 x Yellow wires. Thick wire to dynamo. Thin wire to ignition light.
E – Black wire to earth.

Working on the driver's side of the car, feed the long cable along the inner wing behind the inner wing support plate and secure it in position using the steel strip-type plates. Next, focus on attaching the wires with bullet connectors for the offside horn making sure that the metal contacts are fully inserted and that they do not project outside the rubber casing. Doing so will prevent the possibility of creating a short circuit. The wires are coloured purple and purple with a black stripe. Still working on the off side of the car, identify the folded steel clip located on the inner wing, which is used to hold two earthing bullet connectors. There is a hole for the wiring for the lighting to go through the inner wings. It is advisable to protect the edges of this hole with a hollow rubber grommet of the right size to sleeve the wires to both the headlamp and sidelamp units. It is also worth considering at this stage adding an extra earth wire to all the sidelamp holders to ensure a good electrical connection.

For reference purposes the wires here are:

Red – Sidelamp
Black – Earth
Blue + white stripe – Main Beam
Blue + red stripe – Dipped beam
Green + white stripe – Indicator

Continuing downward to where the loom meets the front crossmember, two wires connect the brake pressure switch, Green + green – purple stripe. These can be connected either way round. With the loom positioned on top of the front crossmember and firmly secured using the metal clips the connections for the off side of the car can then be made. The connections at the end of that part of the loom include the connections for the lights with the Green–red striped cable for indicator and two wires for the nearside horn. The same arrangement is adopted using the earth bullet connectors in a folded steel clip and the rubber grommet in the inner wing to protect the wires for the lighting from chafing where they pass through.

Returning to the bulkhead, identify the section of loom that runs down towards the gearbox bell housing. Four wires will be seen, which are associated with the flasher unit, including a black earthing wire located under the top securing tab that the flasher unit can utilise. There are three other connections on the bottom of the unit.

B – Green feed supply
P – Light-green indicator lamp
L – Green + brown stripe to indicator stalk

The explanation included here assumes that the engine and ancillary components are fitted.

Proceed to the starter solenoid. The thick Brown wire with a large Lucar connector fits next to the bolt on terminal to the battery lead and the Red + white stripe Lucar connector fits to the solenoid coil. The other bolt-on connection takes the lead to the starter motor. Usually, these large connections are protected by rubber boots, which slide over the wire and cover the securing nuts.

A thinner section of loom that comprises six wires goes towards the engine and dynamo. They connect as follows.

Dynamo – Brown + green stripe small spade connection
Brown + yellow stripe large spade connection
Oil pressure – Green + yellow stripe shorter wire to pressure switch
Oil filter – Green + yellow stripe longer wire to oil filter housing

Ignition

On some coils the contacts can be identified as CB +ve and SW – ve. The following information is applicable to positive-earthed vehicles.

Ignition – White wire – SW (-ve) contact
White + black stripe – CB (+ve)
White + black stripe – Distributor

If the polarity of the vehicle has been changed to negative earth, the wiring circuit needs to be:

White wire CB (+ve) contact
White + black stripe SW (-ve)
White + black stripe Distributor

Work on connecting this section of the loom is almost complete by this stage. Three wires need to be fitted to the dip-switch to control the lighting circuit. They are identified as:

Blue – feed wire to the common terminal
Blue + white trace – main beam
Blue + red trace – dipped beam

Connecting to either of the other terminals is not a problem, provided the common terminal is the feed.

The remaining part of the loom needs to be routed to the rear of the car. From the engine bay this section of the loom runs along the inside edge of the chassis rail and through the gearbox crossmember and the central crossmember before entering the boot floor through a protective grommet. It is important to adequately clip the loom to the vehicle body using the metal clips provided so as to avoid contact with the clutch linkages and reduce the risk of snagging when the vehicle is in use. With the loom in the boot area, it can then be positioned and secured using the metal clips provided and routed, first towards the offside boot corner and then along the rear of the boot floor ending up by the light cluster on the near side of the car.

The green and black trace wire for the fuel gauge should be connected, while the wire for the number plate light on the inside of the boot lid, which loops under the boot hinge and is clipped to the rear parcel shelf, needs attaching to the red feed wire on the multi-way connector on the loom. The black wire needs to be suitably earthed. Attention can then turn to connecting the light units on both sides of the car.

For reference purposes, the wires here are:

Red wire – sidelights
Green + purple stop lamps
Green + red left-hand indicator
Green + white right-hand indicator

Additional earthing for light units is recommended.

Returning to the inside of the car and the central part of the dashboard, where there are wiring clusters with bulb holders adjacent to the speedometer: switch connections need to be made for the ignition, lights and wipers.

Ignition

On the ignition switch a brown + blue trace wire should be connected to the main terminal along with a white wire that leads to the bulb holder and a twinned brown + yellow trace and a white wire that goes to feed the right-hand fuse in the engine bay. The last wire to the ignition switch is a white + red trace from the starter motor position on the switch.

Lights

When connecting the light switch, it is important to first establish the common terminal for all three positions before fitting the brown and blue trace wire. The first position terminal should then be fitted with the red wire before the blue wire, which feeds down to the dip switch. It is important to note that there is another red wire feed to the panel light slider switch under the dash, which goes to the two red + white trace-wired bulb holders used for instrument illumination.

Wipers

The wiring for the wiper motor consists of a light-green wire from the fuse box to the top of the motor. Wiring to the switch consists of a green + black trace wire to one terminal on the switch along with a black earth wire, which is grounded to the body to the other terminal. The light-green wire, which is the switch live feed from the ignition, goes directly to the wiper motor. The earth return is switched to complete the circuit, with a second earth to enable the self-park facility.

The voltage stabiliser unit, recognisable as a small rectangular block on the back of the speedometer, has two double terminals identified as 'B' the input and 'I' the output. Three green wires go to the 'B' input, one of which is fed from the right-hand fuse. The other two feed the wiper motor and the two oil-related sensors. On the output side 'I' a light-green wire goes to the fuel gauge while the wire to the other connector, a green with black trace, goes to the sender unit in the fuel tank.

Interior Light

The interior light is supplied by a constant live feed from the left-hand fuse by a thin purple wire and connects to a length of wire by the driver's door pillar. There are two earth connections associated with the circuit, one to a screw on the light itself. Two courtesy switches on the 'A' pillars that provide the earth connection are linked together at a double bullet connector. Additionally, a black earth wire follows the feed wire up to the lamp.

The last of the wires to be connected are associated with the steering column, the indicator stalk, and the horn push. A short section of wiring harness runs down the outside of the column to a group of bullet connectors. The coloured wires need to be paired with each other. They consist of:

Green + brown trace – feed from flasher unit to common terminal.
Green + white trace – feed to right-hand indicator.
Green + red trace - feed to left-hand indicator.
Light-green – to green light on the indicator stalk.
Black – steering column earth.

In the case of the purple + black trace wire, this needs to be connected to a matching purple and black trace wire from the horn push, but in some instances a brown and black trace wire may be present from the horn push.

The final step to complete the task involves fitting the bulb holders into the back of the speedometer before securing it in place. It is important to make sure the main beam is in the top position.

Additional Note

From 1969 onwards the oil filter warning light was discontinued. However, the wire is often retained in replacement looms. If present, it is surplus to requirements and needs to be safely stowed away.

Additional Components

All the ancillary electrical components as fitted to the last saloon that had been removed were checked and assessed to determine whether they could be retained following refurbishment, overhauled or used as they were. The original wiper motor proved serviceable without the need for major overhaul, however, other components such as the fuel pump were rebuilt (*see* Chapter 11). Other items such as the coil and the light units were replaced with new items where necessary. One item that was fully stripped and overhauled was the C40 dynamo. The procedure outlined here may prove helpful in servicing an existing unit or determining whether further work using the services of a specialist company might be required to replace bearings or overhaul other component parts.

C40 DYNAMO

With the unit removed from the vehicle and placed on a workbench, begin the strip-down by removing the two long securing bolts from the back of the unit. This will allow the back cover to be removed and provide access to the two carbon brushes. Separate the front plate from the round body and check the front bearing for smooth running when it is rotated. If it is smooth in operation, simply clean the assembly. If not, further work may be required to replace the bearing. Next,

Electrical System

focus on releasing the tension on the brush springs and slide the brushes out of the housings, checking for tightness and wear. It is recommended to fit new brushes in any case and when doing so to check and refit the springs. Check the spigot bearing in the shaft and the bearing housing for wear, noting that it should be a smooth sliding fit. It is useful at this stage to lightly polish the segmented commutator with fine emery paper, making sure to clear the segments and wipe clean afterwards. With all checks complete, reassemble the front plate and armature to the body and locate in position before placing the rear cover in position over the bearing. Then, using a thin screwdriver, push the brushes back to allow the commutator to slide past and locate against the body. Finally, secure everything in position by refitting the two long screws. Reference to other technical publications may be necessary if further checks prove necessary on details such as coil resistances and methods of testing.

C40 dynamo with long screws removed.

C40 dynamo internals showing commutator.

C40 carbon brushes illustrating uneven wear when removed.

C40 dynamo and coil. Final fit.

11
Fuel System

INTRODUCTION

The key components of the fuel system include the fuel tank, the petrol pump and the carburettor. Slight variations in the fuel tanks' size, changes to the fuel gauges, sender units and carburettor size occurred during the production run of the Morris Minor. Different fuel filler arrangements applied to certain models.

FUEL TANK

The fuel tank is located under the boot floor on saloon and convertible models and under the rear load area of the Traveller and LCV variants. All have a filler neck on the left-hand side. LCV models have a filler neck that is located slightly further forward, and consequently the tank design differs slightly from that used on passenger vehicles – meaning that they are not easily interchangeable. For all models the capacities are 5.0 gallons (23ltr) up to March 1957 and 6.5 gallons (30ltr) thereafter. After-market, 9.5-gallon (43ltr) capacity tanks are available. They have a similar plan area but hang lower and have a higher lid, which projects into the space occupied by the spare wheel. All the tanks have a fixed suction pipe, which has a gauze filter fitted, and is not accessible for maintenance. The outlet has a ¼-inch BSP female connection at the front left-hand side of the tank.

Early fuel tank.

Later saloon fuel tank.

FUEL GAUGE SENDER UNIT

The fuel gauge sender is located in the central part of the lid and is electrically connected to the gauge on the dashboard by a single (green/black) wire. The sender is grounded to earth by the six hex-headed/slotted screws that connect it into the tank. The sender has a wound resistor with a rotating 'wiper', which is fixed to a polythene or brass float on the end of a rigid wire. The fuel gauge is basically a voltmeter and the sender is a variable resistor. As the fuel level rises and falls, so the electrical resistance offered by the sender varies, causing corresponding changes in voltage.

Two types of sender units were used on the Morris Minor. The changeover point was October 1964. Before that date, the system used un-damped display needles, which worked directly from the unregulated battery supply. The voltage available would naturally fluctuate by up to about 25 per cent due to the variables of battery condition and generator output. Since the gauge measures voltage, so the needle position indicating remaining fuel would fluctuate in sympathy. To overcome this, the 1964 upgrade introduced a voltage stabiliser, which reduced the voltage to a constant 10v. This is mounted on the back of the speedometer and is utilised as a 'junction box' for the supply to various other services – hence there are several green wires on the 12v side. The gauge was also changed to a 'damped' type. The two types are easily distinguishable as the change coincided with the change to the black faces of the speedo and fuel gauge. These improvements gave an enhanced accuracy to the system. The sender unit was also upgraded and now had a design that 'reversed' the signal, meaning that it could not be used with the old-type gauge. Anyone who has tried this will confirm that it shows 'F' when empty and 'E' when full! Replacement later-type senders are available, but early-type ones are more difficult to source.

FUEL GAUGE TESTING

The test procedure to diagnose a non-working or inaccurate gauge is as follows: remove the green/black wire that connects to the sender unit in the boot of the car. Whilst observing the gauge, switch on the ignition and ground the green/black wire to a clean earth on the car. The gauge should now show a full-scale deflection ('F'). If it does, then the fault lies with the sender, which could be stuck and requires it to be removed and the arm freed off. It can then be tested out of the tank (ensuring the sender unit is grounded to earth). If the fault persists under the above test, then the fault lays with the gauge itself or the wiring. The best way to test the gauge itself is by substitution. Remember that the gauge needs to be earthed to the car to work properly. Check that the regulator output has 12v in and 10v out.

DELIVERY PIPE

The original rigid fuel pipe was a $^{5}/_{16}$" drawn steel pipe with a brass tube-nut connector. These are often replaced during maintenance or restoration with a similar-sized copper or Kunifer (copper/nickel) pipe. These are not prone to corrosion. Original steel pipes are prone to corrosion and often rust through, initially leaving tell-tale damp patches on the pipe. Copper pipes are often frowned upon in use as brake pipes due to their inherent defect of 'work-hardening'. Since the fuel pipe is not designed to move (as are some of the brake pipes) this is not regarded

Later-type sender unit.

Early-type fuel gauge.

Later-type fuel gauge.

Fuel System

as a particular problem in this application. However, the better-quality copper/nickel pipes are recommended. The pipe has a soldered brass nipple on the end and a brass tube nut to secure it into the female connection in the tank. The fuel pipe is fixed to the underside of the car with simple metal 'tags', which are deformed around the pipe to secure them.

The pipe emerges into the engine bay on the left-hand side of the car close to the chassis leg and passes up to the fuel pump in a 'swan-neck', which has a diameter of about 15cm. This is necessary since the fuel pump outlet points upwards at an angle of about 45 degrees. The end of the pipe has another soldered brass nipple and a brass tube nut, which fixes to the fuel pump.

PETROL PUMP AND CARBURETTOR

The petrol pump is mounted in the engine bay and is fixed with two ¼" UNF machine screws to the left-hand side of the battery tray. There is a 'live' connection (white wire) from the wiring loom to the thumbscrew on the end of the pump. There is also an earth connection (black wire), which fixes to a 2BA or 4BA screw on the side of the pump, which 'piggy-backs' on to one of the fixing machine screws. The standard points pumps are dual polarity, so the pump, will work with either positive or negative earth. If a more modern electronic pump is fitted, then a specific 'positive earth' or 'negative earth' model will be needed depending on how the car is wired. The pump is designated as 'LP' (low-pressure), and the delivery pressure is about 1.5psi. The dual polarity AUA66 pump specified for the Morris Minor should not be exchanged for other similar-looking models such as AUF214, which is specified for the ADO16 range (Morris/Austin 1100/1300) and is designated 'HP' (high pressure). Whilst the pumping capacity is about the same, the delivery pressure is higher, and the pump is designed to 'push' the fuel as it is mounted near the fuel tank.

The outlet of the petrol pump is connected to a flexible pipe, which will deliver the fuel to the carburettor. This will be either rubber or stainless-steel braid covered rubber. These hoses should be regarded as 'consumable', since rubber components inevitably have a limited life. There are various grades of fuel hose (for example SAE J30 R6, which is suitable for unleaded fuel and SAE J30 R9, which is suitable for ethanol-laced fuel). This hose should be inspected regularly for signs of perishing/cracking and consideration given to replacing with R9 grade hose, which will give protection against the deleterious effect of ethanol additive – currently 10 per cent in the UK.

The majority of R9 hose is now supplied with an inside diameter of 5.6mm. The spigot diameters will be imperial ¼". The metric equivalent is 6.4mm. This is not a problem, since the end of the flexible pipe will be expanded to fit over the slightly larger spigot. When the correctly sized (10–12mm) stainless-steel clips are fitted, it will form a very tight, safe joint. The specification for the pipe states that it is suitable for fuel injection systems in which fuel pressures are much higher than found in a Morris Minor.

The penultimate destination for the fuel is, of course, the carburettor, which is described in detail elsewhere. It is mounted on the left-hand side of the engine above the exhaust system. The throttle-return spring is anchored via a steel 'banjo'-shaped bracket from the exhaust manifold clamp – where the manifold joins the exhaust system (on the later models). The choke cable emerges from the upper part of the bulkhead near the battery and has a pinch bolt trunnion to secure it to the relevant lever on the carburettor. The throttle cable is attached to the back of the pedal and is connected to the carburettor via a short length of cable, which fits into a small, fixed ferrule on the carburettor body. The throttle cable is secured to the lever on the carburettor by a ¼" pinch bolt. Since the carburettor is close to the hottest part of the engine, the exhaust, certain measures are taken to keep the heat build-up to a minimum. The carburettor is mounted on a black insulating spacer made from Bakelite or phenolic tufnol. Its use helps avoid transferring excessive heat into the fuel, which can cause fuel vaporisation. The air filter mounted directly onto the carburettor is a wire mesh filled oil-bath arrangement on cars up to about 1960 and a conical disposable paper filter thereafter. The oil bath type should be cleaned, and the oil replaced during servicing. The paper element filter should be replaced regularly, particularly where vehicles are used regularly in dusty conditions.

Later HS2 carburettor.

Helpful Tips

- A persistent smell of petrol in the car – particularly after filling the tank – is often due to failure of the cork gasket on the fuel tank. This is easily replaced.
- Although not originally fitted, it is good practice to 'insulate' the fuel pipe from the metal tags that hold it in place to eliminate possibility of 'fretting' caused by vibration inside the metal tags. To prevent this – when replacing the pipe – a short (20mm) length of PVC pipe of suitable diameter, split down the side and slipped over the pipe, can be inserted where it passes through each of the tags.
- When replacing the fuel pipe with a new part, ensure that there is an air-tight connection between the pump and the new pipe. Air leaks will *not* be obvious – other than by a continuously ticking fuel pump. If necessary, use some PTFE tape to improve the joint.
- Avoid the temptation to fit an in-line filter since the fuel pump has one fitted inside anyway. These filters make it harder for the pump to 'suck' fuel up from the tank by increasing the 'negative' pressure. This, in turn, increases the tendency for the fuel to vaporise in hotter weather. It also introduces another pair of unnecessary joints to the pipework.
- Avoid stainless steel braided hose. This is often fitted for aesthetic purposes. However, it is difficult to inspect for cracking and the rubber pipe under the braiding will deteriorate just as quickly (and invisibly!).
- In hotter climates or where vehicles are prone to use in slow-moving traffic, an after-market heat shield can be fitted to help prevent fuel vaporisation.
- The paper element filter should be replaced annually as it will clog up, so less air is drawn in, which artificially affects the fuel/air mixture. It creates a similar situation as driving with the choke on.
- There is something of a dilemma when it comes to winter storage. There have been recommendations to leave the tank full (if using E10 – which it is assumed will eventually be dominant). Modern fuel is far more volatile than it used to be. As a consequence, the volatile fractions will reduce by about 15 per cent in just five weeks. This will obviously result in the vehicle having a tank full of stale fuel when it is removed from storage. It is recommended to drain the fuel in cars that are stored for long periods. This will give the more corrosive fuel less opportunity to rust through the fuel tank. Even a very small amount of moisture in the fuel will combine with the hygroscopic ethanol, drop to the bottom of the tank and start the corrosion process.

SU Fuel Pump Identification and Operation

SU fuel pump.

The electric solenoid fuel pump, originally made by SU (Skinners Union) dates back to the early 1930s, just before the company was acquired by the Nuffield Organisation. The 12-volt type used in post-war Morris Minors, designated AUA 66, is easily identified by the specification tag and the black end cap. The SU fuel pump is mounted in the engine bay adjacent to the bulkhead. It is relatively simple in its operation and uses a linear action powered by an electrical solenoid. When energised, the pump action is not continuous and works on demand in conjunction with the carburettor. The carburettor contains a needle valve in its float chamber, which regulates the flow and when the fuel level drops, the needle valve opens and pressure in the delivery pipe drops. This causes the pump to actuate and operate as many cycles or strokes as is necessary to replenish the float chamber with fuel and to replace the lost pressure in the pipe between the pump and the chamber.

The fuel pump remained essentially unchanged throughout its production life with only relatively small differences in the design. The diaphragm uses brass or plastic spacers to maintain a central position within the solenoid body. Three different arrangements were used: small brass washers; a linked set of four nylon spacers; and individual 'dumbbell'-shaped nylon spacers. It is helpful to note that in 1985 a second type of diaphragm was introduced. Consequently, two types of diaphragm remain in use. All factory-fitted pumps will have the earlier type, whereas replacement pumps made post-1985 utilise the later type. Unfortunately, the early and late types must be matched with the appropriate solenoid body. They cannot successfully be mixed. Fortunately, it is possible to tell the difference without dismantling – so that the correct servicing parts can be ordered. They can be distinguished by the size of the screw securing the earth eyelet on the flange of the casting nearest to the alloy pump chamber. The early pump bodies use a short 2BA cheese-head screw that screws into a blind, threaded hole in the casting. The post-1985 unit uses a smaller 4BA cheese-head screw. Later pumps also incorporate a blue ceramic varistor (labelled as a 'suppressor') fitted between the points' contacts, which has the effect of reducing the spark generated by the fluctuating current flow to almost nil – thus prolonging the life of the points. Early pumps had single contact points and no current smoothing and consequently had a shorter life.

Fuel System

SU FUEL PUMP RESTORATION

Introduction

Over the past decade Brian Wood has restored over 350 SU fuel pumps used on the Morris Minor. In this section he describes and illustrates the process he has perfected to re-commission individual units. Fortunately, there is still a ready supply of new components, the most common of which are listed below. The recommended minimum of new parts is as follows (together with their SU part numbers):

Rocker and blade assembly	AUB 6106
Brass valve discs (2)	AUA 839
Outlet spigot fibre washer (red)	AUA 1442
Filter housing fibre washer (same as above)	AUA 1442
Inlet spigot fibre washer (thicker, red)	AUA 1405
Valve cage washer (black)	AUA 1479
Solenoid to sandwich plate gasket	AUB 809X
Sandwich plate to pump chamber gasket	AUA 4082
Lead washer	AUA 1662
Insulating washer	AUB 609
Suppressor Assembly	CZX 1004

It is assumed that all the other component parts will be reusable. However, if this is not the case, parts availability remains good.

Dismantling

At the outset care needs to be exercised when attempting to remove the six 2BA screws, which hold the solenoid to the alloy pump chamber. Sometimes the steel screws corrode into the aluminium pump body and when attempts are made to release the screws they often shear off, usually flush with the surface. If this occurs salvage may be possible by carefully drilling out the screw remains and installing a Helicoil-type repair thread.

Before attempting to remove the solenoid from the pump chamber it is advisable to secure the pump in a vice before attempting to remove the inlet and outlet bosses and the filter nut using a ³⁄₈th Whitworth ring spanner.

The points are removed from the pedestal by sliding out the thin steel pivot pin. Sometimes this suffers from corrosion and the upstands, which contain the pivot, can sometime snap off as they are not very strong. If this occurs a replacement pedestal will be required. It is advisable to refit new points, although on occasion the originals can be reused. The tungsten contact discs on the points can be carefully smoothed, if sufficient thickness remains, using an oil stone or suitable wet and dry abrasive paper. They need to be as flat and as smooth as possible.

The next stage involves the removal of the two cheese-headed 2BA screws holding the pedestal to the solenoid. It will be found that the pedestal will still be attached to the pump via one of the black wires going into the solenoid; the other wire can be separated by releasing the screw holding down the upper points contact blade. The wire going to the pedestal can be released by unscrewing the brass 2BA nut and carefully removing the old lead washer, which is shaped around the eyelet by a 'dished' underside of the brass nut. There should also be an insulating washer on top of the nut. Often at this point the eyelet will break off from the black wire. Whilst this does make it easier to dismantle, it means that a new eyelet will need to be soldered on it.

Unscrew the diaphragm until the threaded rod is released from the rotating 'trunnion' on the points assembly. Pull clear and set aside with the coil spring ensuring that the brass or nylon spacer discs are retrieved. The condition of the diaphragm is quite important, as it separates the fuel from the electricity! Although they do vary, most diaphragms consist of two black rubber/nitrile discs. Some also have a thin, clear plastic membrane at the end. The two black membranes are usually stuck fast together and should be carefully separated. It will be found that this step improves the flexibility of the diaphragm, which should then take less energy to push it up and down – thus theoretically increasing the efficiency of the pump. It is crucial at this point to carefully inspect the condition of the diaphragm and replace it if there is any doubt as to its condition. Reassuringly diaphragms tend to be quite long lasting and it is unusual to see damaged ones.

> **Tip:** Putting a small quantity of talcum powder between the two leaves of the diaphragm may help stop them from sticking together.

The brass valve cage assembly under the outlet spigot should be carefully dismantled and inspected. There should be two small, thin brass discs – one in the brass valve cage itself and the other loosely fitted just beneath it. Carefully remove the thin black washer upon which the valve cage is seated, taking care not to damage the alloy seat underneath. The 'U'-shaped spring clip should be popped out of its retaining ring in the valve cage to release the second brass disc. The discs can either be cleaned and polished with fine wet or dry paper or replaced with new. Replacement is advised.

Remove the nut retaining the filter and withdraw the filter itself. This can then be cleaned and inspected as required.

The alloy valve chamber should now be cleaned to remove the silt and rust deposits drawn up from the petrol tank. The mating surface should be inspected for damage but can usually be successfully sealed as a relatively thick paper washer is fitted upon re-assembly. If access to a compressed air blast cabinet with glass bead media is available, this will allow for a gentler cleaning process to the alloy parts and provide a pleasing uniform finish. The sandwich plate, valve cage and other parts can be treated in the same way. The solenoid can be cleaned using a rotary wire brush (or similar) to remove loose paint or rust deposits. It can then be painted if required.

Reassembly

For the reassembly process, the electrical pedestal assembly will be referred to as the 'dry' end and the pump chamber assembly as the 'wet' end.

Having inspected and cleaned all the parts to be re-used and obtained any new parts required, the process of rebuilding the pump can begin. Check that the electrical eyelets on the ends of the solenoid wires are secure, as they are only single-core wire and they tend to break.

The wet end should be prepared first. Fit the filter and one of the thinner red washers – securing with the filter nut. Make sure the tubular filter is not twisted or squashed by the filter nut. It is sometimes necessary to fit an extra washer as a spacer to ensure that this does not happen. Alternatively, one end of the plastic filter can be carefully 'shaved' to make it slightly shorter so that it does not distort. Care must be exercised not to remove too much, otherwise the filter will 'leak' unfiltered fuel into the pump.

The brass valve cage needs to be re-assembled and a new or good condition brass disc fitted in the top. Carefully insert the 'U'-shaped spring clip and ensure it engages in the small recess near the top of the cage body.

Filter components.

> **Tip:** Shake the cage and listen for the 'rattle' caused by the disc, which should be free to flop up and down between its seat and the spring clip. If the disc is restrained by the clip, the pump will not work.

Next, put the second brass disc into the lower, stepped part of the outlet hole in the alloy chamber housing. If the disc has one smoother side – then this should face inwards – towards the seating (which should be inspected for damage). The thin, black washer should then be installed, and the assembled valve cage placed on top of it. Then fit the remaining thin red washer. Fit and tighten the outlet spigot down onto the red fibre washer. Fit the inlet boss to the remaining hole in the pump chamber using a new (thick) red washer and then set the pump chamber assembly aside.

> **Tip:** The tungsten contact points are sometimes reluctant to start working, particularly if the pump has been stored prior to fitting. To avoid this eventuality the contact faces should be polished before fitting with very fine wet and dry paper (1200 grit).

Fit the new points rocker assembly to the pedestal, sliding the steel pin carefully through the four holes in the

Fitting the filter.

Fuel System

Lower valve disc and thin black washer fitted.

rocker and each side of the pedestal. The pin is not held in by anything other than the end cap, which is fitted last of all – and this is the only deterrent to the pin sliding sideways. It tends to very quickly migrate one way or the other when operating and fall out either partially or fully – with consequences that can be easily envisaged. *It is important to be aware of this when testing the pump later.* Do not fit the top contact blade at this stage.

> **Tip:** At this point, it pays to be methodical in the reassembly process to make sure that everything is correctly aligned so that the completed pump as installed in the car will offer up the various connection points in the right places. A 'clock-face' method can be applied to achieve this.

Outlet boss components.

Place the pedestal on the work surface with the tungsten points contacts at 12 o'clock. Fit the 2BA threaded brass contact stud through the hole in the pedestal located at 4 o'clock. Fit one of the small spring washers first, followed by the larger of the two electrical eyelet connections from the solenoid. Then fit the new lead washer followed by the 2BA brass nut with the concave 'dish' facing the lead washer. Carefully tighten this down so that the nut deforms the lead washer over the electrical contact.

> **Tip:** Due to the short length of electrical wire, it is easier to achieve this connection before the pedestal assembly is fitted to the top of the solenoid.

Pump chamber with inlet boss.

Completed valve chambers.

Fuel System

Contact points assembly.

Fitting the points rocker assembly.

Fitting the terminal pin and lead washer.

Next, fit the pedestal assembly to the top of the solenoid to complete the 'dry' end assembly. There should be two 2BA steel cheese-headed bolts, which secure the pedestal to the solenoid. Using the above layout convention, the one on the right can be fitted with just the spring washer while the one on the left must go through the brass earth eyelet contact from the points rocker assembly (and the closed eyelet for the suppressor assembly). Again, the spring washer should be fitted first.

> **Tip:** The two cheese-headed bolts should be just tight enough. Bear in mind that if they are over-tightened, there is a risk of snapping the plastic pedestal across the middle.

The small 4BA screw can now be fitted to secure the points top blade. Firstly, pass the screw through the smaller electrical eyelet on the second solenoid wire and then fit the screw loosely into the pedestal. Then fit the top contact blade (which has a forked end) by sliding it into position followed by the open (also forked) terminal of the suppressor. Align the contact points end of the top blade in the centre of the rectangular hole above the rocker assembly and check for correct alignment of the upper and lower tungsten contacts prior to tightening the 4BA screw.

Setting the upper and lower limits for the rocker assembly is a vital step in the reassembly process, as this will determine whether the pump will work to its full capacity and that the 'throw over' occurs at exactly the right time at each end of the cycle. The lower limit must be set by bending the small brass 'tang', which now sits just above the solenoid; there should be a gap of 2.3mm between it and the solenoid top.

Bend the tang up or down to obtain the correct clearance. The upper adjustment stipulates that there should be a 0.9mm clearance between the top surface of the pedestal and the spring steel part of the blade (not the contacts themselves). Again, there is a small projecting brass tang just below the top plate of the pedestal, which can be adjusted (bent) slightly with a

115

Fuel System

Fitting the contact blade.

Checking the lower rocker clearance.

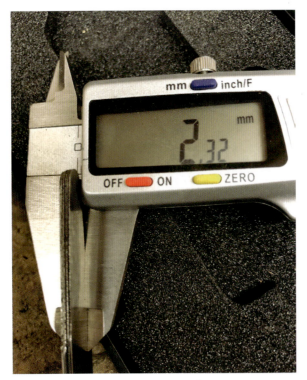

Checking thickness of feeler gauge for lower rocker.

Checking the upper point contact clearance.

pair of thin-nosed pliers to achieve the desired clearance.

The diaphragm assembly must now be fitted. Make sure the coil spring is fitted in the recess in the solenoid with the smaller end of the spring facing the diaphragm. There are three types of spacers employed (as outlined above), which serve to maintain the diaphragm assembly in the exact centre of the solenoid. The easiest one is a square plastic unit with four equally spaced 'lugs', which are fitted to the diaphragm prior to installation. The second alternative is a set of loose nylon 'dumbbell'-shaped spacers, which are inserted when the diaphragm has been fitted (*see below*).

Fuel System

Checking the thickness of the feeler gauge for upper contact.

Fitting of the nylon or brass spacers.

'throw-over' can no longer be achieved by pushing up the solenoid. Then turn the diaphragm the other way – lining up the six holes in the perimeter with those in the solenoid body flange until the holes align. It should be possible to achieve the throw-over manually by placing a thumb on the diaphragm. If not, unscrew by one further set of holes (i.e. 1/6th revolution) and check again. Next, unscrew the diaphragm 1/3rd of a revolution (four more holes). The adjustment of the pump is now set and this position should not be disturbed pending fitting the body to the wet end.

Adopting the previously explained alignment convention, place the assembled pump chamber (wet end) on the work surface with the open side uppermost and the long outlet spigot at 12o'clock. Now fit the solenoid to sandwich plate gasket with the two small holes at the top and concave face uppermost, taking care to align the small holes at the top with the ones on the pump chamber. Now place the sandwich plate followed by the solenoid to sandwich plate gasket – lining up all six screw holes visually.

The two assemblies (wet and dry ends) are now ready to be joined back together. The six cheese-headed screws originally supplied can be reused. Alternatively, new ones can be utilised. Carefully place the solenoid on to the sandwich plate and gasket taking care not to disturb the alignment. The 2BA threaded brass stud should be in the 4 o'clock position when the assemblies are brought together. Fit the cheese-head screws in the six holes and just nip them up for now.

The third (and oldest) method is a set of brass washers – which again must be fitted later.

The next stage is a little difficult and may take a while to achieve at the first time of asking. Insert the threaded end of the diaphragm spindle through the centre of the solenoid. The aim is to screw it into the threaded trunnion in the rocker assembly. When this has been successfully achieved, screw it in far enough so that the spacers (if necessary – *see* above) can be inserted without them falling out. Test the action of the points by pushing the diaphragm manually from the bottom and check that the points throw over and back as the diaphragm goes up and down. It is possible, with care, to test the electrical integrity of the pump if a 12v power supply or battery is available. The pump should burst into life – but care must be taken not to lose the diaphragm spacers in the process. Checks for an electrical short circuit or broken wires should be undertaken at this time. If a suppressor is fitted there will be little or no electrical arcing at the points.

The next steps are quite important and a critical part of the setting-up process. Continue to screw the diaphragm up into the points assembly until the

Tip: It is believed that the pump will work slightly better if the diaphragm is tensioned in the 'solenoid energised' position. This does make some sense and is relatively easily achieved by inserting a small screwdriver into the central part of the rocker assembly between the brass frame and the steel pivot pin. (This will be at 6 o'clock). Then gently depress the screwdriver and the points rocker assembly will 'throw-over', by manually pulling up, the diaphragm. This should be maintained whilst tightening up the screws.

Fuel System

Correct orientation of the pump chamber and the solenoid.

Paper gaskets between the pump chamber and the sandwich plate.

Offering up the solenoid to the valve chamber assembly.

Pump ready to be secured together with screws.

Holding the points against the main spring to tension the diaphragm.

Suppressor fitted and connected to the terminals.

Tighten the 2BA cheese-head screws evenly. The screws take a bit of tightening and the best method is to use a 'hit and miss' method – operating on three at a time – tighten one, miss one, tighten the next, then tighten the others. You will need to go around the pump several times to tighten them up adequately and evenly.

Now is a good opportunity to test the operation of the pump. It can be tested on a Morris Minor of course, but paraffin is a good (safer) substitute in the workshop. Sometimes they take a little while to 'draw' the fuel. This is because the valves are dry and probably seal better once in contact with fuel. (Make sure that the pivot pin does not escape if you are running it with the cap removed.)

The insulating washer should now be fitted to the top of the threaded brass contact stud and the end cap can be fitted. There should be a spring washer (internal star type is best) next followed by the plain brass 2BA nut. A little black insulating tape around the joint between the body and the cap will help to keep moisture out. Ingress of moisture seems to cause the points to corrode more rapidly. The black plastic thumbscrew can then be fitted to finish the job.

Make sure that the earthing screw on the solenoid body is present (just adjacent to the flange). If not, it can easily be replaced by a 2BA (pre-1985) or 4BA (post-1985) screw.

SU CARBURETTOR RESTORATION

Introduction

The SU carburettor is one of the simpler carburettors used on classic cars and consequently it is by far one of the easiest to service and repair. Having only a single variable jet and no accelerator pumps, the complexity is reduced. Consequently, it lends itself to home maintenance and repair. The carburettors in most Morris Minors rarely need much attention – due largely to their robust construction. They do, however, suffer from wear over time. The increased ethanol content in fuel is another contributory factor due to its impact in increasing the wear on metal parts, particularly 'yellow' metals. Replacement parts for carburettors are increasingly being made of more ethanol-resistant materials, which should help provide future protection. The gradual degradation of the carburettor over the years may not be noticed, but when a newly built one is fitted, the difference in car performance will be immediately apparent.

Dismantling

Consideration is given here to the HS2 type as fitted to the later Morris Minor models. It is distinguished by the 1¼" choke with side float chamber. Other 'HS' models are essentially similar – as is the earlier model H2 and associated variants. These have a different float chamber connection with the fuel joint in the connection itself – whereas the later model has a more reliable 'dry' joint. The other main difference is the float chamber, which has the lid fixed by a concentric bolt. Disassembly is straightforward. An initial clean with solvent or paraffin is advisable before beginning. Any remaining oil in the dashpot should be drained by undoing the large nut on top of the dashpot and removing the damper. It is advisable to make a photographic record of the orientation of the throttle lever and the choke lever, particularly as the reassembly of the choke lever itself is difficult to envisage when the parts are separated on the bench.

Tip: Photograph the choke lever assembly prior to dismantling.

Remove the two cheese-head screws that secure the dashpot and carefully withdraw the piston and the spring. Note that the piston and dashpot are matched and should not be mixed with other units. There is a close tolerance between the piston and the dashpot, so be careful with any abrasive cleaning. Loosen the slotted screw at the base of the piston and remove the brass needle.

Undo the three cheese-head screws securing the top of the float chamber and remove the lid. Carefully withdraw the float pivot pin with pliers. The float should drop out. Unscrew the brass float seat with a small ¹¹⁄₃₂ AF or 9mm socket and withdraw the assembly complete with the needle. Undo the self-tapping screw at the bottom of the main jet, retaining the screw and the small brass collar between the lever and the jet. Unscrew the brass nut holding

The fully restored SU fuel pump as fitted to the last saloon.

Fuel System

the main jet flexible pipe at the base of the float chamber and remove the pipe.

Tip: Remove the old black grommet that seals the joint. It usually pulls off the pipe and gets 'hidden' inside the hole.

Ease the lock tabs back on the throttle spindle nut and remove and pull off the lever. Unscrew the small self-tapping Phillips screw securing the choke lever to the main jet and take care not to lose the tiny brass shoulder washer. This prevents the screw from gripping the base of the jet, as this joint is intended to allow rotational movement. Undo the bolt holding the choke lever assembly and carefully remove it.

The body of the carburettor can now be separated from the float chamber by undoing the larger bolt, which secures the two units together. Note the raised notch in the body and corresponding slot in the float chamber, which determines the draught angle of the carburettor and ensures that the float chamber is upright in service.

Now is probably a good time to remove the 'lift pin', which is the spring-loaded pin that permits manual operation of the piston during final tuning of the carburettor. There are two tiny 'C' clips that must be removed with fine-nosed pliers.

Tip: Make a note of the relative positions of the clips and the spring on the lift pin and take care not to lose the 'C' clips.

Now remove the main spindle and throttle disc. The screws that secure the disc to the spindle are split to prevent them from working loose in service. Gently close them together and unscrew from the spindle. The screws should not be used again. Note that the disc can only be fitted one way and can generally be re-used after cleaning. The brass disc is slightly oval in outline and has edges, which are not at right-angles to the upper and lower surfaces. The discs are cut from solid brass bar – but at a slight angle. This ensures that the disc 'locks' into position and cannot 'over-rotate' when at idle – sealing the throttle tube of the carburettor.

Prior to removing the spindle, test for play in the spindle/bushes by attempting to move up and down. Unless the carburettor is very worn, the wear is usually borne by the brass spindle rather than by the throttle body itself. It will be a judgement call as to whether you need to fit new Teflon-coated bushes in the body or just replace the spindle. It is advisable to (at least) replace the spindle. New bushes are available but fitting them accurately requires precision drilling and reaming of the holes. If this is attempted the oversized drilling/line reaming operation should be carried out to ensure that the enlarged hole (to take the Teflon bush) does NOT penetrate the throttle 'tube' of the carburettor body. The holes should stop short so that the throttle disc can effectively 'plug' the tube and not permit airflow around the disc and spindle, which will adversely affect slow running. The throttle disc should be as airtight as possible in the closed position. If this does happen, the inner ends of the bushes can be re-shaped to match the circular shape of the throttle tube.

Inspection

The parts can now be cleaned as required. It is best to do the cleaning in two stages. First remove the grease and dirt from the parts that are to be re-used with a solvent such as paraffin. When as clean as possible, further cleaning can be given in an ultrasonic cleaner (if required). The author uses a compressed air-blast cleaning method employing glass bead media, which is less abrasive and kinder to the alloy materials used in the carburettor construction. Clean compressed air should be used to make sure all cleaning media have been removed after blasting.

As a minimum the following items should be replaced (SU/Burlen part numbers given):

- Float needle and seat kit   VZX 1100
- Throttle spindle kit   WZX 1310
- Main Jet assembly   AUD 9098
- Needle (AN)   AN

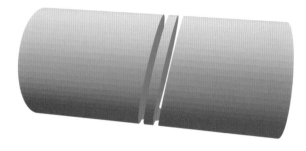

3D illustration of the throttle disc cut at an angle.

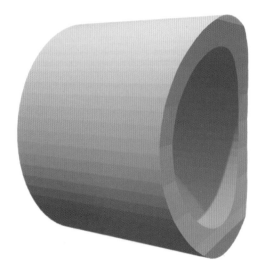

Preferable shaping of end of bush (if used).

The rebuild kit (CRK 104) contains the above items plus the throttle disc. The

Fuel System

above-listed items are supplied as a kit – so the gaskets, screws and lock washer are all included. The service kit (CRK 51) does not include the throttle spindle.

Reassembly

The reassembly is carried out in stages, starting firstly with the fitting of the throttle spindle. It must be inserted the correct way round with the threaded part on the left as you look at the manifold flange. The old throttle disc can usually be cleaned up and reused, although a new one is supplied with the full rebuild kit. Rotate the spindle until the countersunk holes are facing upwards and insert the throttle disc. Note the 'shape' of the disc (as outlined earlier). The disc should now fit snugly within the throttle tube and the spindle should rotate anticlockwise to open. At this point the countersunk split screws should be fitted loosely to assist with positioning the disc in exactly the right position. Gently press the disc into the hole so that it can slide within the slot in the throttle spindle. This ensures it is in the best position to completely seal the throttle when closed. Tighten one screw temporarily, loosen the other and apply some Loctite. Tighten that one permanently and then do the same with the other. Gently prise the forked end of the screws apart as an extra precaution against loosening. Do not bend them too far, or they will snap off. It is possible to trim off the forks from the end of the screws (prior to fitting) so that they are flush with the spindle and then to just rely on the Loctite. This has the benefit of smoothing the airflow over the throttle disc and may improve efficiency by a small percentage!

Next is the float chamber cap. Apply a little Loctite on the brass float needle seat and screw into the lid Insert the new needle. Note the black rubber-type material, which is called 'Viton', on the needle, which is intended to give improved life using fuel with ethanol content. Refit the float to the chamber cap, making sure it has not been perforated.

Tip: It is worth noting that a leaky float usually 'rattles'.

Parts for reassembly.

Insertion of throttle spring.

Split fixing screws.

Fuel System

Gently prise apart the sides.

Screws fixed and 'Loctited'.

Float seat with Loctite on thread.

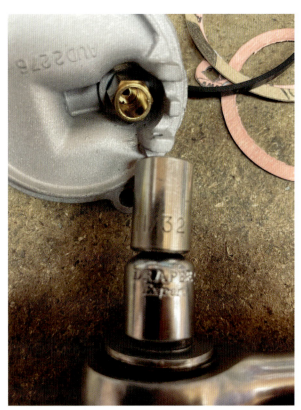
Tightening the seat into the float lid.

It is important to check that the float is adjusted correctly. This is done with the lid inverted. For HS carbs with the early nylon float and steel needle, the gap between the lever and the face of the lid should be between 0.125 of an inch and 0.187 of an inch with the float resting on the needle, but not depressing it. The later type is non-adjustable. Refit the lid to the float chamber using new screws and spring washers.

Fuel System

Inserting the new needle.

The choke lever return spring in position.

The spring-loaded choke lever re-fitted.

the centring of the main jet (*see* later). Screw it in as far as it will go but do not tighten it yet. Fit the mixture adjusting spring and the adjusting nut but leave the adjustment for now.

The next task is to fit the carburettor body to the float chamber, using a little Loctite on the screw while not forgetting the position of the alignment slot. The sequence of tasks outlined here is illustrated below. Make the fuel connection between the main jet and the float chamber ensuring that the small black grommet is in position. Nip up the brass hexagonal fixing collar tight, but not too tight, as the threads are easily stripped! A little petroleum jelly will help with the assembly of this joint. Replace the self-tapper screw and small brass collar that secures the jet to the choke lever, ensuring that the choke lever can rotate freely on the brass collar. There should be some spring pressure trying to keep the jet in the 'up' position. Fit the throttle lever with the new locking washer.

The new needle can be fitted to the piston. The new needle will be a lighter colour than the old one. This is because it is made of a different alloy, which has more resistance to modern fuels. Push the needle into the piston and secure the grub screw. Ensure that the shoulder of the needle is flush with the underside of the piston. Replace the piston, spring and dashpot.

Tip: Make sure the piston slides up and down as it should. Application of WD40 or a similar lubricant will help.

Choke Lever Refitting

At this stage reference to any photographs taken previously is useful as the assembly and orientation of various components illustrated (see below) can be confusing. The return spring and the spring-loaded choke lever is fitted and bolted as illustrated above.

When fitted, check the operation of the lever. The piston lift pin should be re-fitted next, followed by the jet bearing assembly. It is important to note the position of the aluminium washer between the brass tube and the plated nut that secures it and the fact that the brass tube slides around an oversized orifice in the body. This is to allow

Fuel System

Reassembly of the lift pin using the spring and circlips.

Lift pin in position. Insertion of the jet carrier.

Fitting the jet adjuster spring.

Fitting the float chamber to the main body.

Adjustment

With the carburettor re-assembled the next task is to set it up prior to fitting. The most important job on this unit is to centre the jet correctly. It is not the easiest of jobs and requires a little practice and a degree of patience to complete it satisfactorily. The objective is to get the piston (and hence the needle) to rise and fall smoothly with the tapered needle fitted exactly concentrically with the main jet. This is the reason for the oversized hole in the jet carrier. It is vital not to force anything during this process, as doing so could cause the needle to be bent or damaged. In order that this adjustment can cater for the full range of mixture adjustment – screw the lower (spring-loaded) nut in as far as it will go. This will push the jet up to its highest (weakest) position. Since the top nut is still only 'finger-tight', the jet should self-centre itself – to some extent. Using a finger, raise the piston and let it drop under gravity (and spring pressure). It should

Fuel System

Fitting the flexible jet feed to the float chamber outlet.

Fixing the choke lever to the jet using the brass shoulder spacer.

Throttle lever with new locking washer fitted.

RIGHT: Throttle lever with lock tabs bent over.

close with a soft 'clunk'. If it does not, then the best method is to gently tap the base of the assembly. Repeat this process until the piston drops back to the base as described above. When you tighten the securing nut, the jet assembly may move slightly and when you check the 'drop' again, it may jam – meaning a repeating cycle of tapping and re-checking until it operates smoothly.

The fuel/air mixture will need to be finally adjusted when the carburettor has been fitted, but it is helpful to adjust it on the bench to a good starting position. The mixture adjusting nut should be at its highest position and should then be unscrewed 2½ turns. This should be good enough to start the engine and to allow for final tuning adjustments to be made.

125

Fuel System

New needle AN.

Ensure that the shoulder of the needle sits flush with the base of the piston.

Replacing the piston, spring and dashpot.

Centralising the main jet.

Screw in the idle adjustment screw so that it just opens the throttle disc – this, again, should permit the engine to start and run at a reasonable 'idle' speed at first start-up. Also, check the fast-idle screw on the choke lever. It is best to slacken this off so that it does not affect the idle. It can be adjusted later to give an appropriate fast idle when the choke is utilised for cold starting.

Refitting

The carburettor can now be fitted to the manifold with new gaskets and the thick black heat insulator and reconnected to the throttle and choke cables. Refit the throttle return spring, which is usually fixed to a small 'banjo' bracket bolted onto the exhaust clamp. Adjust the spring tension so that it is at the *minimum* force required to close the throttle cleanly. If it is too tight, the spindle may wear prematurely, and the throttle may be harder to open from the foot pedal. Refit a new air filter. Replace the air filter element and the fuel pipe that supplies fuel to the pump. Fill the dashpot with thin (damper) oil, making sure not to over-fill as the excess will squirt out of the breather hole in the top of the damper.

> **Tip:** Check the condition and specification of the flexible fuel pipe from the pump to the carburettor. If there is any doubt about its condition replace it with 'R9' grade hose, which is ethanol resistant. Note that steel braided hoses sometimes obscure the true condition of the rubber hose within.

Switch on the ignition and check for leaks around the fuel joints. If all is well, start the engine and carry out the final adjustments to the mixture and the idle.

TUNING

This process can either be carried out manually or with the aid of a 'Colour Tune' or other suitable tuning device. A fully rebuilt carburettor will be much easier to set up and tune.

With the work completed so far, the carburettor should be sufficiently adjusted so that the engine will start and idle reasonably well. In order to achieve smooth and efficient running, adjust the tick-over so that the engine idles at about 750rpm, or at a slow speed sufficient for it to reach its normal working temperature. The hexagonal mixture nut on the carburettor should be adjustable by hand or with a small spanner if necessary. Gradually screw the adjuster upwards (anti-clockwise looking from the top) until the engine falters. Then screw it back a little to regain a smooth idle once again. The mixture can be checked by pushing up the piston lift pin momentarily. The engine should stutter a little – but not stall. If it does, the mixture is too weak. If it continues at a faster idle, it is too rich. The objective of this process is to establish the weakest mixture that will be adequate for efficient combustion. After running for a while, the colour of the spark plugs should be checked. A sooty black colour indicates that the mixture is too rich. White indicates that it is too weak. A light-brown colour in the centre will confirm the correct setting.

Before and after.

12
Interior Trim

INTRODUCTION

Interior trim refurbishment or replacement can be one of the most rewarding aspects of a full or partial restoration. With Morris Minor models the added benefit of the availability of an extensive range of replacement parts means that, funds permitting, most interiors can be replaced with original specification trim patterns without having to resort to commissioning bespoke replacements using the services of an experienced upholsterer. The only exceptions relate to the non-availability of some original-type materials including 'Karvel'-type carpet and the rexine-type covering used to cover the board-type headlining fitted to split windscreen Series MM and Series II models. In addition, the moulded rubber floor coverings fitted to light commercial and Traveller models are no longer available, though very occasionally new old stock items come to light. Where retaining originality or keeping the original trim parts supplied with the vehicle is deemed a priority, refurbishment using readily available leather recolouring and revitalising kits is an option. Recolouring vynide or vinyl materials is also possible, using Angelus acrylic leather paint, which can be mixed to a colour of choice. Preparation involves washing the materials to be painted with hot soapy water, drying thoroughly before lightly buffing the surface with a Scotch pad. Prior to applying the paint using a 0.8 spray gun, the surface should be cleaned again using an anti-silicone wipe. After painting, the materials should be dry after an hour if left at room temperature.

FMT 265 J

The interior trim on the project car proved to be beyond reasonable repair and though the rear seat coverings could have been salvaged it was decided to replace all the internal trim fittings with new parts. In this endeavour the project team were greatly supported by staff at Newton Commercial, who not only supplied the new materials but, as will be seen later in this chapter, assisted in the recovering of one of the front seats. Further assistance was also given by fellow author Richard McKellar, who shared his experiences in retrimming his Morris Minor Million and gave permission for his previously published guide to fitting a headlining to be updated and supplemented by images of the fitting of a new headlining in FMT 265 J. In respect of the interior trimming this was the first task tackled when the car returned from the paint shop.

HEADLINING REPLACEMENT

Removing and replacing the headlining fitted to post-1956 Morris Minor saloons and Travellers is a very time-consuming job. It is also one that requires patience and care. The removal of an existing headlining is a task not to be rushed, as much can be learned about the way it is constructed, fitted and tensioned.

In the case of the project car, it soon became apparent that not only was the headlining in a dire state of repair but that the supporting metal bows and the front wooden tension board were beyond future use. A new headlining was sourced from Newton Commercial and replacement bows and a front tensioning board were located.

Removal of the Headlining (Saloon)

The initial stage of removing an existing headlining requires the release of the tensioning wires located at the rear of the car. These steel wires are tensioned by Phillips-headed screws and flat washers. They are located directly under the rear window and screwed into the upper rear seat squab support more commonly referred to as the rear shelf behind the back seat (pictured). Access to these screws requires the removal of the rear seat, the inner rear quarter side panel, and the covered card panel under the rear window. With the tensioning screws released, the headlining can be eased away from some very aggressive-looking teeth situated around the top of the rear window. While this process can be completed with the rear screen in place, it is much easier to do if the rear screen is removed.

Additional tensioning wires are located towards the front of the car on the 'B' posts and on the lower sections of both sides of the dash panel. It is worth noting that earlier cars have a tensioning screw located behind the rear quarter panel halfway down each of the 'B' Pillars and that four-door saloons have 'B' post tensioning wires located behind the trafficator covers. On later cars, including the project car, additional 'B' post tensioning wires were dispensed with. With all tensioning screws released, the supporting bows can be removed from the cant rail. Care needs to be taken to retain the spring clips on both ends of each of the bows.

The final task involves removing the front wooden retaining fillet (tensioning board), which is held in place by two clips on either side. This is best achieved by carefully sliding a small steel ruler in between the headlining and roof reinforcement panel (just above the sun visors). The clips are located about 250mm (9.84 inches) in from the sides. By positioning the ruler over these retaining clips and levering upwards and toward the rear of the car, they should release.

HEADLINING REPLACEMENT – A GUIDE

New headlinings come with a helpful set of instructions. As well as paying close attention to these it is advisable to spend some time examining the original headlining, if only to work out where everything fits and how it goes together. It is recommended to wear clean protective gloves when handling and fitting the headlining to avoid inadvertently marking the material.

Fitting the Tensioning Bows

As a first step locate the three sleeves on the headlining that hold the tensioning bows in place. Measure, check and measure again before cutting a 70mm (2.75 inch) section out of each of the sleeves. Do NOT cut the lining. Note that each of the bows is curved differently. Next, make a hole through the sleeve. Tie a string to the end of the tensioning bows to assist with centralising and tensioning the lining across each of the hoops. This will prevent the lining gathering unevenly in the middle of the roof.

Attaching the Tensioning Board

Using the original headlining as a guide, position, glue and staple the tensioning board. This board should be about 40cm (15.75 inches) from the first hoop. Be sure to check that the material is properly tensioned before stapling or bonding it across the length of the board. If stapling, do so close to the front edge of the board as this will not be seen. Next attach the two retaining clips on the front edge of the board with headlining secured. Fasten these using bifurcated rivets.

Fitting Tensioning Wires

Thread the stainless-steel wire along the length of the lining, making sure it is inserted through the spring eyes on the end of all three tensioning bows. Put a spot of glue on the end of the tensioning wire and allow it to dry before attempting to thread it through. This is a helpful way of preventing snagging and possible damage to the lining. Allow plenty of wire at both ends for tensioning. Next, thread the wire around the back window section of the lining once, again making sure there is adequate wire for tensioning.

Fitting the Headlining Inside the Car

Moving to the inside of the car, loosely position the headlining in place and fit each of the tensioning bow edges in the roof reinforcement cant rail. When satisfied with the positioning, insert the tension board in place and fasten the clips into the front reinforcement cant rail, making sure that the board is centred within the windscreen area.

Thread the tensioning wires down each of the windscreen pillars and pull them through under the dash. Working towards the back, carefully stretch and tension the headlining until it is centrally positioned before threading the tension wires down both 'B' posts and pulling them through (pre-1963 cars only). Loosely wrap the wire around the Phillips-head tension screw behind a flat washer.

Final Tensioning

Moving to the back of the car, attention should now focus on tensioning and clipping the back part of the headlining over the aggressive 'teeth' at the top of the window. A bit of pressure can be applied here to get the lining taut. Under tension any creases in the headlining will gradually disappear. The headlining is fully tensioned by carefully positioning the tension wires under the flat washers at each of the fixing points. On pre-1963 cars there are eight fixing points and on post-1963 cars just six, as the 'B' post fixing points were removed. The wires should be evenly tensioned using the Phillips-headed screws. Once the headlining is fully tensioned, attention should focus on fitting the rear finishing board under the rear screen before securing the excess material in each of the rear quarters. Any surplus material will need to be cut, folded, and secured with sprung trim clips.

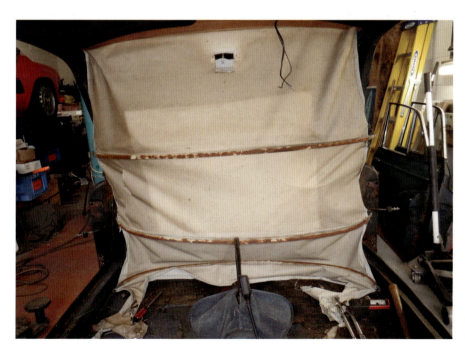

Original headlining being removed.

Interior Trim

Rear location points for tensioning wire screws and flat washers.

New tensioning board and replacement hoops/bows.

Accurate measuring is essential before cutting the sleeves that retain the hoops/bows.

The distance from the back edge of the tensioning board to the first bow/hoop should be 15.75 inches (40cm).

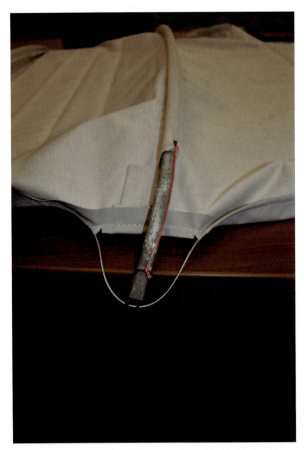

Tensioning wire threaded through the spring clip on the end of the hoop/bow.

High-heat-resistant contact adhesive was used to bond the supplied material to the original rear finishing board.

The recovered rear finishing board.

Interior Trim

Positioning the assembled headlining by running the bows/hoops along the cant rails. It is important at this stage to ensure the courtesy light wiring is in place.

Rear window aperture, with the rear finishing board correctly positioned and secured by cup washers and domed screws. Earlier cars had a full wrap-around finisher secured at the edges by the cant rail.

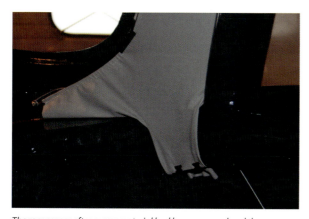

The rear corner after excess material had been removed and the headlining had been secured by clips. All excess wire was removed.

The use of a heater helped smooth out any final wrinkles in the headlining. The job when finished including the wiring for the courtesy light.

Courtesy light wiring.

Courtesy light unit with bullet connectors fitted.

SEATS AND INTERIOR TRIM

For the home restorer the good news is that replacement seat covers and interior trim panels are available for the whole range of Morris Minor models manufactured between 1948 and 1971. Newton Commercial, based in Leiston, Suffolk, England, are a long-established company, well known for providing quality materials produced to original specification for a wide range of British post-war cars and commercial vehicles. The company has the prestigious accolade of being British Motor Heritage Approved.

Throughout Morris Minor production, a wide variety of seat and interior trim patterns were utilised. Featuring different materials including vynide leather cloth, leather facings and in later years heat-formed vinyl, the number of options available are considerable. If originality is a priority when undertaking a restoration, then time spent researching the paint/trim combinations for specific models and year

Interior Trim

Examples of Morris Minor Interior Trim

1. Morris Minor Series MM, 1948–1953

2. Morris Minor Series II, 1953–1956

(continued overleaf)

Examples of Morris Minor Interior Trim *continued*

3. Morris Minor 1000, 1960

4. Morris Minor 1000, 1962

(continued overleaf)

Interior Trim

Examples of Morris Minor Interior Trim *continued*

5. Morris Minor 1000, 1964–1971

of manufacture will pay dividends. (Sample interior patterns as shown in the images above and on the previous two pages, numbered 1 to 5.)

In the case of the project car, it was apparent from the outset that the seat and interior trim coverings would need to be refurbished or replaced. The decision was taken to seek professional assistance with the retrimming of the front and rear seats. A complete interior was supplied by Newton Commercial and the trimming of the driver's front seat was undertaken by experienced Newton Commercial employee Tom Balls. John Carroll photographed the sequence of tasks. His images are included here as a step-by-step guide for the home restorer.

To maintain the high professional standards set during the initial refurbishment, the rest of the seat refurbishment was outsourced to a local upholstery trimmer. Mark Jacklin, MCJ Upholstery undertook the task.

Refurbished seat frame ready for recovering.

Interior Trim

Prior to refurbishment both front seat frames were stripped of all coverings before being thoroughly checked for any signs of weakness or metal fatigue. They were then sent for powder coating to ensure a hard-wearing, high lustre finish. The rear seat base springs – which were in a poor state – were also thoroughly cleaned before being powder coated.

RECOVERING THE FRONT SEAT: A STEP-BY-STEP GUIDE

As-new rear seat springs after powder coating.

1. To protect a newly refurbished seat frame from wear or damage while it is being worked on, cover vulnerable parts of the tubular frame with bubble wrap.
2. Begin by hooking new supporting rubber base straps into place, noting that the hooks have shared locating holes in the frame.
3. Fit seven support straps in the base and five on the back.
4. Spray the outer face of the seat frame base with glue from an aerosol in preparation for attaching the thin padding in place.
5. Carefully position the padding on the seat frame, ensuring it is level along the top edge.
6. Replicate the positioning as illustrated here. This is critical, as it will affect the finished line of the vinyl and piping around the seat base.
7. Next, fit the new foam seat base, which is specially shaped to fit around the tubular frame of the back. Glue around the edges.

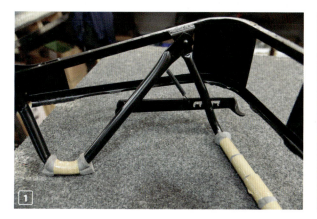
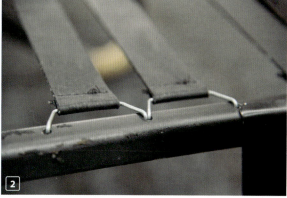

Interior Trim

Fitting the Base Seat Cover

8. Thread the seat base cover under the seat back, making sure it is sitting square on the foam base.
9. Glue the inside of the seat base cover to fix it in position, before pulling the sides down in readiness for fixing them in position.
10. Pay particular attention to aligning the piping on the seat cover around the edge of the seat base.
11. It is recommended to work from the middle to ensure that the piping stays on the corner and does not go out of alignment.
12. Using the spring clips supplied as part of the kit, clip the vinyl onto the seat frame by gently tapping them into place.
13. Trim and fold any surplus material to achieve a smooth appearance with the back cover.
14. Trim any surplus material at the bottom of the seat base, gluing the remainder on to the rail.
15. Success. A finished seat base with neat piping on the corner and the bottom edge neatly folded and clipped.

Interior Trim

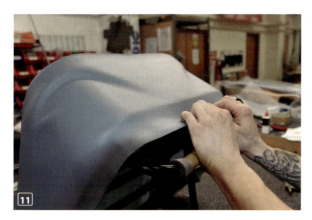

Interior Trim

Fitting the Seat Back Cover

16. Fit the coco mat padding in position on the seat back before gluing to the frame and rolling it around it. Trim off any surplus padding where folds have been made.
17. To help with fitting the vinyl cover, a useful ploy is to cover the coarse padding with a shaped sheet of plastic.
18. Slide the vinyl cover over the plastic-covered padding, making sure that the piping remains square on the seat back and that the moulding on the seat back aligns perfectly with that on the seat base.
19. Clip the layers of vinyl to the bottom rail using the clips provided. As there is more than one layer of vinyl, the clips may need to be opened up a little before being clamped in place.
20. In the event of any creases remaining in the vinyl, the gentle use of a heat gun can help eliminate them.
21. Job done! The completed seat … just as it would have left the factory.

The process was repeated for the passenger seat before attention turned to the rear seat back and base. New covers had been supplied as part of the interior trimming kit. Replacing the rear seat coverings is a much more straightforward task and one that is not always necessary due to the lack of use and wear on some vehicles. With the last saloon, a full interior re-trim was undertaken and the work on the passenger seat and the rear seat squab and back was outsourced to a local professional upholsterer Mark Jacklin (MCJ Upholstery).

REAR SEAT BACK

Removing the cover on the seat back was easily accomplished by extracting

Interior Trim

the staples that secure it in place after the black felt covering had been carefully removed along with the metal locating pins. With the vinyl cover off, the condition of the wooden back and the original padding could be assessed, and decisions made on their re-use. An additional covering of Dacron, a fibre fill material, was added to improve the overall profile of the seat back. Following a trial fit, the critical task of positioning the new cover and securing it in place by stapling the vinyl to the wooden back began. Key to a successful fit is the need to ensure that the cover is evenly tensioned as stapling progresses. For the home restorer, frequent checking is recommended.

With the cover securely fastened, attention switched to refitting the black felt covering to the wooden back. This had been successfully removed without damage and was refitted using black staples rather than being glued in place. The final task was reattaching the metal locating pins on the seat back using the original screws in the easily identifiable original positions.

REAR SEAT BASE

The newly refurbished spring base was covered by the original padding, which required a slight addition before being covered in Dacron. Securing the new vinyl cover required a different technique to that used on the seat back. With the emphasis once again being on evenly tensioning the cover and ensuring an even profile to the piping on the front edge and sides of the seat, extra care was taken with the alignment of the cover before it was secured in position using 'Hog rings' (circular metal clips). These 'C'-shaped clips were passed through the material over the reinforced channel on the bottom edge of the material and attached to the outer edge of the metal spring base before being closed to an 'O' shape using pliers. This process was repeated at evenly spaced intervals with regular checks to ensure that the material was tensioned correctly to provide a smooth even finish to the front and sides of the base.

Seat base complete with wasp's nest as removed from the last saloon.

Powder-coated seat base.

Original seat base covering. The missing piece was replaced!

Both the seat back and squab were covered with Dacron to enhance the profile and provide a smoother additional covering.

Interior Trim

The newly supplied vinyl covers for the seat back and squab.

Edges stapled in position on the seat back prior to refitting the locating pins.

Completed seat back.

Closed C-ring fastenings in position on the seat base.

Completed seat back and squab.

Interior Trim

INTERIOR DOOR CARDS AND SIDE PANELS

As noted previously, a complete range of new interior trim panels is available from Newton Commercial in authentic colours and specification for all Morris Minor models. Some of the individual panels do require additional preparatory work prior to fitting.

Door Cards

While the actual fitting of new door cards in position is relatively straightforward, some preliminary work that involves cutting the vinyl covering requires a degree of caution. Although the hardboard backing comes pre-drilled with apertures for the door handle and window winding mechanism, the extension pieces (shafts) to which the respective handles are attached need to be carefully located, their position measured (and measured again as a double check) before a small incision is made in the vinyl to allow the extension pieces through. The door card is attached to the door frame using triangular-shaped spring clips, which are easily inserted into the pre-prepared apertures in the hardboard backing before being lined up and pressed through the locating holes in the door frame. Fitting the door pulls also requires a degree of precision. Some lining up is required once the previously used holes at the top of the door frame have been located. Care must be exercised with the alignment before making two corresponding holes in the vinyl for the fixing screws to pass through. The chrome finisher can then be attached using chrome-headed self-tapping screws.

For anyone deciding to drill new holes rather than using previously used ones, it is recommended to use a short drill bit to avoid inadvertent damage to the window glass. It is also important to retain the use of the original-style fibre washers when fitting the handles to the door to prevent chafing on the vinyl.

Door cards as supplied with no holes predrilled in vinyl covering.

Door pull with authentic later style finisher.

Fitted door card assembly.

Interior Trim

Rear Inner Side Panels with Arm Rest

Fitting the inner rear side panel is another task that requires careful measuring and alignment. Five factory pre-drilled holes in the body on each side need to be located, as these are the fixed points to which the new panel will be attached using self-tapping screws and cup washers. Like the door cards, the vinyl will have to be carefully pierced at exactly the right point to line up with the pre-drilled holes. It is advisable to locate the centre top fixing as a starting point followed by a side fixing next to the 'B' post. With the panel loosely in position it should then be possible to line up the remaining fixing points more easily before tightening up each of the screws a little at a time. Having extra lighting in the car makes this task much easier.

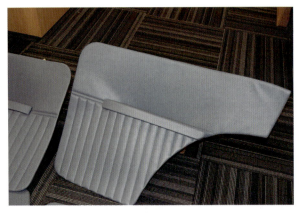

New rear side panel with no pre-drilled holes.

Self-tapping screws with cup washers provide a neat finish.

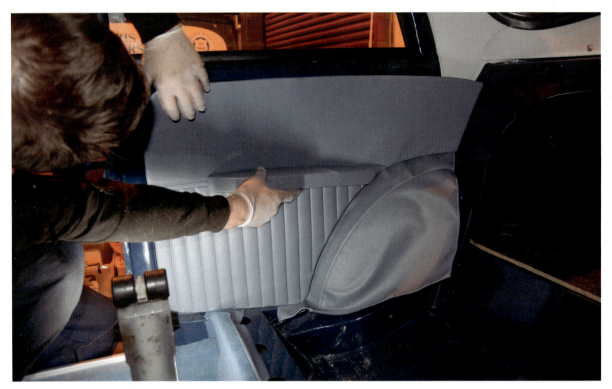

Having in-car lighting proved beneficial for this task.

REAR WHEEL ARCH COVERINGS

These coverings are also supplied as part of the kit and would normally be glued into position. In order to achieve a smooth finish, the underlying wheel arch needs to be in good repair and any previous glue removed prior to refitting. In cases where there have been repairs to the metalwork in this area resulting in unevenness on the surface, applying an additional foam or hessian covering prior to fitting the vinyl cover is a useful method of ensuring a smooth, even outer finish.

FITTING NEW CARPETS

Replacement carpet sets for all Morris Minor models are readily available. For the two-door saloon the set comprises thirteen pieces. Some, like the gearbox tunnel covering, the rear tunnel and the front inner wheel arch covers, are specially shaped or moulded. Where vehicles have been modified, for instance by changing to a five-speed gearbox and adding a changed gearbox cover, additional matching carpet pieces are available to order.

While at first glance changing or replacing the carpet set would seem a straightforward operation, proper sequencing of the tasks involved can save time and the unnecessary repetition of work. Key areas requiring the use of heat-resistant contact adhesive to affix the carpet include the inner sill coverings, front inner wheel arch coverings, the rear heel board, rear tunnel covering and rear seat side infill pieces.

It is advisable to make gluing the inner sill coverings in position one of the first jobs to do if replacing a complete carpet set. It is important to note that the pieces supplied as part of the carpet set do not normally come with an aperture for the seat belt fixing point. Consequently, an aperture will need to be made, preferably before gluing takes place. An additional reason for making the fitting of the sill covering a priority is that the aluminium sill finisher fits over the top edge of the inner sill and over the top edge of the carpet. It is best to have the carpet in situ before fitting the sill finisher. Alternatively, the sill finisher may have to be removed before fitting new carpet, if this is a stand-alone task. Additionally, if a new carpet is being fitted while the front parcel tray is still in position, it will be necessary to remove the scuttle panels as the wheel arch carpet fits underneath them. It will also be necessary to loosen and remove the bolts securing the parcel tray and undo the screws and cup washers holding the panel in place. On each of the wheel arch coverings there is a square cut out that fits around the inner sill and a V-shaped cut to assist with positioning the carpet on the wheel on the curved wheel arch before it is glued in place.

After gluing the front inner wheel arch pieces, the rear heel board covering, the rear seat side infill pieces and the sill coverings, attention should switch to cutting and positioning sound-deadening material on the transmission and gearbox cover before focusing on fixing the front moulded tunnel and gearbox carpet in place along with the metal ring that secures the gear lever gaiter.

Securing the metal ring in position is a task that requires elements of skill, dexterity and patience. There are six locating holes for the screws, which go through the metal ring. These need to match with those on the tunnel. This task is made more difficult due to the screws having to go through the moulded carpet and underlay if this is fitted by choice. Some of the carpet sets supplied use thinner felt pieces cut to shape. These need to be carefully positioned along the full length of the transmission and gearbox tunnels taking account of the handbrake wires and the need to cut out holes for the seat belt anchorages. With the metal ring secured the moulded carpet is likely to remain in position, but applying adhesive to the edges of the moulded sections will help ensure they do not slip around.

With these tasks complete, it is then a case of placing the other mats in position in preparation for the task of fitting the rest of the interior. Care needs to be exercised in the case of the front carpets, particularly on the driver's side, where the carpet that will need to be positioned around the dip switch, foot pedals and steering column in readiness for the fitting of the floor-mounted fixings, which secure the carpet in place. Further adjustments will be required when the front seats are positioned and aligned prior to the fixing bolts being passed through the carpet and underfelt to the position of choice on the threaded adjustment bars, which are integral to the floor.

FINAL FITTINGS

Before permanently fitting the front seats in position, attention switched to fitting the parcel shelf located beneath the dashboard. When initially assessed it was apparent that the original parcel shelf was not serviceable due to distortion caused by damp over a long period of time. Consideration was given to acquiring a kit to recover the crash pad and purchasing a replacement parcel tray. In the interests of saving time, a good replacement parcel shelf was sourced and fitted. New sun visors supplied at the same time and in the same material as the headlining were one of the last items to be fitted, along with new glove box liners. After careful alignment the liners were installed and fastened to the supporting bracket at the rear before being firmly secured using two self-tapping screws on the

Carpet set with moulded tunnel cover.

Securing the metal ring around the gear lever rubber.

Interior Trim

Trial layout prior to seats being fitted.

Job complete.

front edge on each side. The glove box lid was then fitted on the passenger side. Door draught excluder in the correct colour was purchased cut to size and then attached using the metal push-on locating clips supplied. One continuous piece on each side was carefully positioned with extra attention paid to the corner next to the top of each 'B' post. The draught excluder was firmly located using a soft mallet before being evenly pinched all the way round using a specialist padded tool. As is often the case when new draught excluder is fitted, the new rubber moulding prevented each of the doors from closing easily. This was accepted as a temporary position, which was rectified when final checks were made and panels, including the doors, were realigned, as part of the final assembly checklist. It is perhaps worth noting that new-style 'soft' draught excluder is available in a non-standard black colour and is favoured by some restorers who are prepared to forgo 'originality' in favour of a comfortable door fit.

13
Reassembly

When the bodyshell returned from the paint shop, the task of prioritising the sequencing of work to rebuild the car assumed greater importance. Although checks had been made frequently to check the alignment of the outer body panels during the preparation and painting process, they were not secured in their final position when plans were made for transporting the bodyshell back to the workshop.

While work progressed on refurbishing and recommissioning various components simultaneously, one of the first tasks undertaken with the bodyshell was the fitting of a new headlining (see Chapter 12). Part of the rationale for this decision was the assumption that this would be easier to complete with the front and rear screens and the rear side windows removed. With the headlining installed, it made sense to refit the windows at the earliest opportunity.

WINDOW FITTING

In preparation for this task, new rubber window seals were acquired for all the windows and, as a concession to increased safety, a new laminated windscreen was purchased. The side windows and rear screen originally fitted to the car were retained. Considerable work was required to salvage these, as they were heavily coated in grime and mould accumulated over twenty years. Removal required a concerted effort using copious amounts of cleaning materials and the careful use of Stanley blades to remove the worst of the discoloration. The period rear screen demister was removed.

Prior to refitting, the new rubbers were laid flat and left in a warm room for 24 hours in an effort to increase their suppleness. The side windows were fitted first using a window fitting cord and XCP Rustblocker as a lubricant to assist in pulling the rubber into position. Contrary to popular practice, washing-up liquid was not used for this purpose due to its salt content.

With the window glass positioned in the rubber and the window cord carefully positioned around the rubber, the window was positioned on the inside and pressure applied to push it outwards. The cord was used to pull the rubber into position with care being exercised not to tear the rubber by applying too much pressure. Three people were involved in fitting the new rubbers to the rear screen and the side windows.

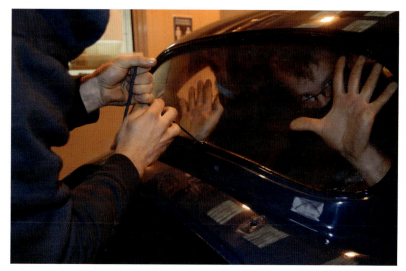
A patient, methodical approach paid dividends when pulling the rubber into place.

A neat even finish was achieved.

Reassembly

FRONT WINDSCREEN

Fitting the front windscreen required the use of a different technique. While the same principle applied in the use of window cord and XCP Rustblocker as a lubricant, the new laminated screen was positioned from the outside and then pulled inwards. (The reverse of the rear screen procedure.) In addition the front windscreen had to have beading inserted into the recess on the outer edge of the moulding. This required the use of a special 'windscreen insert tool' to assist with evenly positioning the beading within the recess. An additional 5mm of extra beading was accommodated within the recess in anticipation of shrinkage that occurs over time, resulting in gapping where the two edges join.

OUTER REAR PANELS

The front and rear wing were fixed to and unbolted from the bodyshell several times during the final stages of the restoration. On occasions this was to allow easier access to other mechanical components and to avoid potential damage to the paintwork. In the case of the rear wings the final fit had to incorporate the accurate alignment and fitting of wing piping. This necessitated careful positioning of the piping to take account of the curvature of the wing before marking and cutting the inner edge to align with the threaded holes for the wing bolts. The technique favoured to ensure even seating of the upper edge of the piping was to cut out V-shaped pieces so as to avoid any creasing or overlapping of the material sandwiched between the inner edge of the wing and the bodyshell. Starting at the centre point at the top of each wing and then working forwards towards the rear quarter panel, the piping was carefully positioned, with particular care being taken to ensure proper alignment at the front bottom edge to take account of both the curvature of the wing and the straight edge. With that objective successfully met, attention then switched to obtaining the correct profile on the rear section of the wing. A good deal of adjustment was required before the wing bolts were fully tightened and each of

Teamwork proved crucial in applying pressure when pulling front rubber inwards.

The special beading tool used to insert the beading into the recess in the rubber.

A job successfully completed.

the rear wings was permanently positioned. Attention was also paid to the area where the edge of the sealing rubber for the rear bumper support bar comes in contact with the wing piping and efforts made to ensure that the seal was seated sufficiently well to avoid leakage into the boot area.

DOORS

On return from the paint shop the unassembled doors had already been carefully fitted and aligned. A decision was made not to disturb them and to complete the reassembly process with the doors already in position on the car. In large part the reassembly process was the reverse of the dismantling process described in detail in Chapter 12. Additional work was required on the door frames and in replacing the window felts, weather strips and sealing rubbers. The door frames presented a dilemma, as questions arose over whether the frames on the doors were those originally fitted at the factory. Reference to the contemporary photographs of the car at the factory on the day of production proved inconclusive and photographs dating from 1994 showed the car with stainless steel door frames fitted. Initially, the stainless steel frames were retained and, as the accompanying photographs show, were present when the restoration was completed in 2020. Observant readers will note that subsequently the door frames were repainted in body colour and refitted to the car.

In connection with the door frames and windows, it is useful to note that when fitting new window felts it is necessary to make an adjustment to the top part of the upright felts by making a cut out to allow the window to pass over a joint. Failure to do this will prevent the window from closing. New sealing rubbers were fitted beneath the quarter light assembly and replacement new old stock weather strips were inserted along with new quarter light rubbers. The original domed quarter light screws were retained.

HINTS AND TIPS

Fitting and aligning doors and achieving even vertical gaps between the

Starting point. Centralising the wing piping in line with bolt holes.

Securing a tight and even fit requires a patient and methodical approach.

Stainless steel door frames were reinstalled but subsequently changed.

Reassembly

door and the front wing and the 'B' post can be a time-consuming and at times frustrating process, particularly when attempted for the first time. It is also a matter of choice whether to fit the cover plates for the inner sills and the outer sill finishers before or after a trial fit of the doors, due to the potential of causing damage to the painted surfaces.

Preparatory work includes locating and aligning the hinge retaining plate in the hinge pillar. Prior to offering the door up to fasten the hinge bolts, a helpful strategy is to take an old hinge bolt, cut off the hexagonal head and then, with the threaded part secured in a vice, cut a groove in the top sufficient to accommodate a flat-blade screwdriver. Insert the threaded part of the bolt into the locating plate through the top outer hole leaving approximately 10–12mm protruding.

With the door suitably supported either on a trolley jack with a piece of wood placed between the door bottom and the jack or wooden blocks with a piece of carpet on top placed at an appropriate height, the door can be manoeuvred into position more easily. Using the protruding threaded bolt as a guide point, the remaining bolts – four on the top and three on the bottom – can be located and fastened. With luck this will simply pull the door into line, but further adjustments may prove necessary. If the door is out of alignment it may be necessary to fabricate some shims. Using the hinge as a pattern make a cardboard template before fabricating a shim using 1mm mild steel. Do not use aluminium to make the shim. With the shim fitted behind the hinge, further adjustment can be undertaken. It is common to find shims being used on the bottom hinge to accommodate raising the height of the door to improve the evenness of the gap between the door and the 'B' post and allow for further checks to be made on the location of the door frame in the door aperture. If fabricating a suitable-sized shim is not an option, it is possible to purchase shims from some specialist suppliers. When working with doors that have been recently painted, a useful precautionary tip is to apply some low-adhesive tape to the edges of the door to protect the paintwork from being damaged while adjustments are being made.

A combination of new and original fitments was used in the final reassembly.

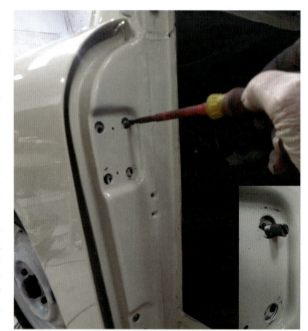

Modified hinge bolts being used to locate the retaining plates for the top and bottom hinges prior to door fitment.

Modified hinge bolt (inset).

Sill finishers and cover plates painted in readiness for fitting.

FRONT WINGS

Unlike the rear wings, wing piping was not used along the top edge of each of the front wings where they are bolted to the inner wing. To aid alignment with the edge of each of the doors and to allow for adjustment before final tightening, bolts were placed loosely at the front top edge, bottom of the back edge and the top back corner before being nipped up once a provisional alignment had been established. New bolts and washers were used and,

Reassembly

before fitting the bolts, were lightly coated with grease. Once satisfied with the evenness of the gap between the edge of the door and the back edge of the wing and the continuity of the curvature from the door into the wing, the remaining wing bolts were fitted and tightened. The final fixing bolt for each wing was the non-caged nut and bolt that fits at the front forward edge. A useful guide point for the alignment of the wings with the door is the rain channel close to the bulkhead. The rear edge of the front wing should be in line with the bulkhead edge of the rain channel.

FRONT PANEL AND GRILLE ASSEMBLY

The assembly of all the component parts of the front panel was completed off the car before the panel was offered up for final fitting. A carefully sequenced approach was adopted to completing this task as evidenced in the accompanying photographs. A new grille surround finisher was fitted at the outset. Securing it in place required the use of sixteen plastic fittings. This was followed by attaching the painted, slatted grille panel held in position by four self-tapping screws. In anticipation of later adjustments, the opportunity was taken while the panel was being prepared for fitment to attach the refurbished bonnet release mechanism and the bonnet locating plate and safety release lever. With the panel still off the car, the outer top chrome bar was added and affixed using seven 2BA nuts along with the inner support panel for the radiator. The reconditioned radiator was added prior to the panel being offered up for final fitting … one of the last and most rewarding tasks associated with the reassembly of the outer body panels.

Front Panel Final Fit

Extra care was taken with the fitting of the front panel, with additional help being used in the initial stages to cope with the extra weight with the radiator being attached. This was also to minimise the risk of damage to the paintwork while the panel was being located over the bumper support bars and the initial bolts were positioned. Prior to offering up the panel, anti-rattle rubber strips were positioned on the front edges of the inner wings. With one bolt on each side located on the top fastening point and one bolt secured on the bottom edge of the front crossmember, small adjustments with regard to final alignment with the holes for the two chromed hockey sticks were made. Once properly aligned, the remaining bolts were added, giving a total of four on the top edge, seven on the bottom along with three 2BA nuts on each of the hockey sticks.

Fixings for the outer grille finisher.

With the grille finisher in position, attention turned to fitting the slatted grille.

With the panel off the car, the opportunity was taken to fit the refurbished bonnet release mechanism.

BONNET ALIGNMENT

Preliminary work undertaken prior to the bonnet being fitted included refitting the internal support bars to the underside and locating the newly acquired bonnet hinges on the bulkhead. This task, which can prove difficult, required each hinge along with the rubber gasket to be positioned on the bulkhead and the nuts and spring washers attached to the hinge studs from inside the car. Initially, these were loosely fastened to the underside of

Reassembly

Anti-rattle rubber strips were attached to the front edges of the inner wings prior to the grille panel being fitted.

The opportunity was taken to affix the radiator support panel and the radiator and offer the whole assembly up for final fitting as one piece.

Final checks prior to fitting the front bumper assembly.

the bulkhead. The actual fitting of the bonnet is a three-person job with one person inside the car and two outside to carefully align the bonnet, place the rubber gaskets and the hinges in position on the bonnet and fasten the nuts and washers on the underside. Extreme caution is needed to ensure that the paintwork on adjacent surfaces including the bulkhead and the front wings is protected. As will be seen in the accompanying images, strategically placed cloths were used for this purpose. It will also be noted that at this point in the restoration the side strips fitted to saloon, convertible and Traveller model bonnets and held in place by spring clips had not yet been fitted. The same applied to the bonnet handle, Morris 1000 side badges and the front badge, as well as the centrally placed sprung bonnet catch fitment fitted on the inside. At this juncture the bonnet stay was refitted using the welded mounting point and new split pins and associated fittings.

BOOT LID

In preparation for the fitting of the boot lid following repainting, a new seal was fitted to the inner edge of the boot lid in accordance with the specification for later Morris 1000 models. Earlier Morris Minor saloons and convertibles had a seal that attached to the outer edge of the boot surround. The original hinges were retained when fitting the boot lid and, in the initial stages of fitting the portion that attaches to the car, attention was paid to locating the earth wire for the number plate light and placing the ringed portion onto the boot hinge stud on the driver's side before fastening. Apart from aligning the boot lid to ensure an even gap all round before finally tightening up the respective nuts, the only other major consideration was the reattachment of the self-locking boot stay as fitted to later models. A chrome boot handle was sourced and fitted along with new Morris 1000 boot badges and a new old stock original-style black number plate light assembly. As a precaution to prevent the ingress of water into the boot area – a common problem – a light application of sealant was applied around the apertures where these items fitted.

Reassembly

FITTING FRONT AND REAR BUMPER ASSEMBLIES

First trials at fitting the front and rear bumper assemblies proved difficult, particularly at the rear where it became apparent that at some stage in the past the original spring bar had been damaged. All efforts at securing even alignment failed and a replacement item had to be sourced. The sequencing of this work was important and was only attempted after the front and rear wings had been fixed in position and alignment with other panels checked. The decision was also taken to assemble the various component parts on the vehicle rather than completing a sub-assembly of the spring bar, metal valance and bumper and then fitting complete assemblies to the vehicle. Careful measurements were made and checked repeatedly to ensure an even height from ground level. One of the reasons for fitting and assembling the components on the car rather than off it is that when tightening the nuts there is a risk of creasing the metal valance. When fitting the bumper and valance, it proved useful to have assistance to hold the bumper and valance together while the two centre bolts were positioned prior to being tightened, finger-tight at first. Once the remaining bolts were located, they were evenly tightened in sequence without causing any damage to the metalwork. At the time when the front and rear bumper assemblies were fitted over-riders should have been added. Unfortunately, they had to be fitted later, due to a delay in the re-chroming schedule.

BRIGHTWORK AND CHROME

The brightwork on the Morris Minor was decorative but not overstated. Most, but not all, of the components that were chrome plated – including external badging, the grille surround, external and internal handles, and the bezels on lighting units – were cast using mazak, a base metal of zinc with alloys of aluminium, magnesium and copper. Mazak was widely used throughout the automotive industry, particularly at the time when the Morris Minor was in production. Unfortunately, over time it became all too obvious that

Initial alignment. Many hands required.

Hinge positions were checked and rechecked before final tightening.

Unadorned bonnet safely in position.

Reassembly

Due to previous damage a replacement spring bar had to be sourced to ensure accurate alignment of other components at the rear of the car.

Repeated measurements were made on both sides of the car to ensure an even gap between the bumper iron and the car bodywork.

This helped to ensure an even fit across the front of the car when other components were added.

there were underlying problems with the original castings. Mazak is prone to pitting and this manifests itself when the plated surface blisters creating unsightly marks and raised edges on the surface. Mazak is also difficult to weld because of its low melting point and, because faults can be difficult to rectify, a lot of damaged chrome work is simply discarded and replacements sought. However, there are specialist companies that offer a restoration and re-chroming service for mazak components. For each individual item the process usually involves grinding out any imperfection in order to achieve a smooth 'pit'-free surface, which is then copper plated. Following polishing the item is then nickel plated and then chromed. Faced with the additional expense of restoration, many restorers tend to look for new old stock items in as near perfect condition as possible. Fortunately, with Morris Minor chrome parts this is still possible. This proved to be the case with the project car, where many new old stock items along with some 'as new' items were sourced and fitted to the car. This applied particularly to external chromed items. The front and rear bumpers and over riders were re-chromed and subjected to triple plating (copper, nickel, chrome). Some internal items, which although not at full lustre, were retained and reused, as they were original components supplied with the vehicle.

Advances in chroming techniques now allow for replica components to be made in plastic and then re-chromed. Examples for the Morris Minor include over-riders and the chrome coverings on the rear light and indicator units on late 1098cc models. For earlier models, including Series MM and Series II models, the split windscreen surrounds that were cast in brass can be re-chromed. Rare items such as the 'short' bonnet hinges and the central windscreen pillar have in the past been cast in brass and chromed as part of limited runs organised by private individuals and clubs.

REASSEMBLY: MECHANICAL COMPONENTS

In preceding chapters various aspects of the build-up of various sub-assemblies have been considered and there

Reassembly

Sequencing the fitting of the chrome bumper bolts starting with the two central ones helped with even tensioning and avoided potential damage to the metal valance.

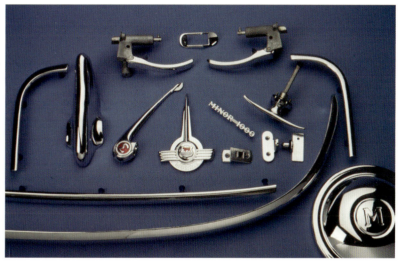

The main chromed components, as fitted to the Morris Minor 1000 two-door saloon.

Frontal arrangement with over-riders fitted.

is little to be gained in referring to them in this final reassembly section. It is worth noting some of the techniques used in refitting some of the major components and acknowledging some of the knowledge gained in doing so.

Engine and Gearbox

Before the rebuilt engine and gearbox were reunited, a new clutch assembly was fitted. In the interests of maintaining originality and reliability, new old stock 7¼ inch Borg and Beck clutch components including a clutch release bearing, a clutch pressure plate and a clutch drive plate were sourced. The original flywheel, which was checked for any signs of previous damage or excessive wear, was reused and fitted on to the back of the engine using four bolts with tab washers. An additional task was undertaken prior to fitting. This involved replacing the phosphor-bronze spigot bush, which is housed in the end of the crankshaft and provides a secure bearing for the end of the first motion shaft.

Before tightening up the six bolts on the outside edge of the clutch pressure plate, a clutch alignment tool was used to ensure that the first motion shaft on the gearbox was accurately positioned so that it could easily slide into the back of the engine. This critical part of the procedure was accomplished much more easily by completing the task on the workbench rather than attempting to align the gearbox with the engine already in place.

With the engine and gearbox reassembled, the task of refitting the combined unit into the car was undertaken with a mixture of joy and trepidation. Joy at the progress that this landmark event marked in the restoration process and trepidation due to the possibility of causing damage to the newly painted engine bay. To assist with the process of installing the combined engine and gearbox, a heavy-duty engine hoist with a tilt facility incorporated was pressed into service.

In preparation for the engine and gearbox being refitted, preliminary work involved fitting the engine mounting towers in the engine bay. Initially these were put in place and just loosely fastened to allow for

153

Reassembly

Chrome embellishments as fitted to the rear of the completed vehicle.

Original new old stock clutch release bearing in Unipart packaging.

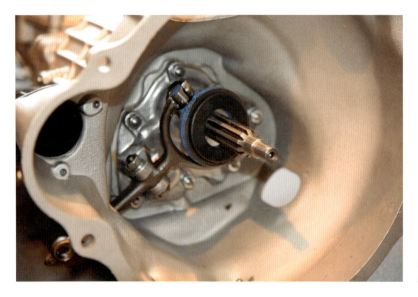

The clutch release bearing fitted on the clutch release fork in the bell housing.

Lining up the first motion shaft with the splines on the clutch friction plate that is held in place against the flywheel on the back of the engine by the black painted clutch cover.

Reassembly

Phosphor-bronze bush being fitted.

movement and adjustment when they were married up to the rubber engine mountings, which were fastened to the engine in advance of it being installed. This was to take account that the single-threaded stud on each mounting must pass through the tower and be fastened in place from the underside using a nut and spring washer. As a degree of flexibility is needed, it is best not to have the engine mounting turrets permanently fixed at this point in the proceedings. Another consideration is, when offering up the four bolts which secure the towers, to do so from the underside so that the nuts are on the top, making them more accessible for tightening and, if necessary, in the

Replacing the Clutch Assembly: Helpful hints

- It is worth noting that while later 1098cc models used a 7¼ inch Borg and Beck Clutch assembly, earlier Series MM, Series II and Morris 1000 948cc models used a smaller 6¼ inch assembly from the same manufacturer.
- When preparing to fit a replacement clutch assembly, take note of the markings on the friction plate that indicates the flywheel side. It is all too easy to inadvertently install this wrongly. Failure to install correctly will result in the radial springs in the clutch friction plate rubbing against the flywheel bolts as they protrude more on one side than the other.
- Ensure that the friction surface of the cover plate is cleaned to remove any transit protection wax.
- It is usual for most clutch kits to be supplied with a small sachet of grease. This should be applied sparingly to the splined shaft only in order to assist with alignment process. Care must be exercised not to apply too much grease, as doing so will increase the risk of contaminating other friction surfaces.
- The use of a clutch alignment tool is essential to make sure that the friction plate is held in the centre of the assembly so that the gearbox will mate up easily.

Flywheel side marking designed to aid correct fitting.

Centre plate alignment.

(continued overleaf)

Reassembly

Replacing the Clutch Assembly: Helpful hints *continued*

- When tightening the six screws that hold the clutch assembly to the flywheel, do so in a way that pulls the assembly in position in an even manner. Evenly tightening opposite facing screws in a sequential pattern is a favoured method.
- If reinstalling the engine with the gearbox still fixed in position, additional care needs to be exercised when aligning the first motion shaft with the centre of the clutch. Clumsy handling at this stage can result in the springs on the clutch cover being 'pinged off'. It is useful to have additional help available when, with the engine still supported by an engine hoist, reconnection with the gearbox is attempted.
- Final tasks include adjusting the position of the threaded clutch rod by releasing the locknut and the spherical nut against the outer end of the clutch fork to achieve the recommended clearance at the pedal and replacing the return spring that connects to the engine back plate and the release fork.

---

future, undoing. In anticipation of the final fitting of the engine and gearbox it is necessary to have a means of supporting the weight of the gearbox prior to it being secured in position. A trolley jack is ideal. Alternatively, some form of roped support from inside the car could be considered.

With the engine and gearbox securely fastened to the engine hoist using lifting brackets fastened by the bolts on the top of the rocker cover, both units were manoeuvred into position and gently lowered using the tilt facility to avoid damage to the paintwork, particularly on the bulkhead crossmember as the gearbox was being carefully guided underneath and on the front crossmember as the engine was being positioned.

Key to the accurate locating of both engine and gearbox is the gearbox crossmember. It is essential to ensure that the crossmember and the associated rubber mountings are offered up for fixing the right way round. Failure to do so will compromise the whole operation. This helpful hint is offered following a time-consuming and frustrating experience encountered during this particular restoration. It is important at this juncture to fit the earth strap between the gearbox and the crossmember.

Detailed explanations of the refurbishment and refitting of many of the mechanical components have been recounted in earlier chapters. The rear suspension and the back axle fall into this category. However, it is worth noting the preparation that occurred prior to installing the back axle and the associated suspension components. In order to provide sufficient clearance for the work to take place, the car body was raised significantly and securely supported on the four-poster ramp by the use of strategically placed wooden supports. The accompanying images show the preliminary stages of the reinstallation of the rear axle and suspension components.

With the axle fitted attention turned to completing the transmission and refitting the propshaft. This original item required no additional work other than being repainted and the process of refitting was quite straightforward. With care being exercised to correctly align the previously greased splines at

The engine mounting tower aligned. Note the advice regarding fitting of the four bolts that secure it in place.

The engine on the engine crane secured by lifting eyes bolted to the rocker box mountings. Note the bespoke bar that allows adjustment to tilt the engine in order to get the gearbox into the car.

Reassembly

The engine mounting fittings with the tower bolts fitted from the underside with the nuts on top inside the engine bay for ease of access.

The gearbox supported by a trolley jack while the crossmember mountings are being fastened.

Additional clearance at the rear of the car prior to fitting the rear axle.

the front end it was easily positioned and pushed into place at the gearbox end. Four new high-tensile bolts and nuts were acquired prior to fitting the back end of the shaft to the nose flange on the differential with care taken to correctly align the bolt-hole positions. Once in position, the opportunity was taken to grease the Hardy Spicer universal joints using the grease nipples fitted.

ANCILLARY ENGINE COMPONENTS

Starter Motor

On Morris Minor 1000 models the starter motor used differed slightly. Early models used the Lucas M35G type, but this was changed for later models when a redesignated M35J type was introduced. The main difference between the two versions includes the following items. The earlier M35G type has a brush cover band fitted and internally there were differences in the commutator design and the earthing arrangements. On the M35G a peripheral contact on which the brushes bear from the side is used while on the M35J version a face commutator where they bear on the end plate is used. The earthing arrangement differed too. On the M35G the field windings are insulated from the yoke and the end plate bushes are earthed directly to the end plate, while on the later version the field windings are earthed to the starter yoke. The brush box end assembly and the commutator end plate are fully insulated. To maintain originality a later M35J type starter motor was fitted to the project car after having been reconditioned and new brushes fitted.

Distributor

Morris Minor 1000 models used a new-style distributor designated DM2P4 from 1956 to 1962. At engine number 604288 an updated version, 25D4, was used in conjunction with the 1098cc engine. The different types are easily identified as the model number is stamped into the casing next to the vacuum advance unit. The distributor bodies differ slightly in shape. The original 25D4 distributor fitted to FMT 265 J was deemed sound enough to be reused.

157

Reassembly

Work in progress fitting rear suspension components.

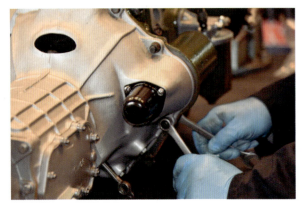

Reconditioned M35J starter motor being fitted as part of gearbox installation.

The original 25D4 distributor and a new LA12 coil.

The main body was subjected to vapour blasting prior to new components including contact breaker points, a rotor arm and new distributor cap being fitted. Prior to installation consideration was given to dispensing with the original ignition set-up in favour of electronic ignition. After much deliberation, it was unanimously decided that at this stage in the restoration and in keeping with the original concept of restoring the vehicle while retaining as much of the original specification as possible that the original 25D4 distributor would be retained and used in conjunction with a newly acquired LA12 coil. However, the option of installing electronic ignition at some point in the future was not ruled out.

Final Fitments

A three-piece stainless steel exhaust system was installed. New radiator hoses complete with new jubilee clips were fitted. Particular attention was paid to the heater hoses to ensure that they were installed correctly. A late edition British Leyland Morris Minor workshop manual was referenced for this task.

Lighting Arrangement

With the headlamps, front indicator and side light units and the combined rear light, brake light and indicator units, new old stock items were sourced where possible. Fitting was straightforward with the only problem encountered in operation being a temperamental indicator switch, which proved so unreliable that it had to be replaced.

Reassembly

AccuSpark Electronic Ignition with Lucas Sports Coil: Key Things to Consider

- A comprehensive set of instructions is supplied with the AccuSpark Electronic Ignition Pack.
- Components can be purchased for either positive- or negative-earthed vehicles. They are not interchangeable, so it is vital to check the polarity of the vehicle before purchase.
- It is usual on Morris Minors to change the polarity from positive to negative.
- For vehicles converted from positive to negative, it is crucial to change the wiring on the coil according to the instructions provided.
- A higher capacity sports coil should be used in conjunction with the distributor provided.
- It may also be helpful to change the existing to silicone or carbon fibre leads, which are more flexible. This can prove useful when fitting.

Advantages of electronic Ignition

- It dispenses with the traditional use of contact breaker points and the condenser.
- There are fewer moving parts to be concerned about.
- The system provides constant reliable service and performance.
- The system is also more suitable for use with modern fuels.
- Ease of installation. The replacement 25D distributor is a direct replacement of the original type fitted and is easily installed.
- There is a proven track record of the system being dependable in use with a wide variety of classic cars.

AccuSpark 25D distributor and Lucas Sports coil.

The familiar later specification frontal lighting arrangement of the 1098cc models.

Some new old stock lighting items were sourced complete with original packaging.

14
Tourers and Convertibles

INTRODUCTION

Open-topped versions of the Morris Minor were built throughout all phases of production during the period 1948–1969.

STRUCTURAL DIFFERENCES

Tourer and convertible models retained the main mechanical and body panels as their two-door saloon counterparts, except for additional strengthening panels to compensate for the removal of the roof panel and modifications to accommodate the fitting of a foldable hood. In the case of early Series MM Tourer models, detachable side screens allowed for a completely open rear aspect. Later Series MM models had fixed side windows and when this change was introduced in 1951, the designation Tourer was dropped in favour of the more familiar convertible model name.

The key structural difference in the convertible bodyshell includes additional bracing on the front scuttle. Two triangular bracing pieces were fitted at either end of the dash panel. These were spot welded in place. Additional strengthening pieces were also added on both sides of the car to the base of the 'B' post. These pieces were welded to the sill at their base and spot welded to the 'B' post. In addition to these features a double strength inner sill panel was added to the bodyshell between the 'A' post and the 'B' post on either side of the car. These panels are concealed by the 'cover plates', which are visible when the doors are open.

SPOT THE DIFFERENCE

The popularity of the Morris Minor convertible in the post-production era led to a situation where demand

Morris Minor Series MM Tourer, 1948–1951.

Morris Minor Series MM convertible, 1951–1953.

Tourers and Convertibles

Morris Minor Series II convertible, 1953–1956.

Morris Minor 1000 convertible, 1956–1962.

Morris Minor 1000 convertible, 1962–1969.

exceeded supply. This led to the provision of a conversion kit to transform a two-door saloon into a convertible. A consequence of this is the need for prospective buyers to distinguish between genuine factory-produced convertibles and post-production models that were originally two-door saloons. It is important to note that a properly converted vehicle is just as safe to use and equally pleasurable to drive as the genuine article. There are a number of checks that can be undertaken to distinguish between a genuine factory-produced convertible and a post-production converted two-door saloon.

1) Researching the history of the car.

   Check the details recorded on the chassis plate and the log book to see if they match. Refer to the advice below regarding the correct designation for convertible models. If time permits, obtain a copy of the original factory record for the vehicle from the British Motor Industry Heritage Trust, which holds the original factory records. These are housed at the British Motor Museum at Gaydon, Warwickshire, England. It will be necessary to quote the chassis number on the log book having first checked to see if it corresponds to the chassis number stamped into the body. Be aware that there have been instances in the past where unscrupulous individuals have sought to change the identity of a converted saloon for that of a genuine convertible. On most cars, this number was stamped into the bulkhead (firewall) near to the battery box. On late Morris 1000 models it was stamped into the floor on the driver's side front floor area (RHD models). Due to the age of the vehicles, the ravages of rust, and replacement floors being fitted, this is a more difficult number to find.

2) Establishing if it is a late production saloon.

   Convertible production ended in June 1969 with Chassis Number 1254328. Any vehicles with a later chassis number than this purporting to be a genuine convertible will be a converted saloon.

161

Tourers and Convertibles

3) Checking the vehicle identification code.

Chassis plates containing the vehicle identification code and vehicle-specific chassis number were fitted to the bulkhead. The information should correspond to that recorded in the log book.

Two types of identification were used on Series MM models from 1949 to 1953. Sequential numbers with the letters MNR to identify the vehicle as a Morris Minor, followed by S or SYN to denote the type of paint, were used on early vehicles. No specific model identification was used on these vehicles. In April 1952 a new-style chassis plate and revised form of identification was introduced. The code, made up of three letters and two numbers, had a body style identifier included. The second of the three letters was used for this purpose. For convertible models, the letter C was used. This style of chassis plate and coding system remained in use during Series II production and continued for Morris 1000 models until 1958.

From 1958 until Morris Minor production ended in 1971, a different style of chassis plate was used. Changes were made to the coding to include the production Series to which the vehicle belonged, and new body style codes were introduced. From 1958 until 1962 when the 1098cc models were introduced, the designation was changed to MAT3 for convertible models, the T being the identifying letter for convertibles. MAS3 identified four-door saloons, MA2S3 two-door saloons and MAW3 Traveller models. The number 3 indicated the production Series.

With the introduction of the 1098cc models in 1962 the designation changed to represent Series 5 models, but the same letter was used to identify convertible models (MAT5).

4) Check key structural components.
The following checklist is a useful guide to determining the authenticity of Tourer or convertible models.
- Spot welding versus seam welding on bracing panels and 'B' post supports.

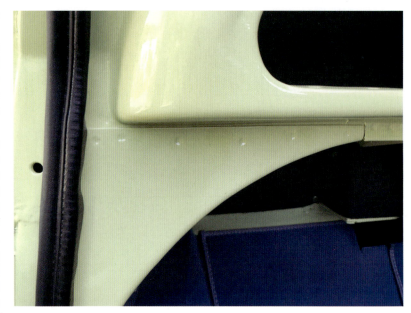
Original spot-welded strengthening panel fitted to the dash.

Original spot-welded strengthening panel attached to the inside of the 'B' post.

Original factory-produced convertibles will have evidence of spot welding where these items have been fitted. In most cases where two-door saloons have been converted these items will have been seam welded into position.

- A key item in the structural integrity of any convertible is the presence of the additional strengthening panels in the inner sills. Checking this area of the car requires the removal of the cover panels. Time taken in doing so or having photographic evidence that the work has been done may pay dividends in the long term.
- Another tell-tale sign that a vehicle has been converted is the slightly different profile on the outer edges of the windscreen top rail compared to that of an original convertible. Some conversions may have incorporated a windscreen surround from an original convertible, however.

Tourers and Convertibles

Original profile of top edge of the Tourer and convertible windscreen.

- A fool-proof way of determining the origins of a saloon or convertible is to carry out an examination of the bottom edge of the inner panel beneath where the hood fits when folded and which is visible with the boot lid open. If the vehicle is a converted saloon, this panel will have several dimples in it. If it is a genuine convertible, the panel will be perfectly smooth.
- Another tell-tale sign is the slightly different profile in the frame of the fixed rear windows. On those supplied as part of a conversion kit the frame is slightly thinner and straighter than those fitted at the factory to original convertibles.
- Convertible models did not have an interior light fitted. Saloons did, and on the 'A' posts an activation switch was fitted that operated the light when the doors were opened. Though inoperative on converted saloons, these are often left in position when the conversion is undertaken.

TOURER AND CONVERTIBLE HOODS AND HOOD FRAMES

During the production period for Tourer and convertible models, the design of the hood frames changed as did the range of colours, the type of material used for the hood covering and the size of the integral rear window.

On early Series MM models, the hood frame was constructed using four hood sticks, but this was increased to five on later Series MM models. The majority of hood frames were painted in a gold colour to correspond with that used on the steering column and the metal edge on the parcel shelf, though on some models a contrasting maroon colour was used. The hood covering was beige and depending on the colour used for piping on the interior either brown, green or maroon piping was added to the edge of the hood covering.

Early Series MM Tourers had detachable side screens at the rear. These continued in use up to chassis number 100920, when fixed rear side windows were introduced. It was at this point that the model designation changed from Tourer to convertible. Little changed with the introduction of Series II models in 1952. Beige remained the main hood colour until May 1956, when Grey was adopted as an additional hood colour. Hood frames were painted gold. With the introduction of the Morris 1000 models in September 1956 when the split windscreen was dispensed with in favour of a one-piece windscreen, the design of the wooden front rail changed due to the revised windscreen surround pressing. For a time, as a temporary measure, presumably to use up existing stocks, the revised front rail was simply added to the Series II hood frames. The hood frame had four hood sticks and in August 1957 at chassis number 524944, the hood covering changed from canvas to a plastic-covered material that was available in grey and maroon. At the same time a much larger rectangular rear window was incorporated into the hood design and the painted hood frame was finished in Pearl Grey. Further changes were adopted from 1962, when the integral rear screen shape changed to what is often referred to as the kidney-shaped design. Pearl Grey and Maroon remained the dominant hood colours at the outset of this

Tourers and Convertibles

period of production, with Black being added later.

FITTING A NEW HOOD COVERING

Fitting a new hood is an intricate process requiring patience and skill. Best results are often achieved when the services of a skilled and experienced fitter are employed and the hood is tailor-made to the correct specification for the individual vehicle. It is advisable for the work to be undertaken in a warm environment, as this will make the hood material more pliable and easier to work with, particularly when tensioning the hood. The use of a heater positioned inside the car is useful in this regard.

CASE STUDY

In the case of the illustrated example, a 1961 Highway Yellow convertible was fitted with a Dark Blue American Mohair hood. The original repainted Pearl Grey hood frame along with the original wooden front rail and covered wooden rear sections were re-used. Preparatory work included covering the front rail with base material, ensuring that the holes for the stainless-steel locating pins and accompanying wing nut fasteners could be easily identified. This was followed with the fitting and trimming of the weather strip at the front of the rail, with care being taken to ensure a snug fit at the top of the windscreen. With the front rail covered in matching hood material, the rest of the hood, which had been tailor-made with the integral rear window fitted along with the matching edging strip finishers to the side and rear, was loosely placed over the hood frame, which had been placed in the upright position. Prior to any further work being undertaken a heater was deployed to provide some warmth. Attention then switched to the rear of the car, where the inner section of the rear of the hood was stapled to the wooden framework.

With continuous tensioning of the hood material, particular care was taken when tucking the inner part of the hood inside the rear window frame and checking the gap above the doors on both sides of the car. With the rear of the hood fully tensioned, a

Original front rail attached to correctly painted Pearl Grey hood frame.

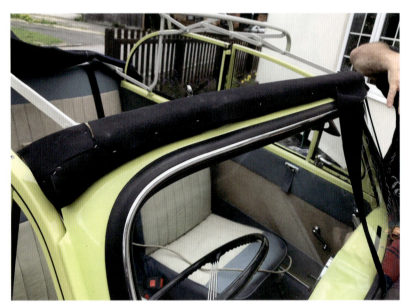

Base covering on front rail cut and stapled in position.

Weather strip attached to front rail and carefully positioned to match the contour of the windscreen surround.

Tourers and Convertibles

critical stage in the fitting process was undertaken. This involved locating the two holes on the back rail of the hood frame and then marking the corresponding position on the inside of the hood cover before fitting the cup washers and self-tapping screws from the outside.

Working inside the car, other locating points for positioning and tensioning the hood were identified and a stud fixing attached. These fixing points are on each of the side window frames with two located on each frame, one positioned to the rear of the bottom edge and the other on the top edge close to the 'B' post. One of the most visible fastenings on the outside of the car is the 'lift dot' fixing, which is located on the lower rear side of the hood on each side. Both need to be unfastened when the hood is lowered and put in the stowed position. A heavy-duty specialist tool is required for fixing these in place on the new hood.

The final task tends to be the fitting of the finishing strip called the 'hidem', which is attached to the front edge of the front rail above the weather strip. It performs a useful function in covering up the staples previously inserted into the rail. Two triangular-shaped finishers, each held in place by a single flat-headed tack, complete the job.

With final checks to see that the hood is appropriately attached to the hood frame, that the material is fully tensioned and that the hood frame is properly aligned with the locating pins on the front rail, the heater should be left in the car for 20–30 minutes after work is completed. Thereafter, it is recommended that the hood remains in the fixed position for a few days and when possible during that period be left in the open in warm conditions.

Original covered rear rail.

Rear inner section of the hood stapled in position.

Rear corner stud-fixing point on rear window frame.

Tourers and Convertibles

Upper rear side window stud fixing point.

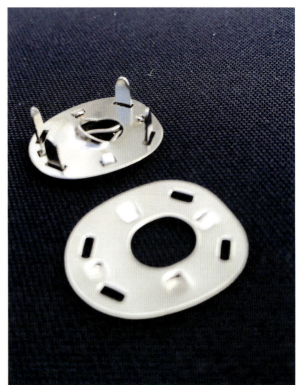

External fastener used for attaching the hood to the exterior of the car body.

Specialist tool used for fitting the 'lift the dot' fastener.

External 'lift the dot' fastener fitted.

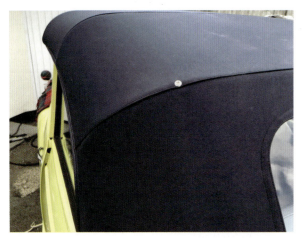

Self-tapping locating screw attached to pre-drilled hole in the rear hood rail.

Frequent centralising and alignment checks are advised when fitting and tensioning the hood prior to stapling.

Tourers and Convertibles

Front edge of hood being tensioned and stapled in position (using an air-fed staple gun).

Hood fully tensioned and ready for the 'Hidem' strip to be attached.

'Hidem' strip being attached. It is nailed in position using fine pins, which are easily concealed.

Metal corner finishers held in position by a single tack conceal the corded ends of the 'Hidem' strip.

Task completed, but the advice from the professionals is to leave the hood in place for a few days before attempting to lower it.

15
Light Commercials 1953–1971

Morris Minor vans and pick-ups were introduced to the model range in 1953. They differed from other models in that they used a separate chassis on to which the front cab, van back or pick-up bed was attached. Being for commercial use, the internal specification was lower than of the saloon and convertible models. Even a passenger seat was an optional extra! The early models utilised the 803cc A-series engine and mechanical components mirrored those used in other models. This trend continued throughout production, with mechanical upgrades and styling changes keeping pace with the Morris Minor 1000 models introduced in 1956 and 1962. Specification changes from 5cwt to 6cwt occurred in 1962, and from 1968 customers had the choice of either 6cwt or 8cwt vans or pick-ups. Austin variants were also introduced in 1968 and were distinguished by a crinkle-type front grille as opposed to the slatted one used on Morris models. Additional Austin features included the colour of the engine block, which was painted black, and Austin badging on the bonnet and on the horn push in the centre of the steering wheel. Along with Traveller models, vans and pick-ups had the distinction of remaining in production until the Morris Minor was phased out in 1971.

Commercial models differed in several respects from other models in the range. Changes to key components were aimed at coping with the anticipated heavy loading. These included the use of telescopic shock absorbers on the rear coupled with stronger leaf springs. Extra strength front suspension uprights, stronger steering arms and wider 4½ J wheels were features of 8cwt models. There was also an option for a low-compression engine to be supplied. This option was taken up by the GPO and other fleet users. GPO Engineers vans and Royal Mail vans had numerous adaptations and differed significantly from standard Morris Minor vans in terms of specification.

Commercial variants of the Morris Minor remain popular both for private and business use. Full-scale restoration is a viable option given the wide range of mechanical and body repair panels available. Several specialist companies provide repair and restoration services specifically for van and pick-up models and a wide range of fabricated repair panels is available. Many surviving commercial vehicles requiring restoration exhibit signs associated with extended use as well as the ravages of time and the presence of rust. Decades after production ceased it is reassuring to know that solutions exist in addressing the common problem areas specific to commercial variants of the Morris Minor.

Introduced in 1953, Morris Minor Commercial variants proved popular with private owners and fleet users (1954 van pictured).

Austin variants were introduced in 1968 (1971 Austin pick-up pictured).

Light Commercials 1953–1971

CHASSIS

The separate chassis fitted to the Morris Minor commercials was quite robust and many original, factory-produced chassis are still in use. Problems with the chassis are confined to the front chassis legs, rusting in the areas where the cab is attached and towards the rear where the chassis curves. Swelling can occur on the top edge. Repair sections are available and with the cab, van back or pick-up bed removed to provide easy access fitting, these can be tackled with confidence. For anyone not wishing to undertake such repairs, a completely new chassis built to original specification can be purchased.

Royal Mail Vans differed significantly in specification from standard production models.

VAN AND PICK-UP SIDE PANELS

Complete new replacement van and pick-up side panels are not available. Occasionally new old stock items emerge but when they do, they invariably attract premium prices. Various options exist to repair existing panel work. The lower half of a van side can be purchased as can various repair panels including outer wheel arch, rear light panels for single and double light fittings and fabricated lower repair panels. With pick-up models, if the side panels require extensive repairs and a better second-hand replacement is not available, one solution is to remove the top part from each side and then fabricate a new side panel either using the new lower van panel mentioned previously or the lower half of a van panel salvaged from another vehicle.

INNER WHEEL ARCHES

New inner wheel arches are available either as individual items or integral to a full-sized rear inner side floor panel. Partial repair panels are also available. In addition, front inner floor panels and replacement outer sills for the cab are readily available. It is important to note that the profile of these items on commercial vehicles is slightly different to those used on saloon, convertible and Traveller models. The inner boxing plates on commercial models differed in design to those used on other Morris Minor models. Until recently, original

Modern replacement chassis are readily available.

Light Commercials 1953–1971

Many refurbished or repaired chassis like this one remain in service.

A wide range and increasing number of repair and replacement panels are still being made for commercial variants of the Morris Minor, as shown in this selection available from Fairmile Restorations.

Repair rather than replacement is an option with this inner wheel arch repair panel.

Front inner floor pressings for commercial variants.

Inner sill boxing plates as fitted to commercial variants differed from those fitted to other Morris Minor models.

Light Commercials 1953–1971

design versions were not available. Consequently, some restored commercial vehicles have the saloon-type inner boxing plates fitted.

VAN ROOF GUTTERING

One of the common problem areas associated with the van back is the roof guttering. Rusting out in this area is easily spotted and until recently not easily repaired, due to the flat nature of the side panel and the profile of the guttering itself. A substantial repair kit, comprising of fifteen separate pieces, has been developed to completely replace the metalwork around the whole of the edge of the van back roofline. Fitting it requires a fair degree of competence and experience in the use of different welding techniques.

PICK-UP TAIL GATE

The hinged pick-up tail gate is renowned for being in a poor condition due to the years of continued use for loading and unloading goods. Repairs using fabricated parts are feasible. This usually involves cutting the welds to take the top rail off, drilling out the spot welds and turning up the folded edge in order to separate the inner and outer skins. With this completed, necessary repairs can be undertaken with bought or fabricated pieces, prior to reassembly. Alternatively, a new tailgate can be purchased.

VAN REAR DOORS

Two types of van rear door were used during production. Up to September 1962, the doors were fitted with small rear windows. After this date, larger rear windows were fitted to improve rearward visibility. New van doors are not available. However, there is a plentiful supply of second-hand doors, and this tends to be the favoured option if a replacement is needed rather than engaging in extensive repairs.

PICK-UP TILT/TONNEAU COVER

Replacement canvas pick-up tilt covers that were originally supplied as an optional extra are available from specialist suppliers, as are custom-made tonneau covers for use on pick-up

Replacement inner boxing plates to the original design are available.

Complete fabricated repair kit for van roof guttering repairs.

Light Commercials 1953–1971

Original specification fabricated pick-up tail gates made by 'Wills Company' are available by special order.

models to provide protection from the elements when the hoops and tilt are not being used. The wooden roof capping fixing can also be obtained from specialist suppliers, as can replacement metal hoops and associated side fixings for the tilt.

Original-style canvas tilt with side-panel fixings.

1971 Austin Pick-Up Restoration

The restoration of this 1971 8cwt Austin-badged Morris Minor pick-up took place over an eight-year period with meticulous attention being paid to every facet of the work. Some key elements are highlighted in this pictorial representation of the work completed.

New wheel arch and inner side floor panels were fitted to the pick-up bed.

Note the additional cross bracing used while work was in progress.

(continued overleaf)

Light Commercials 1953–1971

1971 Austin Pick-Up Restoration *continued*

Temporary fixtures were put to good use to avoid damage to the finished paintwork and provide ease of manoeuvrability when in the workshop.

Repainted restored cab with rebuilt 1098cc engine complete with unleaded cylinder head ready for installation.

Cab mounted on original restored chassis. Note inner sill design, which differed from other Morris Minor models.

A replacement original specification metal cab back was sourced, refurbished, and fitted.

The paint colour of choice for this restoration was 'Bedouin'.

The heel board area is integral to the floor pressing and the upper edge is a key location point for the pick-up bed.

(continued overleaf)

Light Commercials 1953–1971

1971 Austin Pick-Up Restoration continued

Location points for the pick-up bed on the lower heel board.

Handbrake assembly location with cables passing through the heel board.

All suspension components were thoroughly overhauled and where necessary, new original specification parts were sourced.

(continued overleaf)

1971 Austin Pick-Up Restoration continued

Side panel repairs included welding in new rear light cluster panels on both sides.

New corner bracing panels were fitted along with the original storage brackets used for securing the metal hoops when the canvas tilt is not in use.

A new three-piece wooden front rail used for locating the front edge of the canvas tilt was acquired.

(continued overleaf)

Light Commercials 1953–1971

1971 Austin Pick-Up Restoration continued

Spring hanger mounting point arrangement differed from the more familiar arrangement used on monocoque Morris Minor models.

Stainless steel exhaust – a departure from the original in the interests of longevity.

Factory finish interior, including rare rubber floor covering.

Original style tool kit and correctly positioned spare 4½ J wheel add to the as-new perception.

Austin badging and late-model steering lock are distinguishing features of this late-model commercial.

(continued overleaf)

1971 Austin Pick-Up Restoration continued

Authentic black finish to the engine block and rocker cover as per Austin specification.

Picture perfect. Fully restored to concours condition after eight years of painstaking work.

RESTORATION ADVICE

Removing the Pick-Up Cab Back and Releasing the Van Back

At first this may seem a daunting task. However, with advance planning and prior knowledge of the location of the approximately 80 bolts and screws that need to be undone plus some additional help to lift the front cab and the van back or pick-up bed clear of the chassis, this is an undertaking well within the capabilities of the home restorer. Most of the bolts are $^5/_{16}$ BSF.

Working from inside the cab, begin the uncoupling process by locating the captive bolts on the rear side of the B posts. There are twelve in total, with six on each side. Next unclip the rear part of the head lining to expose the ten nuts and bolts that hold the cab back to the front cab (pick-up) and the front cab to the van back (van). With this complete, turn attention to releasing the eight screws that hold the bottom of the cab back and the cab floor together. In the case of the pick-up models, it will then be necessary to release the corner brackets that are situated between the cab back and the pick-up sides. To do so, a total of fourteen bolts and screws will need to be unscrewed (seven per side). At this point the pick-up cab back can be lifted out and removed.

Pick-up Bed and Van Back Removal

Moving to the rear of the van and pick-up, begin the removal process by undoing the 22 screws that hold the centrally positioned wooden floor panels in place before locating the two nuts and bolts at the rear of the chassis. Undo these, taking care not to lose the rubber packing strips situated between the body mount and the chassis. Next, remove the nine nuts and bolts situated across the top of the heel board before releasing the four captive bolts at the bottom of the 'B' post (two per side). Disconnect the rear part of the wiring loom along with the earthing points. With all the nuts and bolts released, removing the van doors and the pick-up tailgate will help reduce the weight before any attempt is made to lift the van back or pick-up bed from the chassis. Ideally, this is a three- or four-person job for a van back and a minimum of two people for a pick-up bed.

Tip: Pre-treating nuts and bolts with penetrating fluid can aid release and may help prevent bolts snapping off. This is something to be avoided, particularly in the case of the bolts held by captive nuts in areas such as the 'B' posts. Subsequent repairs can be difficult and time consuming.

Removing Cab from the Chassis

In order to remove the cab from the chassis a lot of preliminary work needs to be undertaken. One option is to leave the engine and gearbox in situ, an approach favoured by those wishing to avoid any heavy lifting of the engine and gearbox. Experienced restorer, Chris Nuttall, describes the tasks involved:

Position the van or pick-up on level ground in an area with sufficient headroom to allow for the cab to be lifted off. Jack the front of the vehicle up and place two axle stands under the front chassis legs rearward of the front tie-bar mounting points. As an additional precaution, chock the rear tyres in preparation for when the handbrake is removed. Prior to locating and undoing the bolts and screws securing the cab and other components to the chassis (*see* sidebar overleaf), a considerable number of items will need to be disconnected or removed to allow the cab to be lifted clear and separated from the chassis.

SUSPENSION

Remove front wheels and release track-rod ends from steering arms on both sides before turning attention to releasing the tension created by the torsion bars. Place a jack underneath the bottom trunnion, taking care not to damage grease nipples. Jack up slowly until

Location of Nuts and Bolts Securing the Cab to the Chassis

Four nuts and bolts at the rear of the cab bolted to chassis (two per side).

Two bolts inside the cab on the floor either side of the tunnel where inner seat belt mounts are (one per side). Two bolts inside the cab at the front of the hand brake holding hand-brake lever to floor.

Six nuts and bolts located in the engine bay at the bottom of the bulkhead that hold the bulkhead to the chassis (three per side).

Five nuts and bolts around the front panel. Two where the radiator is located (one per side) and three on the outside of the front panel at the bottom where they hold the front panel to the chassis. (They are the middle three of seven.)

Twelve nuts and bolts holding the front engine mountings (six per side).

---

the shock absorber arm is clear of the bottom bump stop. Additional help may be needed at this stage to apply weight to the front wing to prevent the vehicle lifting off the axle stand. Next, remove the top trunnion by first knocking back the lock tab and undoing the nut and then twisting the trunnion off its pin before lowering the jack down slowly until it is clear of the shock-absorber arm. Repeat the procedure on the other side. Note that it will be necessary to support each suspension upright when lifting the cab from the chassis.

Brakes

Disconnect the main brake pipe that comes from the master cylinder to the three-way union, which is located on the off side of the radiator where the brake light switch is mounted. Blank off the end of the main brake pipe to stop fluid leaking out. Disconnect both front brake pipes (steel) from the flexible brake hoses before removing the flexible hoses from their mounting brackets on the inner wings. It will also be necessary to disconnect the hand-brake cables. With the cables released from the lever and both cable guides removed from the cab heel board/crossmember panel, the loose cables should be pushed through the holes to clear the cab. Prior to lifting the cab clear, it will be necessary to move the brake pipe that runs from the three-way union to the master cylinder down the inside of the chassis leg and unclip the brake pipe from the front chassis crossmember, which runs from the three-way union to the near side.

Engine Compartment

With the engine still in position it will be necessary to disconnect or remove several components to allow for the cab to be lifted clear and to avoid any inadvertent damage.

Checklist

- Disconnect and remove battery.
- Drain the radiator and remove along with hoses.
- Disconnect all wires/cables and heater hoses from the engine and cable-tie them to the bulkhead.
- Remove engine stabiliser, starter motor, dynamo/alternator, radiator fan and pulley, distributor cap/leads and rotor arm.
- Remove the exhaust front pipe, inlet/exhaust manifold and carburettor.
- Disconnect speedo cable from the gearbox end. Roll up and cable tie to bulkhead.
- Disconnect the fuel feed pipe to fuel pump. Unclip the pipe from bulkhead and blank off.
- Unclip rear wiring loom from chassis and fuel tank then feed through hole in bulkhead near to driver's side shock absorber. Roll up and cable-tie to the bulkhead to clear the chassis.
- For easy access and reduced weight when lifting cab, front doors should be removed.
- Inside of cab, remove seats, seatbelts (if fitted), the gear lever boot and the gear lever.
- Remove the gearbox cover by undoing the 27 screws that secure it.

Removal of Cab

In preparation for the removal of the cab, it is advisable to place a jack underneath the sump to take the weight of the engine. To prevent damage to the sump the use of a piece of wood placed between the jack and the sump is advisable. With all preliminary preparations complete, attention can now be focused on removing the 31 $^{5}/_{16}$ BSF bolts that secure the cab to the chassis.

With all nuts and bolts undone, it should be possible to lever up the cab from the chassis in a few places to check if it is free to lift off. Having made sure that nothing is still connected that could foul the cab and with the suspension uprights supported clear of the cab, final checks before lifting should include the clearance at the side of the engine and the area around the brake and clutch pedals. With one person at each corner, the cab can be lifted clear.

Wheels and Tyres

Later van and pick-up models were fitted with wider 4½ J wheels, which have the designation LP 917 stamped on them. This marking is located in the central part of the wheel normally covered by the hubcap. Tyres such as the Firestone F560 155R × 14 80S are ideally suited for use with these wider rims.

Interior Trim

The interior trim used in commercial variants differed from that used in the rest of the Morris Minor range. Brown and black were the dominant colours for seat coverings, which differed in pattern from those used in contemporary saloons, convertibles and Travellers. In the interests of practicality due to the anticipated heavy-duty usage, moulded one-piece rubber floor coverings were used in both vans and pick-ups. Replacements are difficult to source and as a compromise carpet is widely used in modern restorations.

16

Traveller Restoration

The Morris Minor Traveller remains one of the most popular models in the Morris Minor range. Mechanically it shares the same components as other contemporary Morris Minor models but its construction is unique. Introduced in 1953 as the Morris Minor Station Wagon, it underwent several name changes, including being designated as the Morris Minor Travellers Car. Colloquially it was also known as a 'shooting brake', but this was never an official designation. Commonly referred to as the Traveller, it remained in production until 1971 when, along with the commercial models, it was discontinued.

From the outset the construction of the Traveller differed from other Morris Minors. Unlike the commercial models, which used a separate chassis on which the van and pick-up bodies were mounted, the Traveller models retained the use of an integral floor pan to which a separate ash frame was attached. In an effort to reduce the overall weight of the vehicle, the frame was infilled with aluminium panels and rearward of the steel cab, a full-length aluminium roof panel was affixed to the top of the frame. Two ash-framed rear doors were also infilled with aluminium panels at the bottom and glass at the top. Forward of the wooden framework the cab was identical to other Morris Minors and utilised the same doors as four-door models.

It is important to note that even though the Morris Minor Traveller models are no longer subject to a statutory annual MOT (though it is still advisable to have one) the wooden framework is structural and as such is an MOT checklist item. Weakness in the wooden frame due to water ingress causing softness in the wood is a recognised MOT failure point.

In this chapter, the emphasis will be on preserving and maintaining existing Traveller wood and the replacement of the wood frame. Other aspects of restoration equally applicable to the Traveller models are covered in previous chapters. Reassuringly all materials including replacement 'ash frames' made to the original specification are readily available and some specialist companies offer a fitting service. However, replacing the Traveller woodwork is well within the capabilities of

The Morris Minor Traveller remained in production for eighteen years.

179

Traveller Restoration

a competent home restorer. Advice in the form of specialised publications, guidance advice from parts suppliers and shared information from individuals who have tackled the job before is readily available on forums and online.

Steve Foreman, who has been in the business manufacturing ash frames as well as restoring hundreds of Travellers over the past 40 years, has shared the following advice for would-be restorers and those wishing to preserve the woodwork on their vehicle.

PRELIMINARY CHECKS

Determining the extent of the restoration work that may be required on the wooden frame on the Traveller is important, as a lot of time and effort can be expended in attempting to preserve the existing wood only to find that it may have been better to have replaced it in the first place.

One of the key tell-tale signs of potential problems is where the wood is showing signs of discoloration and softening. This is caused where fungal infestation has attacked the inner fibres of the wood, resulting in the overall structure being weakened. Applying pressure to affected areas using a blunt screwdriver is a useful way of determining the extent of the problem.

There are certain key areas where the problem is likely to occur:

- The central waist rails, particularly where they are joined to the front and rear pillars. These rails on either side of the car also carry the window runners. The window runners tend to retain moisture, so it is worth checking at either end for signs of discoloration and weakness.
- Rear pillars. These upright pillars are prone to weakness,

Assembled side frames can be purchased separately.

Complete ash frame kit, packaged in readiness for despatch.

particularly in the area at the top where they come into contact with the roof. The bottom of the pillars where the underside picks up road spray and dirt is also prone to softening.
- The foot rails, which are located between front of the rear wheel arch and the front pillar, can be affected, particularly where they are jointed. They often show signs of water staining, but because they are quite substantial pieces of wood they are often salvageable.
- The rear base rail where it is jointed to the rear pillar. This is normally more protected and less likely to be a problem.
- The rear top rail located beneath the roof and the two rear pillars. As moisture can be trapped between the rail and the rear door sealing strip, examining the area beneath the rubber strip is advisable.
- The wheel arch panels where they are jointed. This is a common area for surface discoloration to occur and if not too serious can be treated and the pieces salvaged. Note, because the original wheel arches used threaded sleeves for the wing bolts, discoloration called 'bluing' may be visible. This will be impossible to remove, but might be capable of being disguised by using a suitable finish.
- The cant rails that run the full length of the frame underneath the roof can be problematic, particularly where the roof has been tacked down. If required these can easily be re-commissioned.
- The rear doors. In practice the rear doors tend to last longer than the rest of the frame. The main problem area tends to be the middle rail on each door, particularly where it is jointed to the main doorframe. The only other potential problem areas are the sections behind the door lock and the hinges on the rear pillars.

REFURBISHMENT OR REPLACEMENT

With all the preliminary checks completed, it should be possible to make an informed decision on whether to attempt to refurbish the existing woodwork with the frame on the car or to remove the existing wood and replace with new. It is also possible to replace individual sections of the frame, but this can be more complicated and not necessarily cost effective in terms of the time spent doing it, or satisfactory with regard to getting a satisfactory colour match when finished.

REMOVAL OF COMPONENTS

Assuming the wood frame is basically sound and that any discoloration is not too deeply engrained, it should be possible to remove most of it using a scraper with a sharp blade. Before getting to that stage and to allow easy access to all of the wood surface, it will be necessary to remove various components, including the rear doors, side windows, and the light units, reflectors and door hinges located on the rear pillars. The three lower bolts on each of the front pillars, which secure them to the 'B' post, should also be removed.

Removing the door hinges should simply be a matter of undoing the nuts and removing the bolts. It may be that some of them are rusted on and need cutting through with a hacksaw or grinder. Either way, it is advisable to replace all the bolts with new zinc-plated ones. In order to gain access to the hidden areas of the middle rail it is necessary to remove the side windows: this is best done by removing the inner capping rails. After taking out all the retaining screws the middle capping will need to be levered off to break the seal. The windows can then be lifted out by inserting a screwdriver under the lower runners and removing both the runners and the windows at the same time. Although the runners are screwed down it is likely that the screws will be ineffective. The runners can be easily removed from the wood once the windows are out. Depending on the condition of the upper runners, a decision will have to be made whether or not to remove and replace them. The uprights in the front and rear pillars are likely to be decayed and it is advisable to remove and replace them. The lights and reflector in the rear pillar should be taken out to make stripping and sanding easier. This also applies to the three lower bolts in the front pillar. If these do not turn easily then a sharp tap with a hammer on the screwdriver should loosen them. The sides should now be ready for stripping back to the bare wood.

REAR DOORS

The doors can either be restored with the panels and the glass in place or, for a thorough restoration, they can be removed. It is advisable to leave the glass in to retain the shape and strength, but with the aluminium panels out of the way the inner faces of the lower sections are much more accessible. The aluminium panel on the nearside door is easily removed by taking out the screws. The offside door has the added complication of the locking mechanism. This only becomes a problem when the door handle becomes corroded in its housing. To facilitate removal, liberally spray with freeing fluid where the shaft is located on the inside of the door. After removal of the two outer screws and the single one on the inside, several hard strikes with a hammer and punch should shift it. If this does not work, then the only option is to drill out the shaft where it is held by the inner mechanism. A new handle will be required. However, it is worth exercising care not to damage the main mechanism and rods, as these are not readily available.

TOOLS AND EQUIPMENT REQUIRED

In preparation for stripping and restoring the wood, having the following tools and equipment to hand is recommended. An electric hot-air gun, a scraper with replaceable blades, 70/100 grit paper and a sharp chisel. A suitable wood preservative such as Cuprinol 5 Star will also need to be sourced.

WORKING CONDITIONS

It is imperative that the work is completed undercover and in dry, dust-free

Traveller Restoration

Cuprinol 5 Star wood preservative is suitable for use on the ash frame.

Removing the Existing Finish

- Use the hot-air gun over a small area at a time so that the previously applied coating will soften and bubble out from the grain in the wood.
- Use the sharp blade in the scraper to remove the residue by working with the grain in the wood.
- Work in one specific area at a time until that section is complete.
- Resist the temptation to use paint stripper to remove the original wood finish in order to avoid potential damage to the paintwork on the adjacent aluminium panels.
- Avoid the use of two-part bleaching applications to remove discoloured markings from the wood. These applications weaken the surface of the wood.
- After thoroughly cleaning the wood, soak the whole frame including the doorframes with one or two coats of Cuprinol 5 Star preservative or similar.
- Leave the frame to dry for two or three days in order to allow all active toxins to escape.

conditions. It is also important to set aside adequate time for all the tasks to be completed and for various applications to dry thoroughly. Setting aside at least one week is recommended.

TYPES OF FINISH

Ultimately the type of finish applied will be a matter of personal choice. If a clear, light-gloss finish is preferred, a clear varnish will be required. Provided an exterior gloss with ultra-violet protection is used, this is perfectly acceptable and, for Travellers that are regularly garaged, provided a top up is applied every one or two years this is a feasible option.

After years of experience and experimentation with different finishes the preferred and recommended option from Steve Foreman of Woodies is:

> 'If durability is required, first apply a base cat of Sikkens HLS in light oak. This can be lightened if required by mixing in approximately 20 per cent clear preservative. Follow this up by applying two coats of Osmo clear UV Protection oil which is microporous, flexible and durable.'

REPLACING THE WOODEN FRAME

If a full-scale restoration is being undertaken of a Traveller, including full replacement of the wooden frame, attention will need to be

Applying preservative to all parts of the wood frame including inward facing surfaces is critical to ensure longevity.

Work in progress with the ash frame pre-assembled.

Traveller Restoration

paid to specific aspects, not only to ensure accurate fitting but to avoid having to repeat the process in years to come. Time spent preparing the new wood frame and refurbishing or replacing the metalwork to which it is attached will pay dividends in the long term.

STRUCTURAL REPAIRS

With the frame removed the full extent of the metalwork repairs necessary will become apparent. With luck the inner wings and the flange on the rear wheel arches will be sound and only show signs of surface rust. However, given the age of even the newest Traveller (1971), it is likely that some welding work will be required, either to repair the existing inner wings or replace them. Replacement parts including complete inner wings and separate inner wing flanges are available and fitting them is well within the scope of the amateur welder. Once fitted, the wings need to be treated with a rust inhibitor, primed and painted with a protective gloss coat in the appropriate body colour.

Attention also needs to be paid to the boot-well floor area. As this area is prone to rusting due to leaking back doors and condensation, it is likely that the rear boot floor well will need to be replaced or repaired. This area of the vehicle is particularly important, as it is the part to which the base rails of the frame are bolted.

Other areas, worthy of attention at this stage are the 'B' posts. These are normally sound except for the lower edges, which will either need a repair section fitted or a limited amount of fabrication. If the car is to be re-sprayed as part of the restoration, it is advisable to spray the inner and outer faces of the 'B' post. This will give a better and longer-lasting finish. Occasionally the outer top edge of the 'B' post will have signs of metal corrosion and it is well worth checking if there is inherent weakness there and if repairs are required.

Time taken to repair and ensure accurate alignment of the rear inner flanges will pay dividends when fitting the ash frame.

Restored boot floor area showing location of mounting brackets.

183

Traveller Restoration

Aluminium Panels

Close examination of the aluminium door and side panels should be undertaken after removal from the original frame or doors. At this stage there is an opportunity to strip each panel to bare metal, etch-prime and spray in body colour to the edges normally covered by the wooden frame.

A number of options exist relating to the painting of the roof panel. If the paintwork on the roof is sound it may be that once the drip moulding has been fitted after the frames are in place that only the drip moulding will need etch-priming and spraying. If the whole roof is being painted it will need stripping and etch-priming before being painted.

Restored and repainted sill, 'B' post and inner floor area.

Wooden Frames

The sides must be fitted as an assembled frame and the wood thoroughly preserved and finished before being bolted on. The inside faces need special attention, as once the frames are on the car further protection is difficult. The previous section outlined the various options available to preserve the wood and the pros and cons of different finishes. Whatever system is adopted follow the manufacturer's instruction meticulously. Complete the full process on the frame, inside and out, leaving only one topcoat to be applied once the frame is fitted to the car.

One area worthy of note relates to the middle rail on the frame.

Etch primed and painted aluminium infill panels.

It is important to pay special attention to the drain holes in the middle rail. It is recommended that these are not drilled until after other preservative coats have been applied to the rest of the frame. Failure to do so will cause two problems. First, the hole size will be diminished and second, a topcoat will eventually peel and allow water into the end grain. It is better to fill the drain holes with a powerful preservative by taping up the bottom of the holes and allowing it to soak in overnight or until they will not accept any more. The advantage of this is that during later yearly maintenance, the same process can be repeated by pouring preservative along the

Roof panels are not immune to corrosion, as shown here.

Traveller Restoration

window runners, thus allowing the preservative to soak into the end grain of the middle rail. This will not only protect the wood but also prevent a build-up of fungi on the window runners.

Tip: Under no circumstances sleeve the holes with metal or plastic as this has been found to accelerate rotting in the area adjacent to the drain holes.

Fitting Aluminium Side panels

With the frames prepared the aluminium side panels should now be fitted. A bead of sealant should be run wherever the face of the metal comes into contact with the wooden frame. The panels are secured in place by ¾-inch screws. Zinc-plated pozidrive screws are preferable as they can be fitted using a power screwdriver, which has the advantage of saving a considerable amount of time.

Fitting Rear Wings

Prior to offering up the wing, wing-piping needs to be fitted to the wheel arch on the frame. Patience is key to this task. The piping should be secured in position either by using small tacks or by staples using a staple gun. Starting at the front edge, the piping needs to be evenly positioned on the outer edge with small cuts being made on the inner edge of the piping to take account of the curvature of the wheel arch and the angle of the foot rail. The rear wing should be fitted to the side frame before it is offered up to the car. Experience has shown that this task is accomplished more easily if the frame is in an upside-down position. Originally wings were fitted using bolts positioned in a threaded sleeve. Over time this arrangement proved to be unsatisfactory, as it resulted in dark areas appearing on the wood. Plated or stainless screws and washers are a better alternative. Ten screws are required for each wing.

Tip: Start from the front bottom edge of the wing and work backwards only using a screw where necessary to pull the wing neatly behind the beading of the wing.

Wood frame masked off in readiness for final coat being applied to the roof panel.

FITTING THE FRAME

It is best to begin the process of fitting the new frame by concentrating on the rear base rails. If they have been removed and the original set are being refitted, then it is a matter of bolting them through the original holes using new coach bolts. If a new set is being fitted, they should be centralised, and the bolt holes marked and drilled. The metal rear valance, which is tacked to the base rails using 1-inch sherardised nails, needs to be fitted at the same time. Coach bolts run through the valance into the base rails. The base rails are also bolted through the extreme rear of the boot-well floor. Originally no sealant was used. If a decision is made to seal this area then drain holes will need to be drilled in the boot-well floor, as water will undoubtedly find its way in through the rear doors at some point. Having the drain holes will allow it to escape. A watching brief will need to be kept to ensure that the drain holes do not become blocked in the future.

Tip: It is a false economy to fit an old rear valence where rust is evident on the inner face as this will very quickly cause deterioration of the base rails.

FITTING THE SIDE PANELS

The sides can now be offered up to the car. Assuming the holes have been drilled in the front pillar of the frame, they will need to be checked for alignment and adjusted accordingly. Holes that have been drilled undersized on the new frame will allow greater

Traveller Restoration

New rear valence being aligned with frame fitted.

flexibility when fitting. Note that at the top of the front pillar a small cut-out will need to be made to allow the edge of the roof to slot in.

FITTING THE ROOF

If the roof has been removed, it is much easier to refit it at this stage. Trying to fit it with the wood in place can be problematic. If the T-rubber between the cab and roof is in good condition, then the bolts holding the roof can be fully tightened and the roof will be self-supporting. If, however, the roof is to be sprayed after the wood and new guttering have been fitted, then it is advisable to fit the roof without the T-rubber in place. It will be necessary to leave a gap sufficient to take the T-rubber when under compression – about 5mm should suffice – as this will assist in fitting the guttering into its final position. With painting complete, the top three bolts on the front pillar and the cab roof bolts will need to be loosened to allow the T-rubber to be inserted. Slots will need to be cut into the T-rubber to facilitate this. Adopting this approach means that the paint can be sprayed beneath where the T-Rubber will fit.

FITTING THE SIDE

At this stage having an extra pair of hands available is a bonus. Aligning the side panel up to the 'B' post, having first applied a bead of sealant, will allow for the three bolts to be located and fully tightened. Attention can then switch to the rear of the side panel while making sure that the wheel arch is not fouling the top of the inner wing. It is worth noting that the curve of the wheel arch does not follow the curve of the inner wing precisely. It drifts away about an inch towards the rear.

THE REAR PILLAR

The rear pillar will need to be forcefully pulled into position. A soft rope will help with this or a sash clamp on the side of the rear pillar to the bumper stay. This will hold the pillar in place while the coach bolt that goes through the base of the rear pillar into the hole in the metal framework is located. Should any vertical adjustment be required, the use of a jack under the rear corner is a useful ploy. The rear pillar should butt up to the rear valance on the base rails. Even though it was not done originally, it is helpful to apply a line of sealant in this area. If both sides are being replaced the process must be repeated. With both sides bolted to the front and secured at the base of the rear pillars there will still be some vertical movement on the rear pillars. The next stage is to line them up and fit the rear top rail.

THE REAR TOP RAIL

With the rear doors evenly placed on the rear base rails the rear pillars should be moved until an even ¼ inch gap is achieved on both sides. If new rear doors are being fitted it may be necessary to trim the outer lip to achieve a perfect fit. The rear top rail needs to be put in position at the same time and the height adjusted to leave an even gap of ½ inch. This should allow for the doors to be raised when being bolted on and provide adequate clearance on the base rails and room for the fitting of the top and bottom rubber seals.

Traveller Restoration

The metal brackets, which hold the rear pillar to the rear top rail and cant rail, should now be fitted. For structural rigidity the metal brackets are essential. Simply gluing the joint will not suffice. Plywood fillets should also be fitted to the lower inside face of each of the rear pillars between the metal rear corner bracket and the wood. These are held in place by two screws initially and are further secured when the door hinge bolts are fitted. These items are important, as they allow space for the door mechanism to fit behind the metal cross bar of the load-bay floor.

THE ROOF PANEL

Before turning attention to securing the roof panel in position, it is important to make sure that the wood frame is secure and that it is sitting square.

Tip: Before attaching the roof panel, the headlining support beams with the headlining attached need to be secured in place. Attaching the headlining whether original or new is best done off the car.

With the roof rails screwed in place in the rebates in the cant rail, the headlining can then be rolled up and covered to protect it while the roof panel is secured in place. Aligning the roof panel is best done with two people present to ensure accurate fitting and to help with adjustment if necessary. Wearing gloves with a non-slip palm is helpful when positioning the roof panel over the rear top rail. Once positioned correctly and held in place, the second person should tack the roof in place.

Tip: Position the roof panel so that most of the wood on the rear top rail is covered.

Moving to the front of the car, check that sufficient space has been left for the fitting of the T-rubber before beginning the process of tacking the panel on to the cant rails using 1-inch galvanised nails. With the roof tacked down and flattened evenly to the wood, attention can then focus on fitting the roof guttering.

THE ROOF GUTTERING

New sections of roof guttering are supplied as 7ft lengths. Two are required, and when fitted they meet in the middle at the rear. Before attaching the guttering, a square section needs to be cut out of the front top edge so that it fits neatly around the rear face of the T-rubber. With the guttering held flat to the edge of the roof, two holes large enough to take the tacks being used need to be drilled through the guttering and the roof panel. Drill one at the front and the other just ahead of the corner at the rear.

Work in progress to fit the roof guttering.

Rear corner lip cut and dressed.

Tip: Use a very thin drill bit (2mm) and drill to a depth of 5mm ($^3/_{16}$in).

With the guttering secured, tacks can be hammered approximately 100mm (4in) apart and fully located using a punch, which easily clears the opening of the drip moulding. With the guttering securely fastened the more difficult task of forming the guttering to neatly follow the curvature of the rear pillar needs to be completed. This is best done by carefully bending the guttering through 45 degrees before making a cut in the bottom lip where it meets the centre of the

Traveller Restoration

corner. This will provide greater flexibility to continue round the corner to the rear of the car. Patience is required at this point to ensure proper alignment and it is recommended to use a wooden or metal drift to get the gutter flat to the roof before tacking into position with a gap of ¾ inch on the corner. Progress can then be made to position the rest of the guttering halfway across the rear of the roof. At this point the guttering, which is supplied over-length, will need to be cut using a hacksaw or grinder. It is best to cut at a slight angle to allow a close-fitting joint when the guttering from the other side is cut to meet it.

To complete the task, the top lip on the guttering needs to be flattened over the tack heads. This is best done using a piece of wood or plastic about 150mm (6in) long. Working from front to back, tap down a small amount at a time making sure not too much force is applied, otherwise rippling will occur. Finally cut about 1½ inches off the bottom lip on each corner before smoothing the edges with fine emery cloth and dressing the bottom edge to ensure a tight fit to the top of the rear pillar.

REAR DOORS

With the wooden frame complete, to fit the doors, first bolt the hinges to the doors in exactly the same place as on the original doors. Then they can be offered up and marked onto the rear pillars, leaving enough room for the quadrant rubber seal. Do not fit the seal before the doors. Final adjustment can be made leaving all the nuts loose, which will allow up to ¼ inch play. If new doors are being fitted, it is better to fit them without the panels and glass. This gives better access to the inner bolt heads and there is less weight.

Once the doors are hung and the panels, glass, mechanism and lock are fitted, the holes to take the locating sockets for the door mechanism need to be drilled in the top and bottom rear rails. If the original rails have been used, this will not be necessary. With these and the door seals in place it may be necessary to make further adjustment to the doors. The resulting fit should be tight, and the doors will need to be closed together. If the doors are too loose at this stage, once they have settled on to the new seals, rattles and leaks will result. It is likely that until they have bedded in some leaks will occur along the top rail. After a few weeks final adjustment can be made.

Fitting of the windows, capping rails, interior trim and other related items is a reverse of the stripping-down process. It is important to make sure that the areas between the capping and the middle rail and where the front pillar and middle rail-capping meet are properly sealed in order to prevent leaks.

Rear doors. Trial fit.

Hinges fitted in readiness for final assembly.

17
Return to the Road

With the restoration nearing completion, an added impetus was provided by the prospect of having the last saloon back on the road in time for the 50th anniversary of it rolling off the production line at the Cowley works in Oxfordshire on 12 November 1970. Morris Minor Owners Club volunteers were up for the challenge and all seemed set for the car to make a historic return to the factory, now the BMW MINI Plant, for a much-deserved celebration with all those who had been involved in the restoration process. Alas in November 2020, Covid-19 restrictions put paid to any large-scale gatherings. A nationally enforced socially distanced 'rule of six', coupled with an impending lockdown meant that activities planned for the much-anticipated return had to be scaled back. Undeterred, the car was prepared and slightly ahead of the anniversary date was transported to 'T' building on the BMW MINI Site for a photo opportunity and a more muted celebration. Amidst the prevailing uncertainty at the time due to the impact of Covid, the car remained at the site in the Historic Vehicle Collection in the hope that once the plant re-opened to visitors post-lockdown, members of Morris Minor Owners Club, supporters and benefactors of the restoration and the public would be able to view the vehicle and appreciate first-hand the transformation that had occurred. Once again, the best-laid plans were thwarted by Covid, as restrictions governing visiting the site remained in force for a considerable period of time.

In the week prior to the anniversary event, efforts intensified to actually get the car running. Due to the condensed timeframe, plans were revised and following a thorough visual check of all the mechanical components and all fluid levels, attention focused on preparing the engine for its initial start up after its extensive rebuild. With all of the elements of the ignition system checked, the much-anticipated turn of the key resulted in the reassuring ticking of the SU fuel pump before the engine sprang into life at the third time of asking. Fine tuning, using Colortune equipment to regulate the fuel mixture, followed immediately under the watchful eye of Alan Scott, who had undertaken the rebuild of the engine. Safe in the knowledge that the engine was running smoothly, tentative steps were taken to test the operation of the clutch and the engagement of the

Historic moment as FMT 265 J returns to 'T' Building in Cowley 50 years later. Note the 12 November 1970 image marking the end of saloon production.

FMT 265 J striking a similar pose to the 1970 production line image.

Return to the Road

gearbox. In preparation for an initial test drive the car was put on the four-poster ramp and a full 'spanner check' was instigated and a meticulous final check undertaken to see that all nuts and bolts accessible from the underside of the car were securely fastened. Particular attention was paid to the front and rear suspension, rear axle and differential, the engine and gearbox mountings and the steering rack.

INITIAL TEST DRIVE

The initial test drive was a short 800-metre trip. Reassuringly nothing untoward emerged, particularly in regard to the original components, which had been given the benefit of the doubt due to no excessive wear or play being detected on inspection. Quiet, smooth running coupled with positive and precise gear selection and no excessive noise from the transmission provided welcome reassurance in advance of the car being taken back to the place where it had been built as a brand new vehicle.

A SPECIAL AWARD

The associated publicity relating to the restoration of the last saloon and the fact that in large part the work had been carried out by volunteer members of the Morris Minor Owners Club, drew the attention of the panel of judges for awards being presented in conjunction with the Practical Classics Restoration Show in 2021. In recognising the efforts of all concerned and that the latter stages of the restoration and reassembly of the vehicle had taken place in trying circumstances due to the pandemic, a unique Judges special recognition award of 'Best Lockdown Restoration' was presented in an online presentation by *Practical Classics* magazine editor, Danny Hopkins.

FINAL STAGES

On return from the Historic Vehicle Collection at the MINI Plant in Cowley, Oxfordshire, further work was undertaken on the vehicle to finish some of the tasks that had not been completed due to the compressed timeframe previously mentioned. Plans were put in place to test the car thoroughly on an extended test drive and to rectify any faults that might emerge in advance of the vehicle being displayed at the Practical Classics Restoration Show held at the National Exhibition Centre in Birmingham.

As well as the essential mechanical checks, additional checks were made on the body panels and associated fittings, the electrical system and other elements contained on a pre-MOT check list. Some rectification work including replacing the choke cable, readjusting the hand-brake, rechecking the headlamp alignment and changing the indicator stalk with a smoother operating second-hand unit proved necessary after the vehicle had been taken for an extended 5-mile drive. The major issue to arise related to the steering and prior to the vehicle being taken for an MOT the tracking was checked and reset. The pre-MOT inspection and the meticulous checks paid dividends, as the car passed the MOT with no advisories. This was a testament to all those who had contributed to the restoration as described in the preceding pages.

In the course of carrying out the final inspections, it was noted that during the course of the restoration some marks and scratches had occurred on the paintwork. This prompted the decision to have the exterior paintwork re-polished.

Deserved recognition for all the hard work.

PRE-MOT TEST CHECKLIST

Registration Mark: FMT 265 J
Make / Model: MORRIS MINOR SALOON
Odometer reading: 16971
Vehicle Identification Number: MA2551288377
Date of First Use:

Items to be tested	Pass	Fail	Defects/Comments
Interior checks			
Seats and seat belts	✓		
Warning lamps	✓		
Switches (position lamp, headlamp, hazards)			Hazards not fitted.
View to front, wipers and washers	✓		
Brake controls, servo operation	✓		No servo fitted
Steering wheel and column	✓		
Doors, mirrors, horn	✓		
Speedometer, driver controls (Class 5 only)	N/A		
Exterior checks			
Registration plates	✓		
Lamps, registration plate lamps	✓		
Indicators, hazards		✓	Intermittent use. Bad earth?
Headlamps & aim		✓	Further adjustment needed
Stop lamps, fog lamps, reflectors	✓		Fog lamps not fitted.
Wheels, tyres	✓		
Shock absorbers	✓		
Mirrors, wiper blades, fuel tank cap	✓		
Glazing (Class 5 only)	N/A		
Doors, boot lid, loading doors, bonnet	✓		
Towbars	N/A		
General condition of body	✓		
Under bonnet checks			
Vehicle structure	✓		
Braking systems		✓	Handbrake requires adjustment
Exhaust systems, fuel system	✓		
Speed limiter (if applicable)	N/A		
Steering & power steering components		✓	Alignment check needed pre MOT
Suspension components	✓		
Under vehicle checks			
Steering including power steering		✓	See above - Power steering N/A.
Drive shafts (if applicable)	✓		
Suspension, shock absorbers	✓		
Wheel bearings	✓		
Wheels & tyres	✓		
Brake systems & mechanical components	✓		
Exhaust system	✓		
Fuel system & fuel tank	✓		
Structure, general vehicle condition	✓		
Emissions			Not checked pre MOT.

MOT pre-inspection checklist.

MOT test certificate

① Vehicle identification number
MA2S51288377

②ª Registration number ②ᵇ Country of registration
FMT265J **GB**

Make and model
MORRIS MINOR

⑤ Vehicle category ④ Mileage
 16,979 miles

 ⑦ **Pass**

③ᵇ Date of the test ⑧ Expiry date
05.03.2022 **04.03.2023**

To preserve the anniversary of the expiry date, the earliest you can present your vehicle for test is 05.02.2023.

③ª Location of the test
5, UNIT 2A NEW INN BRIDGE INDUSTRIAL ESTATE, 998 FOLESHILL ROAD, FOLESHILL, COVENTRY, CV6 6EN

⑨ Testing organisation and inspector name
V102101   PARAGON AUTO TESTING
r. edwards

MOT test number
9545 9381 1807

Duplicate certificate issued by DVSA on 24 January 2023

Check that this document is genuine by visiting **www.gov.uk/check-mot-history**

If any of the details are not correct, please contact DVSA by email at **enquiries@dvsa.gov.uk** or by telephone on 0300 1239000.

Receive a free annual MOT reminder by subscribing at **www.gov.uk/mot-reminder** or by telephone on 0300 1239000.

Driver & Vehicle Standards Agency

Page 1 of 1
VT20/2.0

Issued by DVSA

MOT certificate.

Final Polishing

With the car fully assembled and ready to be displayed, attention once again focused on the paintwork and the decision made to have the vehicle machine-polished to remove any marks or imperfections resulting from the reassembly and installation of specific components. Preparation work in masking-off panel edges, rubbers, brightwork and chrome was undertaken to avoid any further marking or dulling of components. 1-inch and 2-inch masking tape widths were used.

Materials used in the final finishing process included a rotary and dual action polisher, Menzerna Heavy Cut 400 Compound and 3500 Super Finish, along with the appropriate coloured pads for specified use.

With just two small areas requiring special attention wet flatted, the process of polishing the panels back to a high gloss perfect finish began using Menzerna Heavy Cut 400 compound with a Menzerna Heavy Cut Red pad on the polisher. The compound was applied sparingly to the pad using three pea-sized blobs of compound. These were then transferred from the pad to the flatted panel and polished. Regular use of inspection lamps was key here to ensure that no flatting marks were left in the paintwork.

After meticulous inspection of each panel following the use of the heavy cutting compound, preparations for the final polish began. At this stage it was vital to ensure that no 'pad trails' or 'hazing' were left on the

(continued overleaf)

Return to the Road

Final Polishing continued

Essential equipment used for final polishing.

Care was taken to mask off previously assembled components.

3000 grade wet and dry pads were used sparingly in specific areas.

Menzerna Heavy Cut 400 Compound.

A modest amount of compound was applied to the pad...

... before being applied to the painted surface...

paintwork after the application of the heavy cut compound. This was deemed essential if a high gloss finish was to be achieved after the application of the Menzerna Super Finish 3500. Using the Menzerna Green finishing pad, the compound was once again applied sparingly to the pad, transferred to each panel and polished to a high shine and gloss.

On completion, any excess compound was removed before every panel was wiped with an Autosmart Panel Prep Plus panel wipe. This helped ensure that all excess polish and any other residues were removed. With all masking tape removed and the surfaces wiped clean, a final wax using Britemax Vantage wax, a product developed specifically for use with 2k paint finishes, was applied to all the external painted surfaces.

(continued overleaf)

Return to the Road

Final Polishing *continued*

… and evenly polished using the dual-action polisher.

Menzerna Super Finish was used to achieve a high gloss finish using the dual action rotary polisher.

Since the completion of the restoration the car has been exhibited at numerous Morris Minor Owners Club events. In 2022 the opportunity to display the vehicle as part of the Derbyshire-based Great British Car Journey collection was taken and in 2023 it took pride of place alongside the first Morris Minor, built in 1948, as part of the 75th anniversary celebrations to mark the start of Morris Minor production.

In 2022/2023 the car was exhibited at the Great British Car Journey attraction in Derbyshire.

18 Specifications

Make	Morris Minor
Model	Series MM

Engine	Designated type USHM2. Cast-iron block and head. Four cylinders, in line, side-valve		
	Bore 57mm	**Stroke** 90mm	**Capacity** 918cc
	Maximum bhp 27.5bhp at 4,400rpm		**Carburettor** SU horizontal type H1
Fuel pump	SU type L		
Compression	6.5/6.7:1		
Gearbox	Four-speed gearbox bolted to rear engine plate. Synchromesh on 2nd, 3rd and top gears. Clutch, Borg and Beck 6¼ inch (158.7mm) dry plate type AG **Ratios** Reverse 3.95:1, First 3.95:1, Second 2.30:1, Third 1.54:1, Top 1.00:1		
Rear axle	Semi-floating hypoid axle, ratio 9.4:1		
Brakes	Lockhead hydraulic 7in diameter drums (17.8cm). Front: two leading shoes. Rear: one leading and one trailing shoe		
Tyres	14in pressed steel disc. Four-bolt fixings. Tyres 5.00x14		
Suspension	Front: Independent by torsion bars and links. Armstrong double-acting hydraulic dampers. Rear: Semi-elliptic leaf springs. Armstrong double-acting hydraulic dampers		
Steering	Rack and pinion, 2.5 turns lock-to-lock		
Dimensions Two-door saloon (15½cwt), Tourer (14cwt), Four-door saloon (15¾cwt)	**Length** 12ft4in (376cm), 12ft4in (376cm), 12ft4in (376cm)	**Height** 5ft0in (152cm), 4ft9in (143cm), 5ft0in (152cm)	**Width** 5ft1in (155cm), 5ft1in (155cm), 5ft1in (155cm)
	Turning Circle R.H. 33ft 1in (10.09m), L.H 32ft 11in (10.04m)		
Capacities	Fuel 5 gallons (22.7ltr)		

Make	Morris Minor
Model	Series II saloon, convertible, Traveller

Engine	Cast-iron block and head. Pressed steel sump. Four cylinders		
	Bore 58mm	**Stroke** 76mm	**Capacity** 803cc
	Maximum bhp 30bhp at 4,800rpm		**Carburettor** SU type H
Fuel pump	SU type L		
Compression	7.2:1		
Gearbox	Four-speed gearbox bolted to rear engine plate. Synchromesh on 2nd, 3rd and top gears. Clutch, Borg and Beck 6¼in (158.7mm) dry plate **Ratios** Reverse 5.174:1, First 4.09:1, Second 2.588:1, Third 1.679:1, Top 1.000:1		
Rear axle	Hypoid axle		
Brakes	Lockhead hydraulic 7in diameter drums (17.8cm). Front: two leading shoes. Rear: one leading and one trailing shoe		

Specifications

Tyres	14in pressed steel disc. Four-bolt fixings. Tyres 5.00x14		
Suspension	Front: Independent by torsion bars and links. Rear: Half-elliptic leaf springs		
Steering	Rack and pinion, 2.5 turns lock-to-lock		
Dimensions Two-door saloon (15½cwt), Four-door saloon (15¾cwt), convertible (15cwt), Traveller (16½cwt)	**Length** 12ft4in (376cm), 12ft4in (376cm), 12ft4in (376cm), 12ft5in (379cm)	**Height** 5ft0in (152cm), 5ft0in (152cm), 5ft0in (152cm), 5ft0in (152cm)	**Width** 5ft1in (155cm), 5ft1in (155cm), 5ft1in (155cm), 5ft1in (155cm)
	Turning Circle 33ft (10m)		
Capacities	Fuel 5 gallons (22.7ltr)		

Make	Morris 1000 948cc
Model	Two-door & four-door saloons, convertible, Traveller

Engine	Cast-iron block and head. Pressed-steel sump. Four cylinders set in line with overhead valves pushrod operated		
	Bore 62.9mm	**Stroke** 76.2mm	**Capacity** 948cc
	Maximum bhp 37bhp at 4,750rpm		**Carburettor** SU H2 type, 1¼in
Fuel pump	SU type L		
Compression	8.3:1 (high compression engine)		
Gearbox	Four-speed gearbox bolted to rear engine plate. Remote control gearchange. Synchromesh on 2nd, 3rd, and top gears. Clutch, Borg and Beck 6¼in (158.7mm) dry plate		
	Ratios Reverse 4.664:1, First 3.628:1, Second 2.374:1, Third 1.412:1, Top 1.000:1		
Rear axle	Three-quarter floating rear axle. Hypoid final drive		
Brakes	Lockheed hydraulic 7in diameter drums (17.8cm). Front: two leading shoes. Rear: one leading and one trailing shoe		
Tyres	14in pressed-steel disc. Four stud fixings. 5.00x14 tubeless		
Suspension	Front: Independent by torsion bars and links. Rear: Half-elliptic leaf springs		
Steering	Rack and pinion, 2.5 turns lock-to-lock		
Dimensions Two-door saloon (15½cwt), Four-door saloon (15¾cwt), Convertible (15cwt), Traveller (16½cwt)	**Length** 12ft4in (376cm), 12ft4in (376cm), 12ft4in (376cm), 12ft5in (379cm)	**Height** 5ft0in (152cm), 5ft0in (152cm), 5ft0in (152cm), 5ft0in (152cm)	**Width** 5ft1in (155cm), 5ft1in (155cm), 5ft1in (155cm), 5ft1in (155cm)
	Turning Circle 33ft (10m)		
Capacities	Fuel 6½ gallons/30 litres		

Make	Morris 1000 1098cc
Model	Two-door & four-door saloons, convertible, Traveller

Engine	Cast-iron block and head. Pressed steel sump. Four cylinders set in line with overhead valves pushrod operated		
	Bore 64.58mm	**Stroke** 83.72mm	**Capacity** 1098cc
	Maximum bhp 48bhp at 5,100rpm	**Carburettor** SU HS2 type, 1¼in	
Fuel pump	SU type L		
Compression	8.5:1 (high compression engine)		
Gearbox	Four-speed gearbox bolted to rear engine plate. Remote control gearchange. Synchromesh on 2nd, 3rd and top gears. Clutch, 7¼in single dry plate		
	Ratios Reverse 4.664:1, First 3.628:1, Second 2.172:1, Third 1.412:1, Top 1.000:1		
Rear axle	Three-quarter floating rear axle. Hypoid final drive		

Specifications

Brakes	Lockhead hydraulic front 8in diameter drums. Rear 7in diameter drums. Front: two leading shoes. Rear: one leading and one trailing shoe
Tyres	14in pressed-steel disc. Four stud fixings. Tyres 5.00/5.20x14 tubeless
Suspension	Front: Independent by torsion bars and links. Rear: Half-elliptic leaf springs
Steering	Rack and pinion, 2.5 turns lock-to-lock
Dimensions Two-door saloon (15½cwt), Four-door saloon (15¾cwt), Convertible (15cwt), Traveller (16½cwt)	**Length** 12ft4in (376cm), 12ft4in (376cm), 12ft4in (376cm), 12ft5in (379cm) — **Height** 5ft0in (152cm), 5ft0in (152cm), 5ft0in (152cm), 5ft0in (152cm) — **Width** 5ft1in (155cm), 5ft1in (155cm), 5ft1in (155cm), 5ft1in (155cm) — **Turning Circle** 33ft (10m)
Capacities	Fuel 6½ gallons/30 litres

Morris Motors Ltd
British Motor Corporation Ltd
British Leyland (Austin Morris) Ltd
Paint Colour Reference Codes

A number of options exist when sourcing accurate colour matching for Morris Minor colours. In the absence of any reference codes most suppliers utilise modern technology in the form of a spectrometer to achieve as accurate a colour match as possible using an original paint sample, usually taken from a component from the interior of the vehicle where the paint has not faded. A useful starting point is the contemporary codes issued by Morris Motors Ltd, the British Motor Corporation Ltd and British Leyland (Austin-Morris) Ltd. The known codes for the range of colours used on Morris Minors produced in the UK from 1948 to 1971 are listed below. Many Morris Minors assembled as CKD (completely knocked down) in overseas assembly plants were painted in a range of locally sourced paint colours.

Checks with a number of paint suppliers, undertaken concurrent with the preparation of the text for this publication, indicate that the following reference codes are still used in the trade.

Colour	Paint Code	Colour	Paint Code	Colour	Paint Code
Black	BLK	Sandy Beige	BE15	Old English White	WT3
Platinum Grey	N/A	Dark Green	GN12	Porcelain Green	GN17
Romain Green	N/A	Sage Green	GN5	Lilac	RD17
Maroon A	RD8	Cream	YL5	Dove Grey	GR26
Mist Green	N/A	Turquoise	BU6	Rose Taupe	GR27
Gascoyne Grey	N/A	Pale Ivory	YL1	Almond Green	GN37
Empire Green	GN22	Frilford Grey	GR5	Highway Yellow	YL9
Thames Blue	N/A	Pearl Grey	GR10	Trafalgar Blue	BU37
Clarendon Grey	GR6	Clipper Blue	BU14	Maroon B	RD23
Birch Grey	GR3	Smoke Grey	BU15	Peat Brown	GR30
Smoke Blue	N/A	Yukon Grey	GR4	Snowberry White	WT4

The following codes are applicable to the colours used for late Traveller and commercial models built at the Adderley Park Plant in Birmingham.

Colour	Paint Code	Colour	Paint Code
Cumulus Grey	GR29	Azure Blue	N/A
Glacier White	NMA/059	Yukon Grey	GR4
Bermuda Blue	BU40	Everglade Green	GN42
White	NAB/206	Damask Red	CMA/099
Aqua	JMA/060	Persian Blue	BU39
Limeflower	HMA/029	Connaught Green	GN18
Bedouin	SAA/004	Flame Red	CMB/061
Teal Blue	JMC/018	Antelope	BLVC/007

Specifications

Contemporary ICI codes were also available for all Morris Minor colours. Though not generally referenced by suppliers in the modern era, they are included here as a previously known reference for which Morris Motors Ltd, British Motor Corporation Ltd and British Leyland (Austin Morris) Ltd codes are not available.

Colour	Paint Code
Platinum Grey	ICI 0123
Romain Green	ICI 0095
Mist Green	ICI 2383
Gascoyne Grey	ICI 2783
Thames Blue	ICI 2382
Smoke Grey	ICI 3306
Azure Blue	ICI 7660

Special care was exercised during the first 500 miles when running in the newly rebuilt engine.

Appendix: Specialist Directory

Parts

Name	Leadbetters of Lancashire
Address	329–331 Preston Road, Clayton Le Woods, Nr Chorley, Lancashire PR6 7PY
Telephone number	01257 275314
Email	morrisminorspares@hotmail.com

Name	Tom Roy
Address	Morris Minor Parts, The Workshop, East Long Close, Battersby, Great Ayton, Middlesbrough TS9 6LR
Telephone number	01642 723400
Website	tomroy.co.uk

Name	Minorparts of Oxford
Address	2 The Green, Ascott-under-Wychwood, Chipping Norton OX7 6AB
Telephone number	01993 830349
Website	minorpartsofoxford.co.uk

Name	Andrew Eggleton
Address	Morris Minor Parts, 34 Tyning Road, Winsley, Bradford-on-Avon BA15 2JL
Telephone number	01225 868799
Website	www.morrisminorcarparts.co.uk

Name	Moss Bradford
Address	Unit 12 Acorn Park, Charlestown, Baildon, Shipley BD17 7SW
Telephone number	01274 539999
Website	www.moss-europe.co.uk

Name	Moss Manchester
Address	117 Stockport Road, Stockport SK3 0JE
Telephone number	0161 480 6402
Website	www.moss-europe.co.uk

Name	Moss Bristol
Address	Avonside Industrial Park, Unit 14, Avonside Road, Bristol BS2 0UQ
Telephone number	0117 923 2523
Website	www.moss-europe.co.uk

Name	Moss London
Address	Unit 16, Hampton Business Park, Bolney Way, Feltham TW13 6DB
Telephone number	020 8867 2020
Website	www.moss-europe.co.uk

Appendix: Specialist Directory

Name	East Sussex Minors
Address	Morris Minor Workshop, Battenhurst Farm, Battenhurst Road, Stonegate, East Sussex TN5 7DU
Telephone number	01580 200203
Website	morrisminorspares.com
Email	info@morrisminorworkshop.com

Name	Morris Minor Centre
Address	993 Wolverhampton Rd, Oldbury B69 4RJ
Telephone number	0121 544 5522
Website	abingdonmgparts.co.uk
Email	enquiries@davidmanners.co.uk

Restoration

Name	Ian Allen – Minor Services Classic Restoration
Address	53 Main Street, Witchford, Ely CB6 2HG
Telephone number	01353 662485
Website	minor-services.com

Name	J. H. Evans
Address	Cardeston, Ford, Shrewsbury SY5 9NQ
Telephone number	07811 578936
Email	jhevans@hotmail.co.uk

Name	Chertsey Minors
Address	Unit 6, Stevens Yard, 113 Fordwater Road, Chertsey KT16 8HB
Telephone number	01932 568822
Website	chertseyminors.co.uk
Email	chertsey_minors@btinternet.com

Name	East Sussex Minors
Address	Morris Minor Workshop, Battenhurst Farm, Battenhurst Road, Stonegate, East Sussex TN5 7DU
Telephone number	01580 200203
Website	morrisminorspares.com
Email	info@morrisminorworkshop.com

Name	West Riding Classic Cars
Address	16 Brearley Lane, Brearley, Luddenden Foot, Halifax HX2 6HU
Telephone number	01422 881221
Website	westridingclassics.co.uk
Email	enquiries@westridingclassics.co.uk

Name	Tim Lang Classics Limited (formerly Minor Magic)
Address	Three Bridges, A38, Taunton TA4 1EN
Telephone number	01823 461861
Website	carrestorationuk.co.uk
Email	enquiries@minormagic.co.uk

Appendix: Specialist Directory

Name	The Morris Minor Millennium Company Limited
Address	213 Upper Chorlton Road, Manchester M16 0BH
Telephone number	0161 861 8559
Website	morris-minor-millennium.weebly.com
Email	paulmarcuswood@tiscali.co.uk

Commercial Vehicles Parts Fabrication

Name	Fairmile Restorations
Address	The Green Business Centre, Stanford Bridge, Worcester WR6 6SA
Telephone number	07971 424396
Website	fairmilerestorations.co.uk
Email	enquiries@fairmilerestorations.co.uk

Name	Wills Company
Address	Lytchett Matravers, Dorset
Telephone number	01202 944048
Website	willscompany.co.uk
Email	alex@willscompany.co.uk
Instagram	wills.vintage.engineering

Bodywork

Name	Surface Processing Limited
Address	Unit 20 Sovereign Works, Deepdale Lane, Lower Gornal, Dudley, West Midlands DY3 2AF
Telephone number	01384 242090
Website	surfaceprocessing.co.uk
Email	sales@surfaceprocessing.co.uk

Name	Derby Plating Services Limited
Address	148 Abbey Street, Derby DE22 3SS
Telephone number	01332 382408
Website	derbyplating.co.uk
Email	info@derbyplating.co.uk

Traveller Wood

Name	Woodies
Address	Unit B1-B2, 10-12 Fitzalan Road, Arundel BN18 9JS
Telephone number	01903 885642
Website	morriswoodwork.co.uk
Email	info@morriswoodwork.co.uk

Name	Traveller Timbers
Address	5 The Close, Little Weighton, Cottingham HU20 3XA
Telephone number	01482 846787
Website	travellertimbers.co.uk

Convertibles

Name	Canterbury Convertibles
Address	Preston Hill, Wingham, Canterbury CT3 1DB
Telephone number	01227 720306
Website	morrisminorconvertible.co.uk
Email	sales@morrisminorconvertible.co.uk

Name	Don Trimming Company Limited
Address	2A Hampton Road, Erdington, B23 7JJ
Telephone number	0121 373 1313
Website	donhoods.com
Email	dontrimming@aol.com

Interior Trim

Name	Newton Commercial
Address	Eastlands Industrial Estate, Leiston IP16 4LL
Telephone number	01728 832810
Website	newtoncomm.co.uk
Email	sales@newtoncomm.co.uk

Name	Woolies
Address	Whitley Way, Northfields Industrial Estate, Peterborough PE6 8AR
Telephone number	01778 347347
Website	woolies-trim.co.uk
Email	info@woolies-trim.co.uk

Tyres

Name	Vintage Tyres (Beaulieu)
Address	The National Motor Museum, Beaulieu, SO42 7ZN
Telephone number	01590 431051
Website	vintagetyres.com
Email	sales@vintagetyres.com

Name	Vintage Tyres (Bicester)
Address	Bicester Heritage, Classic Performance Engineering, The Main Stores, Buckingham Rd, Bicester OX26 5HA
Telephone number	01869 879540
Website	vintagetyres.com
Email	bicester@vintagetyres.com

Name	Longstone Tyres
Address	Hudsons Yard, Doncaster Road, Bawtry, DN10 6NX, UK
Telephone number	01302 711123
Website	longstonetyres.co.uk
Email	info@longstonetyres.co.uk

Appendix: Specialist Directory

Electrics

Name	Autosparks Limited
Address	80-88 Derby Road, Sandiacre, Nottingham, NG10 5HU
Telephone number	0115 949 7211
Website	autosparks.co.uk
Email	sales@autosparks.co.uk

Name	Classic Dynamo & Regulator Conversions Ltd
Address	Unit 4A, Bridge St, Saxilby, Lincoln LN1 2PZ
Telephone number	01522 703422
Website	dynamoregulatorconversions.com
Email	info@dynamoregulatorconversions.com

Paint

Name	Car Restoration Paints Ken & Lyn Restoration Factors
Address	Meadow Lane, Buxton, Derbyshire
Telephone number	07778 165 966
Website	carrestorationpaints.co.uk

Name	J K W Refinishing Supplies Ltd
Address	2C Monk Rd, Somercotes, Alfreton DE55 7RL
Telephone number	01773 830078
Website	jkwrefinishingsupplies.co.uk
Email	enquiries@jkwrefinishingsupplies.co.uk

Insurance Companies

Name	Hagerty Classic Car Insurance
Address	The Arch Barn, Pury Hill Farm, Paulerspury, Towcester NN12 7TB
Telephone number	0333 200 5137
Website	hagerty.co.uk
Email	enquiries@hagertyinsurance.co.uk

Name	Footman James – classic vehicle insurance specialist
Address	Castlegate House, Castlegate Way, Dudley, West Midlands DY1 4TA
Telephone number	0333 207 6120
Website	footmanjames.co.uk
Email	enquiries@footmanjames.co.uk

Name	Lancaster Insurance
Address	Lancaster House, Meadow Lane, St Ives, Cambridgeshire PE27 4ZB
Telephone number	01480 484806
Website	lancasterinsurance.co.uk
Email	customerservice@lancasterinsurance.co.uk

Appendix: Specialist Directory

Name	Peter James Insurance
Address	772 Hagley Road West, Oldbury B68 0PJ
Telephone number	0121 506 6040
Website	peterjamesinsurance.co.uk
Email	classics@peterjamesinsurance.co.uk

UK Clubs

Name	Morris Minor Owners Club
Address	18 Shaftesbury St South, Derby DE23 8YH
Telephone number	01332 291675
Website	mmoc.org.uk
Email	info@mmoc.org.uk

Name	Minor LCV Register
Address	17 Felbrigg Crescent, Pontprennau, Cardiff CF23 8SE
Website	minorlcvreg.co.uk

A historic image: the first and last Morris Minor saloons dating from 1948 and 1970, respectively, pictured together to mark the 75th anniversary of the launch of the Morris Minor.

Index

A series engine 8, 47, 52–53, 55, 61
AccuSpark electronic
    ignition 158–159
Adderley Park 8, 198
ash frame kit 180
Ashmore, John 15
Austin 7, 11, 61–62, 110, 168, 172–177,
    197–199
Austin Motor Company Ltd 7
axle ratios 88, 93
axle reassembly 94–95

BMC Ltd 39, 47, 62, 68–69 74
boot 9–11, 26–28, 34–36, 38, 41,
    101–105, 108–109, 150, 163, 185.
Boothman, Mark 19
brakes 96–100
British Leyland Ltd 38
British Motor Industry Heritage
    Trust 18
Bywater, Andrew 61
bonnet 7, 9, 26, 34–36, 149–151, 168
bodyshell 7, 11–12, 27, 38, 198–199

cab removal 177–178
camshaft bearings 53, 56
canvas tilt 172, 175
Carroll, John 134
central crossmember 11–13, 19,
    23–24, 26, 82, 101–102, 104, 156
chassis (LCV) 169–170
chassis leg 22–23
chassis plate 18, 38, 161–162
chemical treatment 26–28, 33–37
chrome 153–154
CKD (Completely Knocked Down)
    models 38
clutch assembly 153–156
commercial vehicles 7, 9–11, 168–169
conrods 52–23
convertible hood
    replacement 163–167
convertibles 7, 9, 132, 160–161, 167
cooling and heating system 57–60
Cowley 6, 8, 15, 38, 189–190
crankshaft 50–55, 57
cylinder head 48–50, 54

distributor 157
door cards 141
door repairs 36–37
Dunlop C41 89
Dunlop C75 89–90
dynamo C40 105–106

electronic ignition 158–159
engines
    803cc overhead valve 7, 52, 56,
        61–62, 64, 69, 168, 196–197
    918cc side valve 55, 196
    948cc overhead valve 8, 52, 56, 58,
        61–62, 64, 93, 155, 197
    1098cc overhead valve 8, 52, 56,
        61–62, 64–66, 72, 89, 93, 96, 152,
        157, 162, 173, 197–198

Foreman, Steve 180, 182
front crossmember 23, 26, 36,
    102–104, 149, 156
front panel and grille assembly 149
fuel system 108–127

gearbox crossmember 62, 104, 156
gearbox lay gear tooth count
    chart 62
gearbox reassembly 68–80
gearbox repair kit 61
gearbox special tools 69
gearbox strip down 63–67
Great British Car Journey
    194–195

half shafts 94–95
Havard, Mark 4
headlining 13, 129–131, 143,
    145, 187
heater 47, 55–61
hidem strip 165, 167
honing bores 52, 54

Ingram, Robert 4
interior light 105, 131
interior trim 128–144

Jacklin, Mark 138

kingpin assembly 83–84

LCV Register 205
lead loading 41–42
Lomax, Dave 4
low-compression engine 168
Lucas starter motors 157–158

master cylinder 96, 98–100, 198
McKellar, Richard 128
monocoque 7, 176
Morris Minor Owners Club 4, 6, 15–16,
    189–190, 194, 205
Morris Motors Ltd 7, 38, 198

Nuttall, Chris 4, 177

paint codes and colours 198–199
paint types 38–39
pistons 52–53
polishing 43, 45, 192–194
Practical Classics 190

radiator 36, 47, 56, 58, 149, 178
rear springs 84–87
rubber boots 95, 98, 104, 178
rustproofing 38
Ryder, Graham 103

Scott, Alan 47
seats 131–140
sender unit 109
Series II 7–8, 56, 57–58, 85, 88–90, 93,
    128, 132, 155, 161–163
Series MM 7, 10, 55, 58–59, 81, 84,
    88–89, 93, 128, 132, 152, 155, 160,
    162–163, 196
shock absorbers 14, 81, 84, 168
Sikkens HLS 182
Smith's heater components 55–57
specifications 196–198
steering column 90–91, 102, 105,
    143, 163
steering rack 62, 90–92, 190
SU carburettor 119–127
SU fuel pump 111–112, 119, 189
Surface Processing Ltd (SPL) 26–28

Index

suspension 81–87
   front 83–84
   rear 84–87

Taylor, Geoff 4, 68
telescopic shock absorbers 81, 168
timing chain 53, 56, 57
tonneau cover 171–172
torsion bars 81–82
tyres 89–90

U bolts 86–87, 93
unleaded cylinder head 52

valences 34–35
valve seats 55
vernier plate 82
voltage regulator 103

water pump 48, 52–53, 57, 58–59
welding methods 20–21
wheel colours 88–89

wheel cylinders 97–98
wheels 7, 88–92, 178
window fitting 145–146
wing piping 146–147
wiring loom
   removal 101–102
   replacement 102–105
Wood, Brian 4, 112
woodwork
   refinishing 182
   refitting 184–188

Related Titles from Crowood

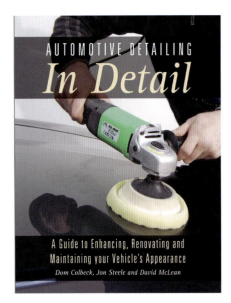
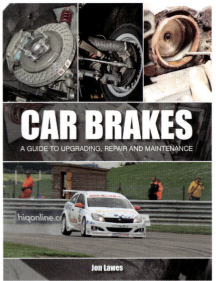
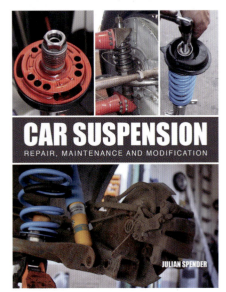
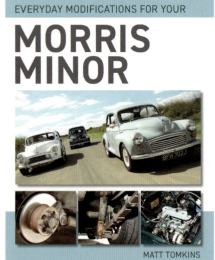
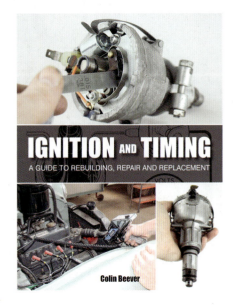
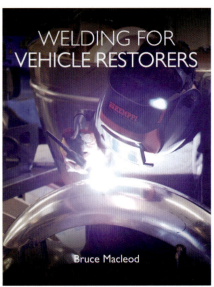